GEOGRAPHIA RELIGIONUM

Interdisziplinäre Schriftenreihe zur Religionsgeographie

Band 5

G. Rinschede and S.M. Bhardwaj (eds.)

Pilgrimage in the United States

Dietrich Reimer Verlag
Berlin

Anschriften der Herausgeber der Reihe:

Prof. Dr. K. Hoheisel
Merler Allee 68
D-5300 BONN 1

Prof. Dr. G. Rinschede
Ostenstraße 26
D-8078 EICHSTÄTT

Prof. Dr. U. Köpf
Liststraße 24/I
D-7400 TÜBINGEN

Prof. Dr. A. Sievers
Römerstraße 118/3308
D-5300 BONN 1

Schriftleitung:
AR Dr. Thomas Breitbach
Ostenstraße 26
D-8078 EICHSTÄTT

CIP-Titelaufnahme der Deutschen Bibliothek
Pilgrimage in the United States / G. Rinschede and S.M. Bhardwaj (eds.).
— Berlin : Reimer, 1990
(Geographia Religionum ; Bd. 5)
ISBN 3-496-00379-0
NE: Rinschede, Gisbert [Hrsg.]; GT

Gedruckt mit Unterstützung der Katholischen Universität Eichstätt
© 1990 by Dietrich Reimer Verlag, Berlin
Dr. Friedrich Kaufmann
Gesamtherstellung: Dietrich Reimer Verlag, Berlin
Printed in Germany 1990

G. Rinschede and S.M. Bhardwaj (eds.)
Pilgrimage in the United States

GEOGRAPHIA RELIGIONUM

Interdisziplinäre Schriftenreihe zur Religionsgeographie

Herausgegeben von
K. Hoheisel, Bonn
U. Köpf, Tübingen
G. Rinschede, Eichstätt
A. Sievers, Vechta/Bonn

in Zusammenarbeit mit der
KATHOLISCHEN UNIVERSITÄT EICHSTÄTT

DIETRICH REIMER VERLAG
BERLIN

Preface

This volume contains ten articles five of which were presented at the "Annual Meeting of the Association of American Geographers" April 1988 at Phoenix, Arizona, and at the "Interdisciplinary Symposium on Religion/Environment-Research" May 1988 at Eichstätt. The other articles were added in order to expand and emphasize the theme of this volume.

The editors would like to thank all those who financially supported the meetings at Phoenix and Eichstätt. Additionally we would like to extend our thanks to the authors who presented their papers and contributed their works to this volume and to the editors of *Geographia Religionum* for accepting this volume for the series.

We would also like to thank the President of the Catholic University of Eichstätt, Prof. Dr. Nikolaus Lobkowicz, and its Chancellor, Carl Heinz Jacob, for their generous financial aid which made this publication possible.

We are also very appreciative of Maria Bernecker for copy-setting, Dipl.-Ing. Karl-Heinz for his cartographic work, and Akad. Rat Dr. Thomas Breitbach who did the technical editing. Last but not least, we are thankful to Gisela Rinschede, and Vinay Bhardwaj for their constant support.

Eichstätt and Kent, October 1989

Gisbert Rinschede   Surinder M. Bhardwaj

Contents

Surinder M. Bhardwaj and Gisbert Rinschede

Pilgrimage in America:
An Anachronism or a Beginning?

1. Introduction

Two sessions on pilgrimage at the 1988 Association of American Geographers Annual Meeting at Phoenix and papers presented 1988 at the "Interdisciplinary Symposium on Religion/Environment-Research" in Eichstätt, Germany, served as the spur to this volume. *Pilgrimage in America?* – with a question mark – was a deliberately chosen title for these sessions. Our understanding of the prevailing perception was that practices, such as pilgrimage, are associated with traditional cultures and people in the Old World. The traditional-sounding "religious" practice of pilgrimage seemed discordant, even anachronistic, in the scientific and technologically advanced society of America. However, having studied several actual and some potential pilgrimage places in America (Catholic and Hindu) over the last few years, it seemed to us that conventional perceptions need to be abandoned.

2. Pilgrimage and Sentiment

Papers presented at the Phoenix Meeting and further exploration of related ideas has brought home two points. First, pilgrimage as a religious activity has to do with tradition, but we should not conclude its disappearance is simply due to advances in science and technology in a society. In fact, these very advances may, in the dialectical sense, cause an upsurge in religious sentiments, and be utilized to articulate and intensify this practice. The second point is that although pilgrimages have religious origin, not all pilgrimages are directed toward the supernatural. A pilgrimage is, after all, the spatial expression of sentiment whether or not strictly religious in origin. It seems to us that pilgrimages are fundamentally sentimental journeys; religious pilgrimages have religious beliefs as the source of sentiment. However, since there are other genera of sentiments that also impel people to undertake a journey, the concept "pilgrimage" should not be confined only to religiously motivated behavior. Even within religiously motivated pilgrimages, some journeys are undertaken for the fulfillment of spiritual aims but others not; for example, those in search of health. To visit a sacred place is not necessarily to enhance spiritually, but may also entail a quest for the fulfillment of worldly desires. Thus, pilgrimages religious and secular, are fundamentally motivated by sentiment. Whereas religious pilgriamges have been studied in some detail, very little attention has been given to the secular ones. If religion has a spiritual and civil dimension, surely sentimental journeys undertaken due to spiritual and civil reasons have a common element in them.

It thus turns out that not only are religious pilgrimages in America (albeit American style) not uncommon, but there is the widespread phenomenon of secular pilgrimages. In the broad category of sentimental journeys travel undertaken for emotive reasons is widespread.

3. About the Contributions

In the opening article, JAMES PRESTON, with the combined perspectives of anthropology and religion, provides theoretical insights into the American style pilgrimage based on, what he terms, "pragmatic spirituality". He rightly warns that American cultural attributes should not obscure the deeper religious motivations of the American pilgrims. Preston considers two fundamental structures underlying pilgrimage; these are "spiritual magnetism" and "sacred trace". Although he has given a more detailed explanation of these concepts elsewhere, they are likely to prove useful in future pilgrimage studies. His eightfold classification of Catholic shrines in America should also be a useful tool to undertake comparative studies of shrines elsewhere, especially in Europe. Characteristics of these shrines bring out both the enduring religious substratum and the impact of strong American cultural traits. Preston's contribution, thus, sets the stage for an examination of American pilgrimage in its many dimensions.

JACKSON, KNAPP and RINSCHEDE analyze contemporary pilgrimage in the Church of Jesus Christ of Latter-day Saints (Mormon), thus providing insight into the pilgrimage of a religion arising from the American soil. The proportion of Mormon adults visiting their major sacred sites is probably higher than in any other religion, partly because of the proximate distribution of Mormon population in relation to the temples, but more due to the pivotal role of the Church in Mormon culture. Their extensive survey reveals that the Temple Square in Salt Lake City is visited annually by more people than Mecca! They bring out the difficulties of precisely defining "pilgrims" and "tourists" and draw attention toward pilgrim-tourist interface. The activity preference of Temple Square visitors, indicates their gravitation towards the sacred, the historic and the natural, rather than secular economic, and recreational. Here, perhaps lies an empirical key to defining pilgrims and non pilgrims.

Five essays following the above deal with pilgrimages in the context of the religions of immigrant groups – three of European origin, and two from South Asia. Although they, unlike the Mormons, were not born in America but they have been significantly influenced by their American experience. These studies implicitly support the current structurationist paradigm which emphasizes the importance of context.

GISBERT RINSCHEDE's "Catholic Pilgrimage Places in the United States", is the first systematic and comprehensive geographic study of the phenomenon of Catholic pilgrimage in North America. Encompassing conterminous United States, and based on field work over several years, this study brings out how the regional distribution of Catholic pilgrimage places is closely linked with the early and recent streams of immigrants into the United States. Thus, pilgrimage sites of the Northeast, the Midwest, the Southwest and the Southern United States are compared in several respects, but especially regarding the ethnic origins of the Catholics. The variety and unity of the Catholic tradition, as modulated by the American milieu, is demonstrated by this comparative analysis. Dimensions of Catholic pilgrimage are examined at various scales, from the national level, down to the microspace of a model shrine.
Rinschede has identified seven significant criteria as bases for a detailed typology of American pilgrimage places. These criteria are useful not only for a general classification of pilgrimage shrines but are especially suitable in the American cultural context, in which it is critical to understand the dynamic role of numerous immigrant ethnic groups. Rinschede also provides an up-to-date, state-wise, list of Catholic pilgrimage places in the United States. This study is part of a forthcoming volume on Catholic Pilgrimage in North America.

FAIERS and PROROK focus upon the evolution of a single Catholic shrine, Carey, Ohio, in "The Pilgrimage to Our Lady of Consolation". They examine the various constituents of the process by which a small church was transformed into an important regional Catholic shrine. They trace how certain meteorological and social events were perceived as miraculous, and the way these perceptions became part of the accepted place mythology. Their argument, in a comparative vein, is analogous to the development of *sthala puranas* (place mythologies) of the Hindu holy places, which narrate legends of the sanctity of these places, and extoll their virtues. Faiers and Prorok see, in the events of this shrine formation, Eliade's classic concept of hierophany, which implies the dramatic detatchment of the sacred from the rest of the cosmic milieu. Since many shrines in the United States are relatively new, and their "mythology" has been systematically recorded and is available, comparative studies of shrine formation might be fruitfully undertaken. Such studies can not only bring out generalizations, much needed in pilgrimage studies, but also provide empirical grounds for Eliade's fertile concepts.

GIURIATI, MYERS, and DONACH's contribution also focuses on pilgrimage to one specific shrine – Our Lady of the Snows at Belleville, Illinois. They provide a detailed, step by step account of the evolution of Our Lady of the Snows at Belleville and its many components as a background for explicating the *meaning* of visiting this shrine. Their major thesis is that although the plan, the layout, the architecture and landscaping of this atypical shrine is clearly designed for the automobile oriented American society, its overall atmosphere exudes a Catholic religious message which is internalized by the visitors. Although Giuriati and his colleagues, like many other pilgrimage scholars, share the dilemma of defining the visitors as pilgrims or tourists there is little doubt that Our Lady of the Snows attracts visitors who experience in it the centrality of religion and the meaning of their faith in God, Mary and the message of the shrine. Thus, although unusual and atypical, Our Lady of the Snows does seem to be a pilgrimage shrine. They argue for a complementarity of various methodologies, statistical and experiential, to more fully understand the phenomenon of pilgrimages.

CAMERON brings out how the Sikh *gurdwaras* (centers of worship) in California became transformed from purely religious places of congregation for early Sikh immigrants, to current arenas of political activity. Starting out as temples of the scattered agricultural communities of the hardy Sikhs, which had taken tenuous roots in the early years of this century, these *gurdwaras* underwent major changes as many Sikhs arrived from India after the liberalization of United States Immigration in 1965. These immigrants brought contemporary religious orientations as well as the current political controversy in India related to the demands for "Khalistan" – a separate Sikh homeland. The essay shows how the homeland politics impacted the Sikh places of worship in California. Although pilgrimage per se is discouraged in Sikhism, many Sikhs do visit their holy places in India. These religious links, and family ties, with the homeland also help infusion of current politics related to Khalistan. An important message of the essay is that centers of worship may also be symbolic of ethnicity, even nationhood, and not only in a passive sense.

BHARDWAJ's contribution, continuation of an earlier work published in Geographia Religionum, shows how several aspects of Hindu religious circulation are in the process of being transferred from the Indian hearth to America, the adopted home of immigrant Hindus. A Hindu sacred landscape is developing in the United States and Canada, nourished by frequent contacts between Indians in North America and South Asia. Hindu pilgrimage in America, however, is primarily temple focused, and lacks its sacred river or mountain orientation. Deities famous for pilgrimage in India are, therefore, the ones attracting American Hindus. There are some interesting similarities between Rinschede's study, and this one. For an example, just as immigrant Catholics from different countries have developed shrines with a distinctive ethnic touch, Hindus from northern and southern India have constructed temples reflecting their regional architectural styles. In each case their temples have become their regional cultural symbols in North America.

The last two essays are concerned not with religious pilgrimage to places whose sanctity is attributable to the divine or to the supernatural act, but rather to profound sentimental attachment to personal idols and national symbols and heroes. Such emotive attraction, or "magnetism" may be due to emotional bond with a person, not necessarily religious, or to a place where deeply felt events of enduring national importance happened. An example of the first type is the contribution by Davidson, Hecht, and Whitney, who examine pilgrimage to Graceland – the home of Rock 'n' Roll superstar Elvis Presley, the second example is provided by Zelinsky's capstone essay which deals with the concept of nationalistic pilgrimages. Both these essays extend the range of pilgrimage studies beyond conventional religions, and thereby invite further scholarly attention.

The interpretive and humanistic, Graceland study of DAVIDSON, HECHT and WHITNEY is based upon a sample of over 200 interviews in Memphis, during Summer, 1984. Their fourfold classification of visitors to Graceland is meaningful because they are freed from the pilgrim/tourist dichotomy. They argue that, religion-like behavior becomes manifest due to the strength of emotional bond, as exhibited by the woman from Toronto who began to pick up litter, to prevent the place from being defiled. They also maintain that it is personal commitment that invests a place with meaning, rather than preassigned sanctity. It is important to note that people visit Graceland not for economic gain, but for giving expression to an emotional bond with their idol, Presley. Such a phenomenon is analogous to the non-Hajj type Muslim pilgrimages associated with the graves and tombs of Iranian Muslim martyrs, renowned poets, and even rulers known for their piety. Likewise, they suggest that sacred places do not acquire meaning necessarily due to the frequency of visits.

WILBUR ZELINSKY's "Nationalistic Pilgrimages in the United States" is premised on the argument that the civil religion of America reflects all the aspects of a fully constituted supernatural church. This includes sacred symbols such as the constitution, the national flag, and the tombs and monuments of national heroes. Thus, by inference there are also, what he appropriately terms, "nationalistic pilgrimages". In this essay Zelinsky identifies many such shrines in the United States. His full argument, of course, is contained in his recent book, *Nation Into State*. Regardless of his "controversial" view that civil religion has replaced the traditional supernatural faiths in the technologically advanced nation states, most contemporary nations share the belief in the sanctity of their respective symbols, and national heroes. Thus, nationalistic pilgrimages constitute a widespread phenomenon in many parts of the world and demand commensurate scholary attention.

4. A Beginning

Pilgrimage, at one time couched in strictly religious terms, may be more broadly viewed as a journey motivated by emotion and attachment, a search for meaning, a quest for the expression of union at an appropriate place. Thus, a pilgrimage place is the locus of communion where the faithful experience an emotional proximity, even union, with the object of their attachment, be it a divinity, a human being, or even a sacred reactualized event. America provides a fertile ground for the exploration of not only Americanized religious pilgrimages and sacred sites but also pilgrimages quite outside of the bounds of strictly divine, and strictly defined concept "religion". In this sense, "Pilgrimage in America" is not an anachronism, but could be the beginning of an exciting new phase in pilgrimage studies – not only in America!

James J. Preston

The Rediscovery of America:
Pilgrimage in the Promised Land

I. Pilgrimage in the Promised Land[1]

In 1492 Columbus set out on a hazardous journey for India. In many ways,
as the promised land, America was a more valuable treasure than India since
it became a place for the transplantation of European populations. Not only
was this exotic new land a material boon for European explorers, it became
the focus of a powerful spiritual quest rooted in rich pilgrimage imagery.

The Protestant settlement of America, with its heavy emphasis on religious
freedom and its ultimate goal of building the "Kingdom of God on earth",
set in motion an archetypal pilgrimage model for the American ethos. All
the ingredients of the classic pilgrimages of Europe and the ancient Middle
East were evident as American pilgrims established themselves a "place set
apart" in the midst of the "wilderness". Death, sacrifice, penance, rebirth, the
renewed bonds of the covenant, all these themes recapitulated pilgrimage journeys that had been made for thousands of years by European ancestors. Unlike
the European Catholic tradition, with its emphasis on journeys to shrines that
house sacred icons, the American Protestant ethos embodied a more ancient,
aniconic quality. Reaching further back in history, Protestants appropriated
the paradigmatic structures of early Judaism. The journey itself rather than
the destination was focal for Americans, a journey that embodied the sacred
movement of an oppressed people who swelled into an unknown territory, cut
off from earlier bonds of comfort and kinship, torn out like pages of history to
stand alone before the lonely chasm of the untamed. The new Jerusalem was
neither a shrine nor an icon; rather it was an idea, an atmosphere, a "place
set apart" for those who dared to take the risk.

This Protestant aniconic notion of pilgrimage abides in much of North America
today. It constitutes a major cornerstone supporting the American way of life.

The European notion of "progress" was successfully transplanted to America because the pilgrimage paradigm is at its root. Even the cult of individualism, and its recent narcissistic variant, is fueled by pilgrimage motifs such as the quest for happiness and the journey to the promised land.

Pilgrimage in North America has taken an equally significant course in its Catholic form, reaching back to the early missionary explorers and the quest for exotic India. The Jesuit martyrs of New France are still venerated today both in Canada and the United States at shrines attracting several hundred thousand pilgrims each year. Many of the founders of Canada were related to the church which was a vehicle for settlement and for the conquest of indigenous Native American populations (see PRESTON 1989). The southwest portion of the United States, Florida and Mexico were equally affected by missionaries. Pilgrimage shrines of considerable antiquity remain active in these places today. The most frequented place of Catholic pilgrimage in the world (outside of Rome and the Holy Land) is the shrine of Our Lady of Guadalupe in Mexico City. Here Catholic syncretism has mixed ancient Aztec traditions with European Spanish Catholicism.

Despite this long history of the pilgrimage theme in the formulation of American cultural traditions, the topic has received little attention in the scholarly community. Until recently geographers, historians of religion and anthropologists have examined famous instances of pilgrimage in Asia, Europe and the Middle East, assuming that in the Americas, and particularly in the United States, the phenomenon is absent or at best secondary. The present volume is a landmark, since it initiates a new field of study, displaying a wide variety of pilgrimage traditions in America and suggesting a set of questions and theoretical issues for examination.

The following discussion shall be limited to prilgrimage in the United States with occasional references to Canada and Mexico[2]. Emphasis will be placed on Roman Catholic pilgrimages, drawing on comparative materials from other religious traditions that have become recently prominent in the United States. Several theoretical questions about pilgrimage in America will be explored. What are the contours of the American variant of pilgrimage? How do American shrines generate "spiritual magnetism" to attract pilgrims? What is the nature of the "sacred trace" in American pilgrimage traditions? Can an interdisciplinary approach shed light on the interpretation of pilgrimage?

II. The North American Variant of Pilgrimage

Pilgrimage takes on a bold and distinctly American flavor in the New World. Even though Hindu, Buddhist, Catholic or Sikh shrines are usually transplanted replicas from the old country, they display uniquely American qualities that penetrate each religion to the core.

In North America there is often confusion about the differences between secular pilgrimages (to places like Graceland where Elvis Presley is memorialized, to the Washington Monument or Plymouth Rock) and religious pilgrimages (to the numerous shrines of the different world religions). This confusion can be attributed to a perceived surface similarity of form and structure among secular and sacred pilgrimages. Disneyland, Epcot Center and Graceland articulate strong American cultural themes like individualism, freedom, and self-actualization. These cultural motifs are evident at all American places of pilgrimage, where devotees demand comfort, a certain amount of entertainment and the benefits of structured learning opportunities. Cultural factors like these should not obscure deeper religious intentions. While American pilgrims engage in sacred journeying with all the trappings of American style tourism, their motives are no less sincere than that of their European or Asian counterparts. They seek spiritual transformation, healing, encounters with the "holy" and renewal through contact with the sacred center. Despite these similarities, something distinctly American is evident in the North American pilgrimage tradition. For instance, most contemporary American Catholics are *not* penitential about pilgrimage. Conspicuous displays of self-effacement are virtually absent. Nor do they rely as much as Europeans on the intercessory powers of saints. American pilgrims are generally *pragmatic* in their religious experience; typically they approach the sacred center to attain inner peace, reconciliation with God, various kinds of favors, or strengthened family bonds. The ritual of pilgrimage is attenuated, utilitarian, individualistic in tone, as well as highly instrumental. Above all else American pilgrims tend to seek direct results from pilgrimage experiences.

Pragmatic spirituality is satisfied through a wide range of sacred centers appealing to a variety of pilgrim needs. There are Hindu, Sikh and Buddhist shrines in America associated with different sects and specializing in particular variants of those religions. Catholic shrines in the United States alone number well over one hundred. These are concentrated in the northeast, midwest and southwest portions of the country where Catholic populations are most dense. Elsewhere I have identified eight types of Catholic shrines in the United States (PRESTON 1985). The following is a brief description of each type.

1. *Shrines devoted to American Saints*: These shrines are not numerous since few Americans have been canonized. In Canada and the United States there are only twelve saints and twelve beatas altogether. Many of the shrines associated with these saints are well attended, often attracting thousands of pilgrims each year.[3]

2. *Historical shrines*: North America has few historical shrines. While the Jesuit settlements of New France and the Franciscan mission shrines of

the southwest are numerous, most of these places are not intended for the reenactment of sacred events from the past. The Mormons, however, attend several pilgrimage sites associated with the founding of their religion.

3. *Ethnic shrines*: The settlement of America by Polish, French, Italian, Spanish and other ethnic groups left strong cultural remnants that retain attraction for third and fourth generations. Ethnic shrines feature festivals, ties of linguistic affinity, sodalities and fraternities, as well as links to the country of origin. Catholic ethnic shrines are numerous throughout the United States and eastern Canada. Although in some places ethnic pilgrimages are waning, particularly in urban areas where ethnic enclaves are disappearing, while in others they continue to flourish.

4. *Marian shrines*: A long standing tradition of Marian pilgrimage has been transplanted from Europe to North America. Marian shrines constitute some of the most numerous and highly frequented places of pilgrimage on the continent. Most Marian shrines are linked to revelations from Our Lady which were popular during the nineteenth and early twentieth centuries. Today Marian shrines continue to attract large numbers of pilgrims of all ages and ethnic backgrounds. Unlike the famous places of pilgrimage in Europe, most Marian shrines in North America are *not* associated with apparitions that have occurred on the spot. Many are replications of famous Marian shrines, such as Fátima, Lourdes or La Salette.

5. *Shrines associated with miraculous cures*: Pilgrimage shrines have often been related to supernatural healings. This phenomenon is rare in the United States due to American *pragmatic spirituality* and the general scepticism about miracles in a predominantly Protestant society. Another reason for this paucity of sacred healings in the American pilgrimage tradition is the fact that these shrines are a recent development, a large majority of which were established in the twentieth century. Most of these shrines were built during the forty years between 1930 and 1970, a period of increasing rationalism, when American social institutions were streamlined to fit the needs of an emerging post-industrial society. Miraculous healings are reported at most American pilgrimage shrines today, but these are rarely exploited by either clergy or laymen to attract pilgrims; indeed, if anything they are underplayed. The Roman Catholic church has been generally quite cautious, in this century particularly, about tauting shrines associated with spontaneous cures or miraculous visions.

6. *Imitative shrines*: Why go to Lourdes, the Holy Land, or La Salette when replicas can be visited in the United States or Canada? Many of these shrines appropiate the entire tradition from the mother shrine, providing a condensed form of the original. Popular devotions often transcend ethnic boundaries. Thus, Our Lady of Lourdes appeals to French ethnicity, yet the Virgin at Lourdes also speaks to the church in a more universal vein. Pilgrimages to imitative shrines reinforce and deepen old family devotions that may reach back several generations.

7. *Conglomerate shrines*: Many American places of pilgrimage incorporate devotions to several different ethnic saints, imitate European shrines, house a relic of the "true cross", or feature a rosary garden. These shrines appeal to a broad spectrum of Catholic spirituality to attract pilgrims. Usually the elements are arranged in layers, with some sort of focus at the core and various strata on the periphery.

8. *Synthetic shrines*: The development of synthetic shrines is unique to American Catholicism. Synthetic shrines typically combine different arrays of sanctuaries, grottos and statuaries in eclectric celebrations of Americanism. These sacred centers are designed deliberately either by individuals or religious orders to fulfill particular devotional needs. Sometimes a gimmick is used to generate pilgrimage, such as the largest cross in the world or the biggest display of Christmas lights. Synthetic shrines are numerous in America. They have wide appeal and often attract large numbers of pilgrims.

III. Theoretical Aspects of Pilgrimage

Since the study of pilgrimage in America is in its infancy, most reports have been exercises in the pure description of individual shrines. Virtually no new theories have been generated. Nor do most studies develop much in the way of interpretation. During the last decade several concepts have been advanced in different disciplines as heuristic devices for interpreting pilgrimage. EDITH and VICTOR TURNER have suggested the notions of *communitas, anti-structure*, and *liminality* to provide an interpretive framework for pilgrimage as process (1978). BHARDWAJ has noted the significance of levels of pilgrimages in the hierarchy of shrines (1973). Clearly, a set of orienting devices is necessary, if we are to make sense out of the large amount of data on pilgrimage presently being collected. Several additional concepts are offered here to stimulate reflection on pilgrimage in North America.

1. Spiritual Magnetism[4]

The power of a shrine to attract devotees constitutes its *spiritual magnetism*. This is *not* an intrinsic "holy" quality of mysterious origins *objectively* radiating from a place of pilgrimage - rather it is derived from human concepts and values, via historical, geographical, social and other forces coalescing at a sacred center. Spiritual magnetism develops at a shrine for a number of reasons. It may be generated by: 1) sacred geography (the location of a shrine in Rome, Jerusalem or Mecca); 2) apparitions or epiphanies believed to emanate at a particular sacred place; 3) reports of miraculous cures; 4) places that are difficult to reach, such as mountain tops, islands or caves that are believed to have powerful spiritual efficacy; 5) the recapitulation of the main events of a religious history; 6) the location of the relics of a saint or holy person; and 7) a focus for the ethnic identity of a particular people. In one way or another all these attributes generate spiritual magnetism. Most shrines encapsulate a variety of them to attract pilgrims.

> The intensity of spiritual magnetism may increase as a shrine becomes associated with additional reported miracles or when it becomes a focus of intensifying cultural activity. Unfortunately, we have too few ethnohistorical studies of pilgrimage to know exactly how this intensification occurs. It would appear, however, that during certain historical periods some sacred centers become increasingly associated with supernatural efficacy. And sometimes the notoriety of a prigrimage shrine seems to develop at an almost exponential rate, as if it were involved in a strong positive feedback system, which eventually peaks, then diminishes as dramatically as it flourished. Perhaps most intriguing is the question of why spiritual magnetism is more intense in one sacred place compared to another, establishing the relative stratification of shrines in the various levels of a pilgrimage network. These questions must await further research to be answered with any degree of certainty (PRE-STON, in press).

The study of spiritual magnetism offers social scientists an opportunity to gain insights into many aspects of human nature, including the social construction of reality, the architecture of civilizations and the variegated expressions of human aspirations. Shrines embody, in condensed formats, the codes of complex societies. Not only do they reflect the sacralization of profane space, they provide also a range of interpretive frameworks whereby pilgrims from a variety of diverse cultural backgrounds become integrated into the sacred center as part of the whole. Pilgrims are attracted to sacred centers precisely because they extend consciousness beyond the ordinary, catapulting pilgrims temporarily toward a larger whole — be it spiritual, social or economic. The centripetal movement into the center lifts the particular to the universal, while the centrifugal movement away from the center returns the pilgrim to the place of his origin, carrying within him a part of the whole. Thus, spiritual magnetism revitalizes local communities through an elaborate and complex multidimensional process.

I once thought pilgrimage could be defined as sacred journeying. I now think differently. Journeys without destinations, no matter how sacred, are not pilgrimages. A pilgrimage must entail: 1) preparation for the journey, 2) the centripetal journey into the sacred center, 3) the multi-layered encounter at the shrine complex, 4) the centrifugal journey home, and 5) the integration back into the community of origin. This five phase peregrination follows the classical pattern associated with all rites of passage noted by ARNOLD VAN GENNEP (1960). Spiritual magnetism is located not in the shrine alone, but in the people who attend it, the journey to it, and the village or town that sends and receives pilgrims. In other words, spiritual magnetism can only be understood as a dynamic processual phenomenon articulated in the context of unbounded communities.

The study of spiritual magnetism reveals a wealth of information about networks of economic exchange, political power, and civilizational change. We are challenged, in both the social sciences and the humanities, to discover the elaborate mechanisms by which spiritual magnetism is generated at civilizational centers (here we may include also quasi-religious or secular pilgrimages). For instance, a large scale multidisciplinary study of pilgrimages to Jerusalem could reveal the whole origin and elaboration of Judaism, Christianity and Islam. It could clarify a number of confusions, conflicts and problems phrased in religious language that stem from this important sacred city. Similarly, a multidisciplinary study of key pilgrimage shrines in the United States could uncover significant elements in the formation of American religion.

2. Tracing the Sacred Journey

Spiritual magnetism represents only the phenomenological surface of pilgrimage. Deeper still is the fire at the core. Using religious language, this might be called *mysterium tremendum* (OTTO 1923), the Otherness of Being, the Awesome, God, or the Unnameable. No description ever seems to do it justice. No matter how it is described this divine essence refers to an invisible transcendent reality emanating up into the pilgrimage. The effect of this perceived invisible Otherness can be studied at three levels: 1) the *communitiy* from which the pilgrim emerges and back to where he will return, 2) the *journey* linking community to shrine, and 3) the *shrine* center itself.

The phenomenon of an invisible reality made visible in the world is what I call the *sacred trace* (PRESTON, in press). Trace is defined in the dictionary "as a visible mark or sign of the former presence or passage of some person, thing or event". It also means, in its archaic usage, "a path or trail through a wilderness". Origins, otherness, quantum leaps into dimensions beyond, a sense of the presence of Christ, for instance, all these come to mind in the phenomenology of the *sacred trace*. Usually the trace refers to something in the past made visible in the present; it may equally acknowledge the caving in of one dimension into another, the rupture of thresholds, or a flooding iridescence that permeates and dissolves all boundaries. The trace refers to all these properties of the religious imagination as articulated in the pilgrimage process.

The term *trace* is used in nuclear physics to mean a methodology for observing the invisible atomic world through traces left in other media. As a religious phenomenon the trace is best illustrated by an example from Hinduism derived from the great pilgrimage shrine of Lord Jagannath at Puri. Here wooden images of the deities are periodically reconstructed every few years (PRESTON 1983). After the deity's image has been carved, the old and new icons are enclosed together in a sanctuary. There a non-Brahmin priest secretly transfers the soul (*brahmapadhartha*) of the deity from the old image to the new one. The soul or "god-stuff" of the deity that is exchanged is top secret. No one knows what it is, though there has been some speculation that it may be a tooth of the Buddha. The sacred images are carved so that there is an inner compartment that contains the *brahmapadhartha* or "god-stuff". The non-Brahmin priest wraps his hands with cloth to avoid touching this trace material with his bare hands, for it would be too potent, even lethal. The lights of the temple are shut out when the transfer occurs. Finally, the empty image is buried in a graveyard where other images of the deity were buried before. The new carved image then becomes the focus of the pilgrimage. Thus, the trace has been ritually preserved in this solemn rite. An apt analogy for modern secularized people is the sense of awe associated with handling radium. Here is a contemporary example of the trace. We handle it with the same extra care, wrapping our hands in asbestos or using robots to manipulate it.

The sacred trace is located at the core of every pilgrimage. It takes many different forms. In some cases it is in the relics or tomb of the saint; it may be the place where Muhammad delivered his sermon, calling together the Brotherhood of Islam or where Jesus of Nazareth rose from the dead. The trace is the source of spiritual magnetism of a shrine, its powerhouse, so to speak. By participating in the epiphany manifested at a particular place of pilgrimage, the pilgrim ingests and carries home the trace of his tradition, then anchors or implants it in his home community. This is part of the reason why sacred objects (sacramentals) of an sorts are purchased and brought home from pilgrimage shrines.

3. Organic and Synthetic Pilgrimages

In the twentieth century the old organic world, rooted in kinship, agriculture and stratified class structures, has given way to a synthetic transformation (PRESTON 1984). The emerging synthetic world civilization is the manifestation of an electric revolution that has torn away older organic roots, replacing them with an increasingly universalized way of life based on computer technology, mass communications, and relationships based on contract rather than kinship. This quiet, all pervasive revolution has been felt most intensely in America where the old cultural core was transformed by the synthetic revolution. Every American social institution has been permeated and changed by the synthetic transformation. Even religion has been invaded by electronic media, the profit motif, and business ethics. Thus, it should be no surprise to discover a number of pilgrimage shrines that have emerged in America to accomodate synthetic cultural traditions. These synthetic shrines appropriate older organic fragments by weaving them into mosaic patterns that appear authentic. Fragments of devotions to various saints, pieces of sacred imagery from older European traditions, bits of religious languages from the past are carefully orchestrated to attract a variety of pilgrims. These synthetic replicas encode pieces of religious experience torn out of context in an almost surreal fashion. This is not to diminish the importance or theological legitimacy of these pilgrimage shrines. No matter what gimmick may be used to attract pilgrims, the important element is the renewal of faith that occurs at a particular place of pilgrimage. Synthetic pilgrimages serve important functions in the religious lives of Americans. They bring people together in a fragmented and highly pluralistic society; forging them, at least temporarily, into a homogeneous entity bonded by ties of religious community. They inspire memories of the roots of people's faith. Most important, synthetic pilgrimages become the building blocks for religious legitimacy in a land where there are few *traces* to link pilgrims back to the long history of their religion.

In North America spiritual magnetism is often generated through the *synthetic trace*. The synthetic code enshrined in world civilization condenses universal consciousness into plastic media that may be easily comprehended by everyone, despite ethnic, linguistic or sectarian differences. Thus, synthetic pilgrimages have an amazing, almost eerie sameness and interchangeability about them. Despite their surface plasticity, the underlying synthetic trace (which is not an organic one rooted in sacred histories) retains powerful elements of awe and mystery for the pilgrim. Beneath the surface plasticity is a sense of awe generated from an emerging cosmic consciousness that creates direct bonds, linking the individual with humanity, nature, and the cosmos. Young pilgrims, on many occasions have told me during interviews that they no longer need the intercessory aid of saints, ethnic ties, or kinship roots celebrated by their elders; instead, the mystery is located in the synthetic webs of a larger cosmic experience immediately available to everyone.

IV. Toward a Higher Synthesis

Why study pilgrimage? What does it tell us about human nature? Not only does the study of pilgrimage offer insights into formal religious traditions, it encompasses a more ambitious task. We are challenged to shift from static to dynamic models for the interpretation of pilgrimage. It can only be understood in processual terms through tracing networks of pilgrims and shrines bonded together by sacred traces. Pilgrimage abides as process in the interstices between formal institutions.

The study of unbounded communities and of pilgrimage as process provides a natural laboratory for the more ambitious task of studying complex social phenomena such as multinational corporations and the vast communication networks that form the infrastructure of the world civilization. While most pilgrimage traditions in the worlds' religions retain an organic quality, they represent prototypes for the universalized type of social organization we see in the contemporary global consciousness. In this sense, all modern peoples are pilgrims, both temporally and spatially, as we become increasingly engaged in the "motion sickness" associated with the synthetic electric superstructure that is presently devouring the world. Our roots are illusory in the impermanence of the fast-paced electric world system. For modern people the only constant is change, movement and the flow of existence. *Movement* is the key to understanding human nature. Unfortunately we have few conceptual tools in the social sciences with which to study it.

Elsewhere I have argued (PRESTON, in press) for a multidisciplinary approach to the study of pilgrimage. Geographers, anthropologists and historians of religion, among others, have unique talents and insights that can best flourish in the context of multidisciplinary research. The study of pilgrimage in America provides an opportunity to launch a well-conceived multidisciplinary project. The pluralism represented in the North American pilgrimage tradition, its frequent articulation in structures associated with synthetic world civilization, and the strong secular nature of America, challenge us to look beneath the surface to deeper levels of analysis. Such a task can be hardly accomplished with any degree of success without the germination of insights provided by a multidisciplinary approach. This volume is a healthy beginning in that direction.

Notes

[1] This paper represents a terse synthesis of over ten years of research on the general theme of pilgrimage. It is based on earlier studies of pilgrimage in India informed by the comparative advantage of recent fieldwork on Catholic pilgrimage shrines in both Canada and the United States. Some of the theoretical concepts and methods advanced here were developed gradually

over the years in a number of formats. I am grateful for insights derived from conversations with Alan Morinis, Surinder Bhardwaj and Gisbert Rinschede. Also, I appreciate the stimulation of a summer session devoted to the theme of pilgrimage at the Center for the Study of World Religions, Harvard University.

[2] For a more general treatment of pilgrimage in the New World, including Latin America, see NOLAN's excellent survey of Roman Catholic Pilgrimages (1986 and 1989).

[3] The current list of saints and beatas (1989) for Canada and The United States breaks down as follows. 1) *United States*: Three canonized Jesuit martyrs, St. Cabrini, St. John Neumann, St. Elizabeth Ann Seton, Bl. Kateri Tekakwitha, Bl. Katherine Drexel, and Bl. Juanipero Serra. 2) *Canada*: Five canonized Jesuit martyrs, St. Marguerite Bourgeoys, Bl. Mother Mary of the Incarnation, Bl. Marguerite D'Youville, Bl. Andre Grasset, Bl. Brother Andre Bessette, Bl. Catherine of St. Augustin, Bl. Francoise Laval, Bl. Mary Rose Durochere, Bl. Louis Zephirin Moreau, and Bl. Brother Frederic Janssoone.

[4] The concepts of "spiritual magnetism" and the "sacred trace" were first developed in 1981 for my keynote presentation at the Conference on Pilgrimage held at the University of Pittsburgh. Subsequently it has been expanded further in several publications (PRESTON 1986, 1988, in press). The version presented here was developed in 1987 for an invited presentation at the Middle East Studies Association.

Summary

This paper explores the contours of pilgrimage in the context of America. The aniconic Protestant pilgrimage motif, so deeply embedded in American history, is contrasted with a Catholic variant that has considerable antiquity and continues to flourish. American *pragmatic spirituality* lends a distinct flavor to the style of pilgrimage in the United States. Three conceptual tools are developed as heuristic devices for the analysis of pilgrimage in the American context. These include a) *spiritual magnetism*, b) the *sacred trace*, and c) *organic vs. synthetic pilgrimages*. Finally, the paper calls for a bold interdisciplinary approach to the study of pilgrimage.

Zusammenfassung:
Die Wiederentdeckung Amerikas: Pilgerfahrt im Gelobten Land

Der vorliegende Aufsatz untersucht die Umrisse des Pilgerphänomens in den USA. Das protestantische, nicht an bildliche Darstellungen gebundene, Motiv der Pilgerfahrt, das tief in der amerikanischen Geschichte verankert ist, steht einer katholischen Variante gegenüber, die eine beachtliche Vorgeschichte hat und auch weiterhin eine Blütezeit durchlebt.

Die pragmatische Spiritualität prägt den Stil der Pilgerfahrt in den Vereinigten Staaten auf eine ganz bestimmte Art. Als heuristisches Instrument für die Analyse der Pilgerfahrt in Amerika werden drei Hilfskonzepte entwickelt. Diese beinhalten a) spirituelle Anziehungskraft, b) heilige Spur und c) organische vs. synthetische Pilgerfahrt.

Schließlich wird zur Untersuchung des Pilgerphänomens ein interdisziplinärer Ansatz gefordert.

Bibliography

BHARDWAJ, S. (1973): Hindu Places of Pilgrimage in India: A Study in Cultural Geography. University of California Press. Berkeley.

NOLAN, M. (1986): Roman Catholic Pilgrimage in Europe. In: Encyclopedia of Religion; Mircea ELIADE; MacMillan Publishing Company; New York; Vol. 11; 332 – 335.

NOLAN, M. and NOLAN, Lee (1989): Christian pilgrimage in Modern Western Europe. The University of North Carolina Press; Chapel Hill, North Carolina.

OTTO, R. (1923): The Idea of the Holy. Oxford University Press. Oxford.

PRESTON, J. (1983): The Hindu Sacred Image: Its Creation and Destruction; Anima; 10 (1); 34 – 50.

PRESTON, J. (1984): World Civilization: An Anthropological Perspective; Cultural Futures Research; 9 (4); 17 – 25.

PRESTON, J. (1986): Pilgrimage in America: An Address to the Catholic Shrine Directors of the United States. In: Proceedings of the First National Shrine Director's Meeting; National Conference of Catholic Bishops; Washington, D.C.; 1 – 10.

PRESTON, J. (1988): The Pastoral Needs of Pilgrims in the Shrines of North America. In: Proceedings of the Second National Convention of Shrines; National Conference of Catholic Bishops; Washington, D.C; 16 – 27.

PRESTON, J. (1989): Necessary Fictions: Healing Encounters with a North American Saint; Literature and Medicine; 8; 42 – 62.

PRESTON, J. (in press): Methodological Issues in the Study of Pilgrimage. In: Journeys to Sacred Places; Alan Morinis; Cornell University Press; Ithaca, New York.

TURNER, V. and TURNER, E. (1978): Image and Pilgrimage in Christain Culture. Columbia University Press; New York.

VAN GENNEP, A. (1960): The Rites of Passage. University of Chicago Press; Chicago.

Richard H. Jackson, Gisbert Rinschede, and Jill Knapp

Pilgrimage in the Mormon Church

Introduction

The Church of Jesus Christ of Latter-day Saints (Mormon) is a uniquely American religion. Organized in 1830 in upstate New York, it embodies the American frontierman's penchant for egalitarianism, democracy and patriotism. Egalitarian because it emphasizes the verity of the equality of each individual. Egalitarian too because its unique holy book, The Book of Mormon, emphasizes the need for communal equality of material goods. It is democratic in that the Book of Mormon and the teachings of the founding prophet Joseph Smith maintain that self-rule by universal suffrage is sanctioned by divinity. The church is nominally democratic in organization since all members vote on appointments to the church hierarchy. Mormons are patriots since the doctrines of the church proclaim America as a land choice above all others, whose particular form of government resulted from divine intervention through the country's discoverers and early leaders.[1]

The religious history and landscape of America is dotted with such "American" religions, ranging from the Quakers to the Shakers, from Seventh Day Adventists to Jehovah's Witnesses (Tab. 1). The organization of the Mormon Church in 1830 was part of a broader social phenomenon which saw numerous new churches established. Over time many of these churches withered away because of self-destructive doctrines, such as celibacy among the Shakers, or because of secularization of their members.[2] The geographic impact of some of these American religions is minimal. Communities such as the Amana Colony; toponyms such as Shaker Heights, or folk art from the Quakers remain as reminders of attempts to create an ideology reflective of the unique place and space of the American frontier. Other American religions, most notably the Mormons and Jehovah's Witnesses, have expanded their numbers and their territorial extent through active proselyting as they have begun to overcome their tie to a specific place. The geographic impact of the successful American

Tab. 1: Churches founded in nineteenth century America
(1986)*

Church	Church Members in the U.S.	World
Advent Christian Church	28,830	33,500
Primitive Advent Christian Church	546	5,700
Seventh-day Adventists	651,954	1,478,000
Christadelphians	15,800	
Christian & Missionary Alliance	227,846	
Disciples of Christ	1,116,326	
Church of Christ	1,051,469	
Churches of Christ	1,604,000	
Churches of God: General Conference	34,870	
Anderson	185,593	
Seventh-Day	5,830	
Church of Christ, Scientists		
Church of Nazarene	522,082	
Quakers	119,000	200,000
Jehovah's Witnesses	730,441	2.3 million
Church of Jesus Christ of Latter-Day Saints ("Mormon")	3,863,598	5,910,496
Reorganized (L.D.S.)	192,082	200,000
Bickertonites	2,654	
United Church of Christ	1,687,777	
Volunteers of America	36,634	
Pentecostalism		
Assemblies of God	556,000	2,082,878
Church of God (Cleveland)	505,776	
Church of God of Prophecy	77,952	
Int'l. Church of Foursquare Gospel	177,787	
Open Bible Standard	46,351	
Pentecostal Church of God	89,508	
United Pentecostal	500,000	
Pentecostal Freewill Baptist	19,700	

* *World Almanac*, 1987, (New York: Scripps-Howard Publishers), 1987, p. 590
– 591

religions is epitomized by the Mormons, whose membership had climbed to nearly 7 million by the end of 1988. (Fig. 1).

The Mormons are a political, economic, and social power in a number of states. Their influence ranges from total dominance at both local and state scales (Utah) to dominance of the local but only minority influence at the state level (Idaho, Wyoming, Arizona) (Fig. 2). The regional concentration of Mormons in the Intermountain West has created one of the most distinct and long lasting cultural regions in the country.[3] (Fig. 3). The geographical impact of the Mormons ranges from community planning and colonization, to architectural styles and social organizations, to perception of sacred space and related pilgrimage.[4]

The Mormon church has grown rapidly, both in the United States and elsewhere, especially in the last three decades as the number of full time Mormon missionaries has rapidly increased (Fig. 4). Growth of the church has created sizable congregations in Canada, Central and South America, Asia and the Pacific (Fig. 5). While the United States still has the majority of members, some small nations have a larger total percentage of their population as members of the Mormon church than any place outside of Utah (Fig. 6). The growth in membership of the Mormon church outside of Utah leads to ever greater pilgrim-like travel to visit the sacred places within Mormondom, even though the only formal doctrine concerning pilgrimage is the mandate for each worthy adult member to visit a Mormon Temple at least once, and preferably, as often as possible.[5]

As an American religion, the Mormons have a complex cosmos of sacred space. These places and spaces are hierarchical in emotive and attractive power.[6] (Tab. 2). Most Mormon sacred spaces reflect the American origin of the religion, but the broader Christian geography also provides sacred spaces that attract visitors, creating pilgrimage flows.

Mormon Pilgrimage and Holy Places

The number of places viewed as sacred by Mormons is quite large, and each attracts pilgrims even though pilgrimage is not a formal doctrine. It includes holy temples in which the Mormons carry out rites sacred to them, as well as places in which important historical events occurred. The specific events leading to designation of a spacial feature as sacred vary greatly from site to site. In each case, for the believer, something occurred or manifested itself at that place to sanctify it, distinguishing it from the surrounding profane world. Sanctity results from the intersection of the plane of mortal profane space and immortal eternal space. Such intersections occur where the Gods

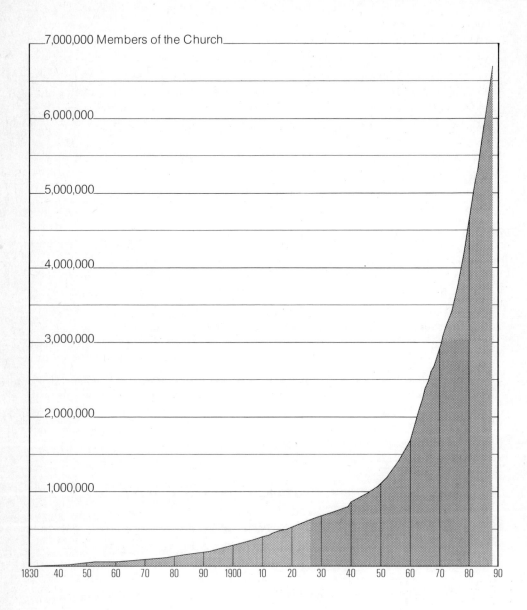

Fig. 1: Growth in membership of the Mormon Church
Source: According to information in the "Church Almanac 1989/90" and
other sources.

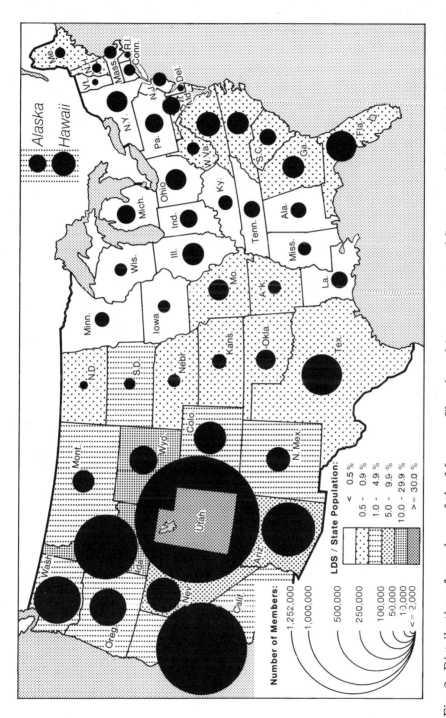

Fig. 2: Distribution of members of the Mormon Church and its percentage of State population in the United States
1988

Source: According to information in the "Church Almanac 1989/90"

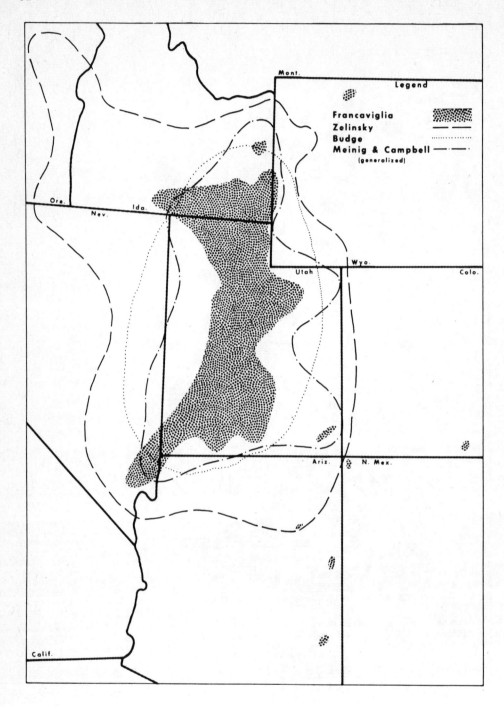

Fig. 3: Representative examples of definitions of the Mormon Culture Region
Source: Map compiled by author after BUDGE, CAMPBELL, MEINIG,
FRANCAVIGLIA, and ZELINSKY

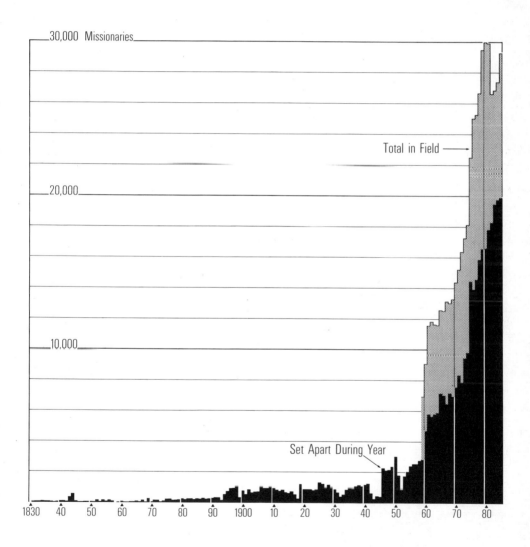

Fig. 4: Growth in number of full time Mormon missionaries
Source: According to information in the "Church Almanac 1987"

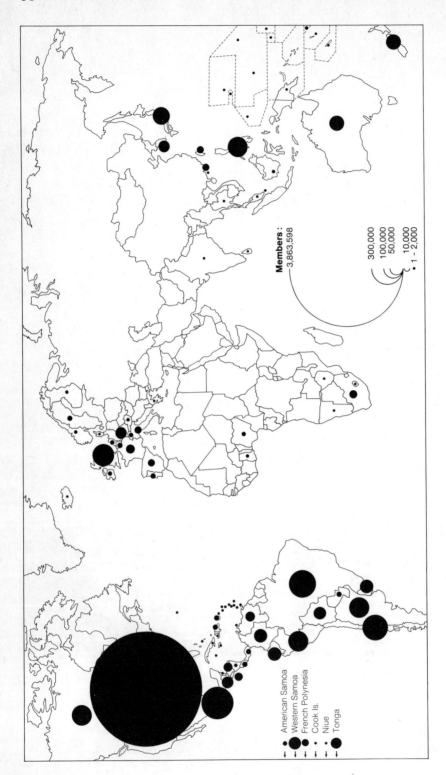

Fig. 5: Worldwide distribution of Mormons 1987
Source: According to information in the "Church Almanac 1987"

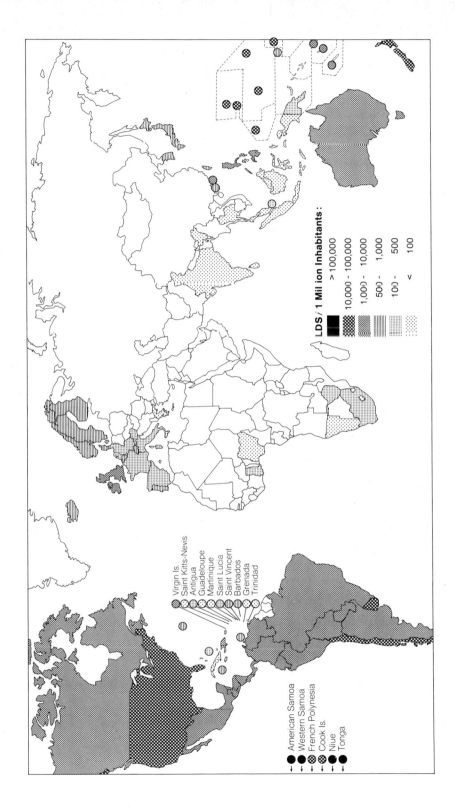

Fig. 6: Ratio of Mormon to total population by country
Source: According to information in the "Church Almanac 1987"

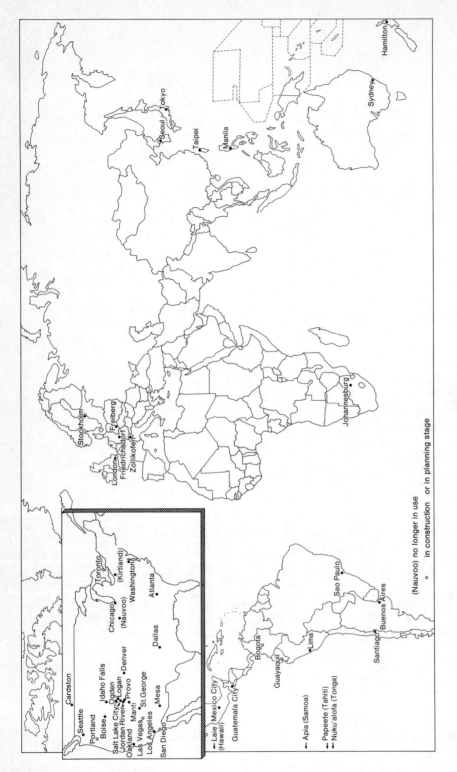

Fig. 7: Mormon Temples in 1989

Source: According to information from the L. D. S. Church

communicate with mortals, as in temples, sacred groves, or other space defined as sanctified.[7] Examination of the sacred space of Mormons in terms of visitor use and importance reflects the relative ranking of sacred places and their apparent attraction for pilgrims.

Mormon Temples

Temples represent the most sacred space in Mormondom both in official doctrine and in the perception of members. The construction of a temple is one of the means by which a specific city is recognized as being complete. Temples are places in which sacred rites are performed by the Mormons if they are adult and worthy. The importance of temples is illustrated by the fact that the church was organized in 1830 with only six members, but by 1836 they had completed their first temple in Kirtland, Ohio.[7] (Fig. 7). This temple was only about 15,000 square feet in size, but its construction, at great sacrifice on the part of the small body of members emphasizes the importance of temples. (Fig. 8)

Tab. 2: Ranking of selected Mormon sacred space

Place	Mean
Salt Lake Temple	1.92
Future City of Zion	2.12
Sacred Grove	2.39
Utah	2.76
Temples other than Salt Lake City	2.95
Bethlehem	3.02
"Holy Land" (Israel)	3.48
Joseph Smith Birthplace	3.70
Nauvoo, Illinois and Kirtland, Ohio	3.70
Chapels	4.63
Carthage Jail	4.65
Present Home	4.74
Present State of Residence	4.79
Utah's Mountains	4.95
Regions Surrounding Utah	4.95
Childhood Home	5.41
Present Day Jackson County, Missouri	5.41
Lincoln Memorial	5.86

Source: Richard H. JACKSON and Roger HENRIE, "Perception of Sacred Space", Journal of Cultural Geography, Vol. 3, (1983), p. 102

Completion of this temple and the migration of Mormon converts to Kirtland combined with the exclusivist nature of Mormon doctrine to cause conflict with non-Mormons in Ohio. By 1838 the Mormons were forced to flee from Ohio and relocated in Missouri. Conflict with residents in Missouri led to their removal to Illinois in 1840 where the community of Nauvoo was established. In 1841 plans for the Nauvoo Temple were elaborated by the Prophet Joseph Smith and the Mormons once again began building their temple. Completed and dedicated in May of 1846, the Nauvoo Temple contained some 50,000 square feet. Located on a bluff overlooking the Mississippi River, it was the site of Mormon attempts to practice their rituals at the same time they were being driven from the city by anti-Mormon mobs. The temple was abandoned in 1846 and subsequently burned by mobs.[9]

Relocating to the Salt Lake Valley, the Mormons established a new hearth and began expanding outward as converts migrated to the Mormon mecca, Salt Lake City (Fig. 8). As in the East, the Mormons once again began the process of temple building. The first temple completed was in St. George, Utah. Dedicated on April 6, 1877, it initially contained 56,000 square feet. (The temple was doubled in size in 1975 when it was remodeled and expanded.)

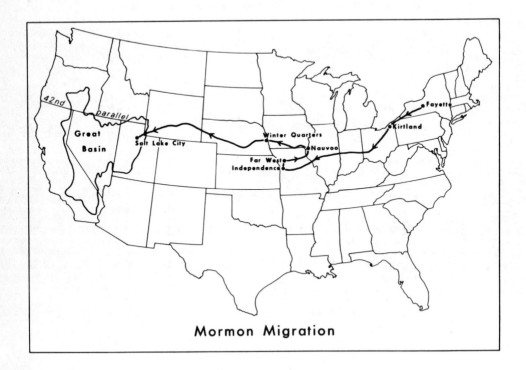

Fig. 8: Mormon migration route and major historic sites

The second temple completed in the West was in Logan, Utah, in 1884. The Logan Temple was approximately the same size (59,000 square feet) as the St. George Temple, and was enlarged to 115,000 square feet during remodeling in the 1970s. The Manti Temple was completed in Manti, Utah in 1888 with 87,000 square feet. The Salt Lake City Temple was the final temple completed in Utah during the early settlement period of the Mormons in the West. Dedicated after Brigham Young's death in 1893, it includes over 250,000 square feet in the main structure and its annex.[10] Other temples constructed in the West date from the twentieth century, including the Hawaiian Temple completed in November of 1919 with 10,500 square feet originally (35,400 after remodeling), and the Arizona Temple completed in 1927 (72,712 square feet) in Mesa, Arizona. Other temples important to the Mormons date from the post World War II era, including those in Idaho, Switzerland, California, New Zealand, London, and elsewhere that reflect the growth of the Church and resultant efforts to provide regional temples to minimize the travel costs for those attending the temple (Fig. 9). The new temples are smaller (averaging less than 10,000 square feet except for the Mexico City Temple) for those built in the last decade, and have fewer individuals visiting to perform their rituals.

Historical Sites

A variety of historical sites are important in Mormon pilgrimage destinations. These reflect both the development of the church initially, and its subsequent growth and spread from its home in Salt Lake City. The most important historical sites are those associated with events occurring in and around Nauvoo, Illinois. Established as a refuge when the Mormons fled Missouri, it emerged as the largest city in the state of Illinois by 1845, with approximately 30,000 people.[11] More importantly, the prophet Joseph Smith was killed by a mob on June 27, 1844 in nearby Carthage, Illinois. The prophet Joseph Smith is viewed as a martyr by the church and is buried in Nauvoo. The Mormons were forced to flee Nauvoo in 1846, leaving behind their recently completed temple for a new home in the Great Basin at Salt Lake. Nauvoo has been partially restored, and is an attraction for both Mormons and non-Mormons in the Midwest. The church maintains a visitor center, restores homes and shops,

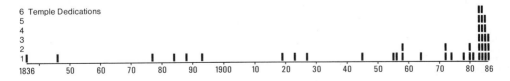

Fig. 9: Temple dedications by year
Source: According to information from the L. D. S. Church

Tab. 3: Visitors registering at Mormon Visitors' Centers,
Information Centers and Historical Sites 1986

	Visitors	
Visitors' Centers	Total	Percent Mormon
Salt Lake Temple Square	2,599,441	68
Illinois Nauvoo Mission	687,384	75
St. George Temple	263,701	95
Arizona Temple	253,399	94
Hawaii Temple	216,095	52
Washington Temple	165,870	88
Oakland Temple	127,422	91
Los Angeles Temple	95,979	91
Mexico City Temple	55,153	71
Independence	41,496	80
Idaho Falls Temple	32,497	92
Manti Temple	13,672	92
Ogden Temple	12,552	83
Alberta Temple	11,309	53
Information Centers		
Church Office Building	84,921	56
San Diego Mormon Battalion	35,204	61
New Zealand	26,628	73
London Temple	14,624	91
New York City	12,942	80
Welfare Square	5,046	64
Historical Sites		
Beehive House	127,206	35
Hill Cumorah	88,214	93
Brigham Young Winter Home	53,266	79
Jacob Hamblin Home	38,915	90
St. George Tabernacle	30,808	93
Liberty Jail	27,007	71
Joseph Smith Home	25,926	95
Winter Quarters	20,902	43
Kirtland	18,399	80
Joseph Smith Memorial	8,166	82
Churchwide Totals	5,276,859	73

Source: Personal correspondence, Church Publicity Office,
Salt Lake City, 1987

and cooperates with a splinter group, The Reorganized Church of Jesus Christ of Latter-day Saints which owns the Joseph Smith home and cemetery. As a destination for pilgrimage, Nauvoo and its associated historic sites nearby is second only to the Temple Square of Salt Lake City for both Mormon pilgrims and non-Mormon visitors (Tab. 3).

The other historical sites that attract Mormon Pilgrims are significantly less important. The Beehive House in Salt Lake City was the home of Brigham Young, and is part of the activity space of visitors to the Salt Lake Temple Square.

The Hill Cumorah is a unique location to Mormons. Geographically the hill is a drumlin left by the advancing glaciers. It is important in the Mormon cosmos as the site where the prophet Joseph Smith found the Gold Plates from which he translated *The Book of Mormon*. The visitors to Hill Cumorah reflect the official numbers who register at the visitors center. An estimated additional 100,000 visit during the month of July of each year when a historical pageant is produced.

The other historical sites where visitors can register reflect a litany of events important to members of the church, ranging from St. George, Utah (Brigham Young's winter home, the home of Jacob Hamblin who was the first permanent Mormon missionary to the local Indians, the St. George Temple and the St. George Tabernacle); to the Liberty Jail in Missouri where Joseph Smith was imprisoned from November 1838 to January 1839 (and where he formalized many of the doctrines of the church); to the Joseph Smith home in New York where he spent his early years; to sites where the Mormons attempted to build communities such as Kirtland, Ohio or Winter Quarters, Nebraska. In each case, the historical sites were important because of the events important to the church which transpired there.

Religious Rites of Pilgrimage

The figures given for visitors to the information centers and historical sites of the Church reflect visitors who may or may not be involved in worship or pilgrimage in the traditional sense. These are visitors who are not involved in a specific or ritualistic religious performance, even though the act of visitation may reflect religious beliefs. The actual rites associated with Mormon sacred sites are confined to the temples of the church. Slightly more than five million Mormons visit the temples each year to practice religious ceremonies. The pattern of religious pilgrimage to these locations reflects the distribution of the church membership (Fig. 10). The most heavily visited are the four temples in the Wasatch front; Provo, Jordan River, Ogden, and Salt Lake City. An

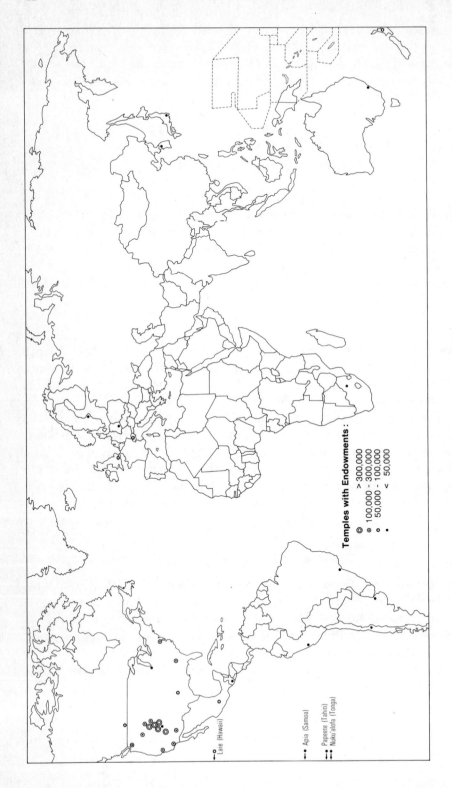

Fig. 10: Numbers of endowments performed by temple 1985
Source: According to information in the "Church Almanac 1987"

estimated 650,000 Mormon adults visit the Provo Temple and perform their sacred ceremonies yearly. The Jordan River Temple with an estimated 450,000, and Ogden and Salt Lake City with between 300,000 to 400,000 visitors per year are the next highest.[12]

Estimates of Visitors

It is important to note that only in the members who visit the temples or register at the visitor center are actual numbers of visitors tabulated. Many visitors to the primary pilgrim sites are not counted formally. The premier pilgrim destination of the Mormons is the Salt Lake Temple grounds and related activity space, and has been for over a century. From the time the Mormons established Salt Lake City in 1847 it has attracted visitors (Mormon and non-Mormon), and the temple square and adjacent administrative activities have been the focus of visits and descriptions.[13] The numbers of visitors to the Temple Square includes those who visit the square during the annual meetings of the church in the first week of April and the first week of October each year. An estimated 100,000 people participate in these meetings yearly. In addition, the Church has an outstanding Christmas lighting display which attracts several hundreds of thousands of visitors during the season from the end of Thanksgiving until the first of January.

Temple Square

The most sacred pilgrimage destination in Mormondom is Temple Square in Salt Lake City. Temple Square was selected by the Prophet Brigham Young the day after the arrival of the pioneer company in the Salt Lake Valley in 1847. He proclaimed that he had seen the site in a vision and designated a forty acre plot for the future temple. The Square was reduced to 10 acres the following day at the insistence of other Mormon leaders who felt that forty acres was too large to care for. The central elements of the Mormon pilgrimage activity space are concentrated on this square, and with the exception of the temple are open to the public (Fig. 11). The sacred nature of the square is symbolically and physically emphasized by the presence of a fifteen foot high wall built in 1857. The wall is constructed of adobe bricks (sun dried clay) on a foundation of cut sandstone. The adobe has been plastered and capped with a stone cap to give the impression of a solid stone and masonry wall. The square is located in downtown Salt Lake City adjacent to the most valuable land of the city.

Inside the square is found the monumental six spired temple constructed of granite stones. The temple was built in a forty year period from 1853 to 1893.

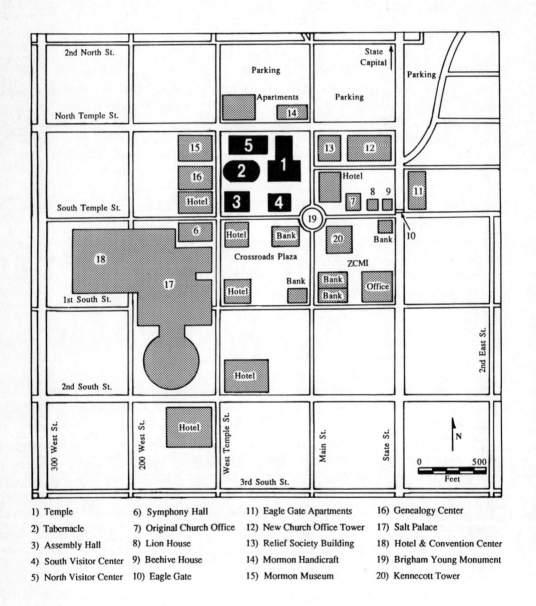

Fig. 11: Temple Square and surrounding area

1) Temple
2) Tabernacle
3) Assembly Hall
4) South Visitor Center
5) North Visitor Center

6) Symphony Hall
7) Original Church Office
8) Lion House
9) Beehive House
10) Eagle Gate

11) Eagle Gate Apartments
12) New Church Office Tower
13) Relief Society Building
14) Mormon Handicraft
15) Mormon Museum

16) Genealogy Center
17) Salt Palace
18) Hotel & Convention Center
19) Brigham Young Monument
20) Kennecott Tower

Of granite quarried in the nearby mountains, it rises 210 feet to a gold leafed statue of the angel Moroni, who Joseph Smith claimed revealed to him the location of the plates from which the Book of Mormon was translated. West of the temple is found the world famous Mormon Tabernacle, home of The Mormon Tabernacle Choir. This dome shaped structure was built at the direction of Brigham Young from native timbers held together with wooden dowels and reinforced with homemade glue and rawhide thongs. The Tabernacle was completed in 1867 and also houses a pipe organ built from local materials. The Tabernacle is a requisite visit to experience its near perfect acoustics, its imposing architecture, and the Tabernacle Choir. The Tabernacle is also the official congregation site for the two annual meetings held by the Church leadership in April and October.

Other important elements of Temple Square include the Assembly Hall, completed in 1882. (The Tabernacle and the Assembly Hall replaced the original meeting place on Temple Square which was an open bowery constructed of upright poles with brush laid over it for shade from the sun.) The Assembly Hall is a multi-spired Gothic style structure reflecting the New England origins of the early leaders of the Church. Two Visitors Centers, an older one on the south and a newer one on the north (opened in May of 1978) also provide information for visitors. The other major elements of Temple Square are related to events of Church history and include monuments to the seagulls who saved the Mormon crops in 1848 when the so called Mormon crickets (mountain locust) were destroying their crops; the handcart pioneer monument commemorating the suffering and death of some fifteen hundred pioneers who attempted to cross the plains pulling handcarts at a late date and encountered early snow storms; the Mormon Battalion Monument commemorating the patriotism in raising a volunteer force in 1846 to go to California to fight against Mexicans, and similar statues and memorials.

Directly east of the Temple Square is a block of ten acres originally owned by Brigham Young which has a group of buildings important to the Mormon pilgrim. The block was originally the site of the tithing office and the affairs of the Church which were operated from the Lion House adjacent to Brigham Young's home, the Beehive House. On this block Mormon migrants camped upon first arrival in the Salt Lake Valley before they were sent by Brigham Young to various areas to settle. Entrance to the Beehive and Lion Houses lots was originally through the Eagle Gate to the East, which provided the entrance into the large compound of Young, from where the Church's affairs were governed.

Growth and improvements in transportation led to the spread of the Mormons beyond the immediate valleys of the Rocky Mountains and culminated in the construction of the first major church building officially oriented towards the Mormon pilgrimage, the Hotel Utah which was completed in 1911. At ten stories, it overshadowed the old structures from the Brigham Young period on the block east of the temple. In 1917, the growth of the Church resulted in construction of the L.D.S. Church Office Building, from which the affairs of the Church were managed. In subsequent years the Hotel Utah has been expanded, and the structure for the Women's Relief Society was completed in 1956. Continued growth of the Church resulted in completion of the 28 story Church Office Building on the north of the block in 1972.

At the intersection between Temple Square and the temple administration block the Brigham Young Monument is located. A number of activities partially oriented to pilgrims are located around Temple Square. Immediately south of Temple Square is the entrance to a large shopping mall, The Crossroads Plaza. Immediately south of the administration block is another shopping mall, the ZCMI, (Zions Cooperative Mercantile Institution). ZCMI was established by the Church in the nineteenth century in response to the movement of non-Mormon merchants into the Mormon Culture Region. Brigham Young, ever the hard-headed conservative Yankee, responded by creating the Church-owned ZCMI to provide goods and services for the Mormons. He argued that the Church might as well obtain the profit from retail activity as non-Mormons who had not participated in the risks of establishing the settlements in the Rocky Mountains. The presence of ZCMI in downtown Salt Lake today reflects the continued commitment of the Church to maintain the area around Temple Square as a scenic and attractive area of the city. Unlike many central city areas, the blocks surrounding the temple square have all been renewed and are a focus of economic activity.

To the west of the Temple Square are another group of church related buildings. One is a new museum completed in the 1980s. The museum displays artifacts of Mormon history and a model of the community as it existed in the nineteenth century. Adjacent to the Museum is the genealogical library, containing the largest genealogical library in the United States which was constructed in the 1970s. Located between the museum and the library is a cabin dating from the first winter in the valley (1847 – 48).

North of the Temple Square the land is primarily occupied by parking lots, although two structures anchor the two southern corners; one an apartment building, and one the Mormon Handicraft Store. The Mormon Handicraft Store is an outlet for goods produced by women in the Utah and Idaho area. These items are high quality handicraft goods which are purchased by pilgrims and tourists. Along the main north south streets approaching Temple Square (Main Street and West Temple) are found the traditional commercial activities of Salt Lake City. Hotels, restaurants and shops designed for the tourist, business visitor, and pilgrim are located here.

The east-west streets that bound Temple Square (North Temple and South Temple) are the location of a variety of commercial activities including hotels and motels, gasoline stations, and the ancillary activities of the Salt Palace convention center and the large new hotels built in the 1970s and 80s. The growth of Salt Lake City as a convention and transportation center led to the construction of a number of large hotels in the area immediately west and south of the Temple Square. Completion of the interstate system (1980s) and the designation of Salt Lake International Airport as a regional hub for Delta Airlines prompted many hotel chains to construct multi-story hotels. Partially in response to over-construction of hotels and resultant economic difficulties the Mormon Church in 1987 closed the Hotel Utah after three quarters of a century as the premier center for pilgrims and tourists in the Salt Lake Valley. The Mormon Church planned to remodel the Hotel Utah to serve as additional offices for the growing church administrative services. Pressure from historic preservation groups, the local business community, and church members presumably caused the church leaders to change their minds, and in late 1988 they announced the hotel would be refurbished and reopened as a high quality "grand hotel".

Nearby are a number of other sites which attract visitors, including the Brigham Young grave two blocks east, the state capital and the original territorial capital building (five blocks north), and the "This is the Place" Monument where Brigham Young reputedly declared that the Salt Lake Valley was the place where they were to settle (approximately 2 miles east).

Pilgrim Characteristics at Temple Square

In order to obtain information about the motivations and characteristics of visitors to Temple Square a questionnaire was administered in 1987. The questionnaire included questions relating to the respondent (age, gender, occupation, education, residence, marital status, income and religion), the visit to Temple Square (source of information, length of stay, number of visits, favorable and unfavorable reactions) and other tourism activities (other places visited, purpose for travel, location and stay before and after Salt Lake City, length of vacation, and preferred types of attractions).

There were 4,100,000 visitors to Temple Square in 1988, more than any national park in the western United States, including Grand Canyon or Yellowstone.[13] Sample results reveal that 93.5 percent were from outside of Utah, with seven western states totaling fifty percent of respondents. (Tab. 4).

Approximately fifteen percent of visitors responding to the questionnaire were from outside of the United States, with Canada (3.3 percent), the German Federal Republic (.9 percent) and Mexico (.5 percent) being the three leading foreign sources.

Slightly more than one-half (51.9 percent) of all visitors to Temple Square are Mormon (Fig. 12) followed by Protestants (21.8 percent), Roman Catholic (8.8 percent) and those claiming no religion (7.9 percent). The majority of individuals visiting Temple Square were part of a family, with husband and wife (33.3 percent), or family with children (32.9 percent). The size of groups visiting Temple Square illustrates the importance of family, with only five percent of visitors coming alone. Over three-fourths of all respondents were presently married while only 1.4 percent were divorced and 17.6 percent had never been married (Fig. 13). More than eighty percent (83.8) of visitors to Temple Square had attended college, and over one-half (52.3) were college graduates.

The income and occupational characteristics of Temple Square visitors reflect the high level of education of respondents. Less than twenty percent indicated incomes of less than 20,000 dollars per year, while one-half earned more than 30,000 per year, and over sixteen percent reported incomes of over 50,000 dollars annually. Forty percent of all respondents listed occupations in business, teaching, or professions such as law or medicine. The largest single occupational group were the retired, constituting 21.3 percent of the sample, with housewives (17.6 percent) being the second largest category. Nearly all respondents to the survey were twenty years old or older (93.8 percent), with the age groups of 40 – 49 and over 60 years being the two largest groups (Fig. 14).

Tab. 4: Major western sources of visitors
to Temple Square 1987

Place	Percent	Place	Percent
Arizona	2.8	Oregon	3.7
California	16.7	Utah	6.5
Colorado	3.2	Washington	6.5
Idaho	11.1		

Source: According to survey administered by authors 1987

Visits to Temple Square tend to be of short duration. Over seventy-five percent of visitors spend at least an hour in Temple Square, but less than fifty percent (42.6 percent) stay for longer than two hours (Fig. 15). Seventy percent of respondents had visited Temple Square on previous occasions, and over one-third (38.4 percent) had visited it six or more times (Fig. 16). The majority of visitors to Temple Square did not stay in Salt Lake City for long, with 46.3 percent staying only one day or less, and only twenty percent staying more than four days (Fig. 17). The reasons given for visiting Salt Lake City explain the short duration of stay in the city, as nearly one-half (47.2 percent) were either just passing through (24.1 percent) or had Utah as one destination among several. Only 7.4 percent indicated Temple Square was their major destination, but an additional 35.7 had Utah or Salt Lake City as their major destination.

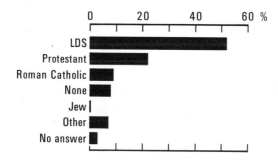

Fig. 12: Religious affiliation of visitors to Temple Square 1987
Source: According to questionnaire in 1987

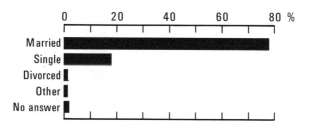

Fig. 13: Marital status of visitors to Temple Square 1987
Source: According to questionnaire in 1987

50

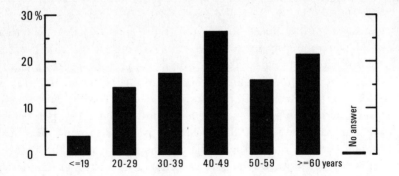

Fig. 14: Age of visitors to Temple Square 1987
Source: According to questionnaire 1987

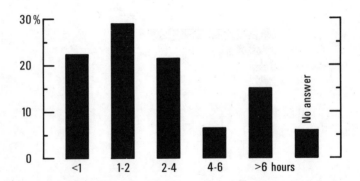

Fig. 15: Length of stay at Temple Square 1987
Source: According to questionnaire 1987

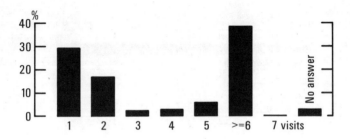

Fig. 16: Number of visits to Temple Square 1987
Source: According to questionnaire 1987

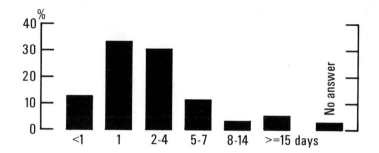

Fig. 17: Length of stay in Salt Lake City 1987
Source: According to questionnaire 1987

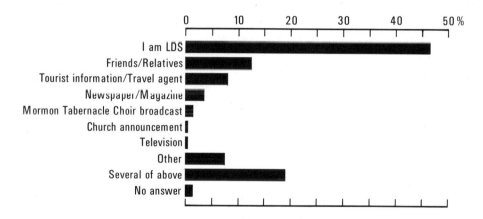

Fig. 18: Source of information about Temple Square 1987
Source: According to questionnaire in 1987

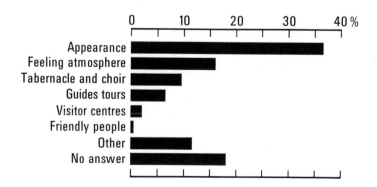

Fig. 19: Most liked things about Temple Square 1987
Source: According to questionnaire in 1987

Visitors to Temple Square learned of it from a variety of sources, with church membership being the primary source of information for nearly one-half of visitors (Fig. 18). For other respondents, no specific source of information dominates, with only friends and relatives accounting for more than ten percent of respondents' information. When asked specifically what prompted their visit to Temple Square, only thirty percent indicated they came because of religious reasons, while thirty-four percent indicated they came because of the historic importance of the Square, to see where the Tabernacle Choir performed (11.1 percent), an interest in learning more about the Mormon Church (8.8 percent), an interest in architecture (6 percent), or because of general interest in the American West (20.4 percent).

When asked specifically about those things that they liked best about Salt Lake City, only 15.3 percent indicated Temple Square. By comparison, 35.6 percent responded that the appearance and friendly people were the things they liked best about the city. In reference to Temple Square, 15.7 percent reported they liked the atmosphere, 36.1 percent the appearance, and 9.7 percent the Tabernacle and Choir (Fig. 19). Nearly two-thirds (60.2 percent) of respondents found nothing that they disliked about Temple Square. Only difficulty of finding parking (6 percent) was selected by more than five percent of respondents as something they disliked about Temple Square.

Tab. 5: Activity preference of visitors to Temple Square 1987

Activity	Percent	
	Like	Dislike
National Parks	74.1	2.8
Historic Sites	68	3.3
Relatives	60.7	7.0
Plays, Concerts	47.7	9.7
Museums	47.8	12.0
Beaches	39.8	15.3
Shopping areas	30.6	22.7
Amusement Parks	26.8	29.1
Sporting Events	21.3	38.5

Source: According to survey administered by authors 1987

To determine if there was any common preference for vacation activities among Temple Square visitors respondents were asked to rank their preference for visiting various types of places on a scale of one to five where one was liked the most, five the least, and three was neutral. Categorizing the responses revealed a high degree of preference for historic sites, relatives, museums and national parks (Tab. 5). Activities with a higher degree of dislike include sporting events, shopping areas, and amusement parks.

To determine the degree to which Temple Square is a focus of pilgrim-like activity for visitors, respondents were asked about a series of other sites that are important to Mormons or are part of the activity space of typical tourist visitors to Utah. Respondents were asked whether they had visited a site, or if they planned a visit (Tab. 6).

Examination of Table 6 reveals the dominance of Temple Square in the activity space of visitors. Other church buildings within a few hundred feet are visited by significantly fewer numbers, and only the Great Salt Lake, (which is a widely known geographical curiosity in its own right) attracts even one-half of the visitors to Temple Square.[14] Other Mormon sacred places had been visited or were planned for visits by an average of less than one-fourth of those who visited Temple Square. Similar proportions are associated with National Parks and other recreation sites in Utah. The dominance of Temple Square in the activity space of visitors is similar to the behavior of pilgrims who travel to a site specifically for religious purposes, and strangely at variance with the reported reasons for visiting Utah and Salt Lake City. As mentioned above, only a small minority of visitors indicate that they came to Utah or Salt Lake primarily to visit Temple Square, yet the majority do not indicate they visited other sites in the city, lending support to the thesis that visitors to Temple Square are pilgrims, even though there is no formal doctrine in the Mormon Church suggesting the need for such a pilgrimage. The importance of the Salt Lake Temple as a symbol of the Mormon Church, (among both Mormons and non-Mormons), and the accomplishments of the Church in settling Utah and much of the Intermountain West, make it a magnet for visitors unrivalled by any other individual attraction in the entire region.

Conclusion

The four million visitors to Temple Square in 1988 is indicative of the Square's importance. As a pilgrimage, the numbers exceed those visiting Mecca; as a tourist attraction it is the most important in the region. By any definition, the presence of such large numbers of visitors at a non-commercial religious site in a sparsely inhabited region indicates the motivation of the pilgrim rather than the recreationist, particularly since other adjacent attractions are not visited

Tab. 6: Familiarity with other Mormon sites or Utah attractions 1987

| | Percent | |
Site	Visited	Plan to Visit
Hill Cumorah	12.5	9.7
Nauvoo	19	9.7
Palmyra	12	9.3
Carthage Jail	16.7	7.4
Sacred Grove	11.6	9.3
Kirtland Temple	10.2	6.5
Jordan River Temple*	11.1	2.3
Provo Temple*	13.0	5.6
Washington D.C. Temple	17.1	6.0
Hawaiian Temple	17.1	4.2
Los Angeles Temple	27.8	4.2
Oakland Temple	20.4	4.6
Winter Quarters Cemetery	5.6	6.0
Arches National Monument	14.4	5.1
Zion National Park	29.2	6.5
Bryce Canyon National Park	26.4	6.5
Canyonlands National Park	10.2	5.1
Capitol Reef National Park	5.1	1.9
Dinosaur National Monument	13.4	6.5
Flaming Gorge Recreation Area	15.3	2.3
Great Salt Lake*	41.2	8.8
Bingham Copper Mine*	6.9	5.6
Park City*	21.8	3.7
Beehive House*	26.9	2.8
Lion House*	20.4	1.9
Relief Society Building*	15.3	1.4
Eagle Gate*	23.6	4.2
ZCMI Mall*	31.5	3.7
Hotel Utah*	19.9	2.3
Utah State Capitol*	26.9	6.0
Salt Palace*	16.2	2.3
Crossroads Plaza Mall*	23.6	4.2
Church History Museum*	20.4	5.1
"This is the Place" Monument*	20.8	5.1
Genealogical Library*	29.6	8.3

* Denotes sites adjacent or near to Temple Square and Salt Lake City.

Source: According to survey administered by authors 1987

by visitors to Temple Square. The continued growth of the church will reflect and lead to even greater numbers of visitors to Temple Square in the future as the informal pilgrimage flow continues to the symbolic center of the Mormon church.

Summary

The number of places viewed as sacred by Mormons is quite large, and each attracts pilgrims even though pilgrimage is not a formal doctrine.

Temples represent the most sacred space in which sacred rites are performed by Mormons if they are adult and worthy. There are about 40 Temples in all parts of the world including the most famous Salt Lake City Temple with about 400,000 visitors per year.

A variety of historical sites are also important in Mormon pilgrimage destinations. The most important are in Nauvoo/Illinois, in Salt Lake City and in other parts of Utah. The central elements of the Mormon pilgrimage activity space are concentrated on Temple Square in Salt Lake City and, with the exception of the temple, are open to the public; for example, the Tabernacle, the Assembly Hall, two visitors centers, and several monuments. Adjacent to Temple Square are situated other church-related buildings important to the Mormon pilgrims.

There were 4,100,000 visitors to Temple Square in 1988, more than any national park in the Western U.S. In order to obtain information about the motivation and characteristics of visitors a questionnaire was handed out in 1987. The questionnaire included questions relating to the respondent, the visit to Temple Square and other tourism activities.

Zusammenfassung:
Die Pilgerfahrt in der mormonischen Kirche

In der Kirche der Mormonen gibt es zahlreiche heilige Stätten, die von vielen Pilgern aufgesucht werden, obwohl die Pilgerfahrt in der offiziellen Lehre der Kirche keine große Bedeutung hat.

Die Tempel stellen die heiligsten Stätten der Mormonen dar. In ihnen werden heilige Riten vollzogen, und zwar nur von erwachsenen Mormonen, die sich als dessen würdig erwiesen haben. Es gibt zur Zeit weltweit über 40 Tempel, von denen der Salt Lake City Tempel mit über 400 000 Besuchern pro Jahr der berühmteste ist.

Auch eine Reihe von historischen Stätten sind Ziel vieler Pilgerfahrten der Mormonen. Die wichtigsten liegen in Nauvoo/Illinois, in Salt Lake City und im übrigen Utah. Auf dem Tempelplatz in Salt Lake City konzentrieren sich die wichtigsten Elemente des Aktionsraumes der mormonischen Pilger, die mit Ausnahme des Tempel öffentlich zugänglich sind. Zu diesen zählen der Tabernacle, die Assembly Hall, zwei Besucherzentren und verschiedene Monumente. In direkter Nachbarschaft des Tempelplatzes liegen weitere, für die mormonischen Pilger wichtige, kirchliche Gebäude.

Mit 4 100 000 Besuchern verzeichnete der Tempelplatz im Jahr 1988 mehr Besucher als jeder Nationalpark in den westlichen USA. Um Informationen über Motivation und Eigenarten der Besucher zu erhalten, wurde im Jahre 1987 eine Befragung am Tempelplatz durchgeführt. In die Befragung einbezogen waren Fragen zur interviewten Person, zum Besuch des Tempelplatzes und zu anderen touristischen Aktivitäten.

Bibliography

BEDELL, G. C., SANDON, L. Jr., and WELLBORN, C. T. (1982): Religion in America, 2nd ed., New York, Macmillan.

BUDGE, S. (1974): Perception of the Boundaries of the Mormon Cultural Region. Great Plains – Rocky Mountain Geographical Journal, Volume 3, pp. 1 – 9.

CAMPBELL, L. D.: Perception and Land Use: The Case of the Mormon Culture Region. Master's Thesis, Brigham Young University, Department of Geography, Provo, Utah.

CHURCH ALMANAC (1987): Salt Lake City: Deseret News Press.

DRAGER, K. (1980): "Latter-day Legislatures. The Mormon Influence on the Politics of California". California Journal, 11, pp. 292 – 293.

ELIADE, M. (1965): Le Sacré et le Profane. Paris: Gallimard.

FLANDERS, R. B. (1965): Nauvoo; Kingdom on the Mississippi. Urbana, Illinois: University of Illinois Press.

HOWARD, M. B. (ed.) (1987): Utah in Demographic Perspective. Provo, Utah: BYU Press.

JACKSON, R. H. (1988): "Great Salt Lake and Great Salt Lake City: American Curiosities". Utah Historical Quarterly, Volume 56, p. 128 – 137.

JACKSON, R. H. and HENRIE, R. (1983): "Perception of Sacred Space". Journal of Cultural Geography, 3, p. 94 – 107.

LAUTENSACH, H. (1953): Das Mormonenland, als Beispiel eines sozial-geographischen Raumes. Bonner Geographische Abhandlungen, Heft II.

L.D.S. CHURCH NEWS Salt Lake City (1988): Deseret News Press, Dec. 24, 1988, p. 8 – 9.

LUNDWALL, N. B. (Computer) (1987): Temples of the Most High, (6th ed.). Salt Lake City: Bookcraft.

MAY, D. L. (1977): "The Making of Saints: The Mormon Town as a setting for the study of Cultural Change". Utah Historical Quarterly, 45, pp. 75 – 92.

MEINIG, D. W. (1965): The Mormon Cultural Region: Strategies and Patterns in the Geography of the American West, 1847 – 1964. Annals, Association of American Geographers, Volume 55, pp. 191 – 220.

MILES, A. O. (1980): Mormon Voting Behavior and Political Attitudes. Ann Arbor, Michigan: University Microfilm International.

PACKER, B. K. (1982): The Holy Temple. Salt Lake City: Church of Jesus Christ of Latter-day Saints.

SMITH, J. (1891): Doctrine and Covenants of the Church of Jesus Christ of Latter-day Saints. Salt Lake City: George Q. Cannon and Sons Co.

Other Sources Referred to in Maps

FRANCAVIGLIA, R. V. (1978): The Mormon Landscape. AMS Press, New York.

ZELINSKY, W. (1961): An Approach to the Religious Geography of the United States: Patterns of Church Membership in 1952. Annals: Association of American Geographers, Volume 51.

Questionnaire

I am a graduate student at Brigham Young University doing a Master's thesis on travel and tourism to Salt Lake City. Thank you for taking a few moments to fill out this survey which will provide essential information to help the city to provide for its future visitors.

SALT LAKE CITY
Temple Square Survey

1. How many times have you visited Temple Square?_____

2. How did you hear about Temple Square?

   a) Television
   b) Friends/Relatives
   c) Church announcement

   d) Radio
   e) Tourist information/
      Travel agent
   f) I am L.D.S.

   g) Newspaper/Magazine
   h) Mormon Missionaries/
      Assoc.
   i) Mormon Tabernacle Choir broadcast
   j) Other (list) _____

3. What were the most important reasons that made you decide to visit Temple Square?
   (Check all that apply)

   a) _____ Came to S.L.C. primarily for other business but included a visit to Temple Square.
   b) _____ Came because I am interested in architecture.
   c) _____ We are Mormons and wanted to see the Visitor Center and the Tabernacle.
   d) _____ Came to Salt Lake City primarily to visit Temple Square or other historic points of interest.
   e) _____ I am here to add to my general education.
   f) _____ Came because I wanted to see the Tabernacle, where the Choir sings every morning.
   g) _____ Curious to see what attracts so many people.
   h) _____ Interested in learning more about the Church.
   i) _____ Missionaries invited me.
   j) _____ Family lives in S.L.C.
   k) _____ Thinking of moving to the area.
   l) _____ Came to do genealogy.
   m) _____ Other (list) _____

4. How did you travel to Salt Lake City?

   a) Private vehicle
   b) Private airplane
   c) Commercial air carrier

   d) Trailer or camper
   e) Train
   f) Bus

   g) Other (list) _____

5. Where did you stay the night before entering Salt Lake City?

   Town _____   State _____

6. How long will you stay in Salt Lake City? _____

7. Where did you stay last night?

   a) Friends/Relatives

   b) Hotel/Motel _____
      (hotel/motel name)

   c) Campground _____
      (campground name)

   d) Other (list) _____

8. Where do you plan to stay the night after leaving Salt Lake City?

   Town _____   State _____

9. How long do you plan or did you stay at Temple Square? _____

10. Did you sign the guest register in one of the visitor centers on Temple Square? _____

11. What other sacred places, historic sites, or other points of interest do you know of, do you plan on visiting, or did you visit in S.L.C.? (Check all that apply)

know of	visited	plan to visit			know of	visited	plan to visit		
			1.	Beehive House				12.	Church History - Art Museum
			2.	Lion House				13.	Brigham Young Monument
			3.	Relief Society B.				14.	Mormon Pioneer Memorial
			4.	Eagle Gate				15.	This is The Place Monument
			5.	ZCMI				16.	Church Office Bldg. and Plaza
			6.	Meridian Marker				17.	Brigham Young Farm Home
			7.	Hotel Utah				18.	Mormon Battalion Monument
			8.	U. State Cap. B.				19.	Hansen Planetarium
			9.	Salt Palace				20.	Genealogical Library
			10.	Crossroads Plaza				21.	Pioneer Museum
			11.	Welfare Square				22.	Other (list) _____

12. What other places do you know of, do you plan on visiting, or did you visit in Utah? (Check all that apply)

know of	visited	plan to visit			know of	visited	plan to visit		
			1.	Arches				13.	National Forests
			2.	Zion				14.	Natural Bridges
			3.	Bear Lake				15.	Alta-Snowbird Resort Area
			4.	Park City				16.	Bingham Copper Mine
			5.	Bryce Canyon				17.	Provo Temple/Visitor Center
			6.	Canyonlands				18.	Ogden Temple/Visitor Center
			7.	Capitol Reef				19.	Jordan River Temple/Visitor C.
			8.	Cedar Breaks				20.	St. George Temple/Visitor C.
			9.	Dinosaur				21.	Logan Temple/Visitor Center
			10.	Flaming Gorge				22.	Manti Temple/Visitor Center
			11.	Glen Canyon				22.	Other (list) _____
			12.	Great Salt Lake					

13. What places of importance to Mormons do you know of, do you plan on visiting, or have you visited outside Utah? (Check all that apply)

know of	visited	plan to visit			know of	visited	plan to visit		
			1.	Hill Cumorah				9.	Washington D.C. Temple
			2.	Nauvoo				10.	Los Angeles Temple
			3.	Palmyra				11.	Oakland Temple
			4.	Liberty Jail				12.	Polynesian Culture Center
			5.	Carthage Jail				13.	Winter Quarters Cemetery
			6.	Sacred Grove				14.	Adam-ondi-Ahman
			7.	Hawaiian Temple				15.	Other (list) _____
			8.	Kirtland Temple					

14. What did you like best about Temple Square?

15. What did you like least about Temple Square?

16. What did you like best about Salt Lake City?

17. Are you on a vacation? _____ yes _____ no   If yes, how long will your vacation be? _____

18. Please indicate the types of things you most enjoy visiting when you are on vacation. (Please circle)

like most	neutral	like least			like most	neutral	like least	
1	2 3	4 5	a) Museums		1	2 3	4 5	f) Amusement parks
1	2 3	4 5	b) Beaches		1	2 3	4 5	g) Shopping areas
1	2 3	4 5	c) Relatives		1	2 3	4 5	h) National parks/Recreation areas
1	2 3	4 5	d) Sporting events		1	2 3	4 5	i) Cultural events
1	2 3	4 5	e) Historical sites		1	2 3	4 5	j) Other (list) _____

19. What is the destination of your trip? (Check the answer that is most applicable)

a) _____ Passing through.
b) _____ Utah is one of several destinations.
c) _____ Utah is major destination.
d) _____ Salt Lake City is major destination.
e) _____ Temple Square is major destination.

20. What ist your current place of residence?

_____

    City   County   State/Zip-Code

21. What category best describes your party?

a) Husband and wife   e) Church charter group
b) Family with children   f) Civic charter group
c) Alone   g) Friends and relatives
d) Couple dating   h) Other (explain) _____

22. How many members are in your party?

a) 1   c) 3   e) 5   g) 10 – 20
b) 2   d) 4   f) 6 – 9   h) 21 – 50

23. Sex of person filling out questionnaire.

a) Male _____   b) Female _____

24. Age of person filling out questionnaire.

a) _____ 19 or less   d) _____ 40 – 49
b) _____ 20 – 29   e) _____ 50 – 59
c) _____ 30 - 39   f) _____ 60 or over

25. What is your religious affiliation? (Please be as specific as possible)

_____

26. Check the highest educational level completed.

a) Less than high school graduate   d) College graduate
b) High school graduate   e) Beyond college graduate
c) Some college

27. What is your occupation? (Check one)

a) Civil service, police or military   e) Other professional   i) Student
b) Clerk, salesman or clerical   f) Factory laborer   j) Housewife
c) Teacher or school administrator   g) Other laborer   k) Retired or disabled
d) Business or managerial   h) Farm owner or manager   l) Other (list)_____

28. What is the annual income of the person paying for the trip?

    a) less than 10,000   e) 25 – 29,999   i) 45 – 49,000
    b) 10 – 14,999   f) 30 – 34,999   j) 50,000 or more
    c) 15 – 19,999   g) 35 – 49,999
    d) 20 – 24,999   h) 40 – 44,999

29. What is your marital status?

30. Please feel free to make any additional comments.

Thank you for your cooperation.

Gisbert Rinschede

Catholic Pilgrimage Places in the United States

Introduction

Whoever takes an interest in the world-wide pilgrim phenomenon would look last for pilgrimage places in the Anglo-American cultural region, primarily because one assumes that North Americans are the least fond of pilgrim activities. The high proportion of U.S. pilgrims in the religious centers of Southern and Western Europe (Rome, Lourdes, Fátima and Medugorje), however, seem to contradict this prejudice.

If one were to search for places of pilgrimage in the United States, one would assume that they can be found primarily in the Spanish-Mexican-influenced South West and in Florida, as well as in French-influenced Louisiana. Far more important and numerous, however, are the pilgrimage places in the East, North-East and Mid-West which have been especially supported by German, Irish, Polish and Italian immigrants.

Until recently, little note has been taken of pilgrimage centers, especially by the national church, and they have not yet been discussed from a geographic, ethnologic and religious studies point of view, except a description of single shrines (THORNTON 1954) and two published papers (GRACIDA 1984 and PRESTON 1986) briefly dealing with theological and religious problems for the first time. Indications of the pilgrimage phenomenon in the U.S. are also absent from relevant works on the religions of America and from general geographic and regional manuals.

When dealing with this subject, some definition and delimitation problems occur in the use of the terms, "pilgrimage place" and "shrine". Both terms are often used synonymously; however, not every "shrine" is a "pilgrimage place".

- A "shrine" is, in its wider context, a place, where religious services are performed for saints or divinities. In this sense, every church and every temple is a "shrine". However, here it usually means a particular place of worship with a particular atmosphere and with corresponding religious activities.

- Only those "shrines" that attract religiously motivated visitors from places farther away than local surroundings are described as "pilgrimage places" here. In this respect, numerous shrines, represented under certain circumstances by important cathedrals and of great historical importance, are excluded, such as, for example, the missionary stations of the South West, which are outwardly similar to "pilgrimage places" because of their heavy tourist streams.

The study presented here is based on four research journeys lasting a total of four months in March/April 1986, April/May/June 1987, March/April 1988 and 1989, in the course of which 65 pilgrimage places in Oregon, California, Arizona, New Mexico, Texas, Colorado, Kansas, Oklahoma, Louisiana, Missouri, Illinois, Indiana, Ohio, Maryland, District of Columbia, Pennsylvania, New Jersey, New York, Vermont, Connecticut, Rhode Island, Massachussetts and Florida were visited.

The goal of this study is an investigation in the spatial dimensions of the pilgrimage places based on the social group of pilgrims; these are investigated according to number, type, origin, seasonality, means of transport, ethnicity, etc. Spatial aspects of pilgrim tourism and considerations for future development and planning of pilgrimage places form the conclusion.

I. Number and Distribution of Pilgrimage Places

1. Number

There are, at present, 126 pilgrimage places in the U.S. visited annually by varyingly large numbers of pilgrims. The Spanish missions in South California, Arizona, New Mexico and Texas are not counted here; although they may still possess national monuments, museums, retreat houses, convents or functional Catholic churches regularly visited by believers of the region, but they are primarily visited by thousands of tourists and therefore cannot be described as pilgrimage places here. Additionally, numerous important cathedrals in the centers of various cities such as New York, Detroit, St. Louis and San Antonio as well as single monumental statues and chapels are disregarded, although they are presented as shrines and pilgrimage places in older works (THORNTON 1954) and in lists of the National Conference of Catholic Bishops (GRACIDA 1984, NCCB 1986).

2. Distribution

Pilgrimage places are distributed in all cultural regions of the United States: in the Northwest, Southwest, West, South, Midwest, Midatlantic and in the New England states. A particular concentration can be found in the Midwest and in New England. In particular, the following federal states are presented by corresponding pilgrimage places:

Alabama 1, Arizona 2, California 3, Colorado 1, Connecticut 2, District of Columbia 3, Florida 3, Illinois 6, Indiana 1, Iowa 1, Kansas 1, Kentucky 5, Louisiana 7, Maryland 2, Massachusetts 10, Michigan 6, Minnesota 3, Missouri 5, Montana 1, Nebraska 1, New Hampshire 2, New Jersey 5, New Mexico 4, New York 13, Ohio 10, Oklahoma 1, Oregon 1, Pennsylvania 10, Rhode Island 1, Texas 4, Vermont 1, Washington 1, Wisconsin 9.

In general, the distribution of pilgrimage places corresponds with the concentration areas of Catholics according to ZELINSKY (1961), NEWMAN and HALVORSON (1980), among others (Fig. 1). Catholics represent the largest single religious denomination in the U.S. with 50 million members. Therefore, 40% of all pilgrimage places are represented in the urban Northeast — with a particularly high incidence in the Northeast (Fig. 2).

The second most important concentration area of Catholics and also of pilgrimage places is the Midwest, especially the area of the Great Lakes and the Mississippi/Missouri area around St. Louis. Particularly the metropolitan and industrial areas around Buffalo, Cleveland, Pittsburgh, Cincinnati, Chicago, Detroit, and St. Louis are strongly represented. This is because the time of urbanization and industrialization of America towards the end of the 19th Century coincided with a strong immigration wave of Catholics from Central and Eastern Europe.

The third concentration of Catholic pilgrimage places corresponds with the Spanish Southwest. Immigration of Mexicans to California, Arizona, New Mexico, and Texas increased the regional importance of the Catholic church and partly originated new pilgrimage places.

French Louisiana forms the fourth concentration area, with a number of Cajun and black Catholics. A series of pilgrimage places in New Orleans stem from the time of French influence.

A last concentration area is in Florida, where at first the Spanish influence was dominant, but where the stream of Cubans, tourists, and retirees from the North has caused an increasing concentration of Catholics and the establishment of pilgrimage places in the last few decades.

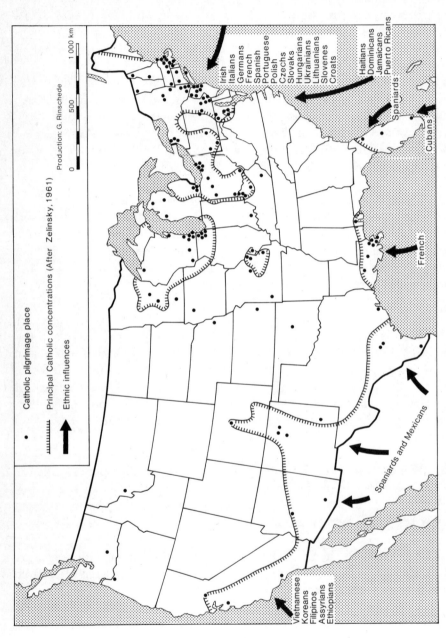

Fig. 1: Distribution of Catholic pilgrimage places in the United States, 1989
Source: Author's investigation 1986 – 1989

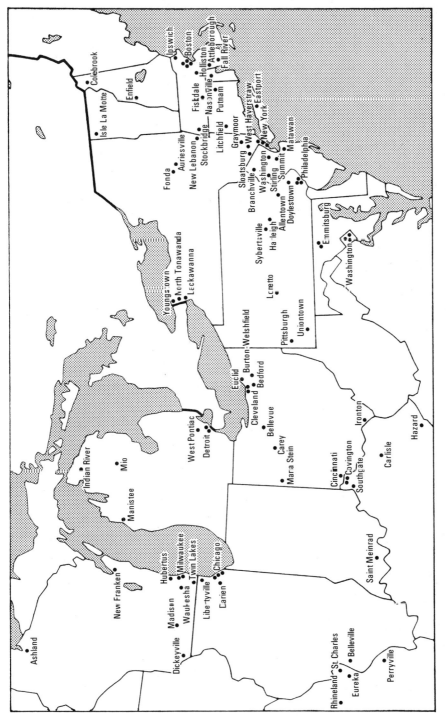

Fig. 2: Distribution of Catholic pilgrimage places in the northeastern United States, 1989
Source: Author's investigation, 1986 – 1989

In the remaining South and West, only a very small number of Catholics and, correspondingly, few pilgrimage places can be found.

II. Pilgrims as a Socio-Geographic Action Group

1. Pilgrim Motivation

Similar to Christian Europe pilgrimages are undertaken in the U.S. for religious reasons. However, there are regional differences, due to cultural and ethnic origins of pilgrims and types of pilgrimage places; these differences are essentially of a gradual nature.

With respect to the Spanish-Mexican inclination, important motives are the fulfillment of a vow, atonement and repentance as well as the search for a healing effect, a miracle, or solution of a personal, family, or work problem, e.g., in Chimayo, New Mexico. Chimayo is also known as the Lourdes of America, because many pilgrims are cured. Above all, families bring their sick children here. Even before the arrival of Spanish missionaries, this locality was worshipped as a holy place. There is still today, in a side room next to the high altar, a hole from which every pilgrim takes some earth in order to mix it with his food when sick (*Geophagy*).

In places of pilgrimage founded and visited by ethnic minorities such as the "National Shrine of Our Lady of Czestochowa" in Doylestown, Pennsylvania by Poles and the Shrine of Our Lady of Charity in Miami, Florida by Cubans, the pilgrimage contains cultural, national, and, in part, also political aspects, because the pilgrims were driven out of their native country or, because of the great distance, cannot make a pilgrimage to the national shrine in Czestochowa or Havanna. Often, just the possibility of being able to participate in services and confessions in their mother tongue alone, is of prime importance.

The pilgrimage place is, as a rule, treasured by established Anglo-Americans as a peaceful and tranquil place and eagerly visited for reasons of prayer, services, and quiet moments.

Social and recreational motives are nearly always combined with these religious motives. Pilgrims traveling in groups spend many hours on the shrine land picnicking and playing within the circle of their group (family, parish group, club, etc.). The recreational aspect of a pilgrimage is evident because large pilgrimage places in the United States were established in the immediate vicinity of major tourist attractions.

2. Number of Pilgrims

The 126 pilgrimage places in the U.S. are visited annually by over 7 million people. This figure is based on this author's studies and calculations. Without taking into account the fact that a number of people visit pilgrimage places several times a year, and that a certain number of pilgrims belong to other denominations, the annual pilgrims total 15% of all Catholics in the U.S.

The largest stream of pilgrims of between 500,000 and over a million per year are received by six places: (1) the "National Shrine of the Immaculate Conception" in Washington, D.C., (2) "Our Lady of the Snows" in Belleville, Illinois, the (3) "Virgen de San Juan del Valle Shrine" in San Juan, Texas, (4) "Our Lady of Czestochowa" in Doylestown, Pennsylvania, (5) "The Cross in the Woods at the Catholic Shrine" in Indiana River, Michigan, and (6) "Shrine of Our Lady of Charity" in Miami, Florida.

About ten other pilgrimage places, e.g., the (1) "Franciscan Monastery" in Washington, D.C., (2) "The Grotto, National Sanctuary of Our Sorrowful Mother" in Portland, Oregon, (3) the "Shrine of Our Lady of Martyrs" in Auriesville, New York, the (4) "Sanctuary of Christ of Chimayo" in Chimayo, New Mexico, the (5) "Our Lady of Fátima Shrine" in Youngstown, New York, (6) "Shrine of Our Lady of La Salette" in Attleborough, Massachussetts, and recently also the (7) "Mary, Queen of the Universe Catholic Shrine" in Orlando, Florida are visited by pilgrims numbering between 100,000 and 500,000 (Fig. 3).

Around 50 pilgrimage places are visited annually by between 10,000 and 100,000 pilgrims; approximately the same number of pilgrimage places are visited by less than 10,000 pilgrims.

Although the total number of pilgrims increases yearly, the development of single pilgrimage places differs greatly. Pilgrimage places, like the "Virgen de San Juan del Valle Shrine" in San Juan, Texas, the "Sanctuary of Christ of Chimayo" in New Mexico and the "National Shrine of Our Lady of Charity" in Miami, Florida, that are visited primarily by new minorities streaming into America, i.e., Mexicans, Poles, Cubans, Puerto Ricans, Filipinos etc., show a continuous increase in the annual number of pilgrims.

Pilgrimage places founded recently by strong religious organizations and orders, too, are experiencing a substantial increase in the number of the pilgrims, for example, the numerous Schoenstatt shrines in Wisconsin, and, especially, the "Shrine of the Immaculate Heart of Mary", established by the "Blue Army of Our Lady of Fátima" in Washington, New Jersey. Since the official opening of the latter in 1978, the stream of pilgrims has increased to 73,858 pilgrims

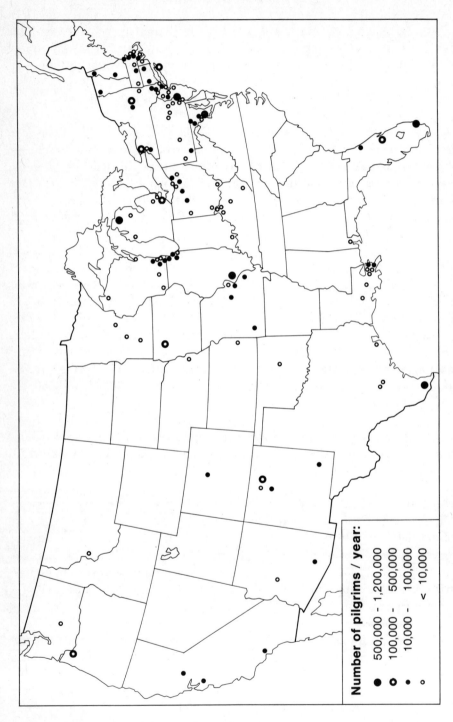

Fig. 3: Size of Catholic pilgrimage places by number of pilgrims per year in 1989
Source: Information of Shrine Offices, 1986 – 1989

Number of pilgrims / year:

500,000 – 1,200,000
100,000 – 500,000
10,000 – 100,000
< 10,000

in 1987, and to over 100,000 pilgrims in the Marian Year of 1988. Within a few years, this shrine will probably be counted among the ten great pilgrimage places of the U.S.

Other places, such as the "National Sanctuary of Our Sorrowful Mother" in Portland, Oregon and the "Shrine of Our Lady of the Snows" in Belleville, Illinois increase the numbers of visitors as ecumenical shrines by gradually attracting pilgrims of other religious faiths. Other pilgrimage places experience a sudden increase of visitors after building or improving access roads, e.g., in Chimayo, New Mexico. Many, such as the "National Shrine of the Immaculate Conception" in Washington, D.C., the "Our Lady of Fátima Shrine" in Youngstown and the new "Mary, Queen of the Universe Shrine" in Orlando also profit from increasing tourism to the federal capital Washington D.C., Niagara Falls and Disney World, respectively. The number of pilgrims rises particularly markedly after the canonization of the person worshipped at the pilgrimage place, as in the case of the "National Shrine of Elizabeth Ann Seton" in Emmitsburgh, Maryland and the "National Shrine of St. John Neumann" in Philadelphia, Pennsylvania.

Conversely, the number of pilgrims has been decreasing in the past few years in some shrines. This can be traced back to changed religious interests of the Catholics concerned. Time-related religious activities such as Novenas (Nine day prayers) in Belleville, among others, attract only a fraction of pilgrims, as compared to earlier days, and therefore had to be shortened to three weekend days.

Pilgrim numbers have declined in a series of places which initially relied mostly on their strong ties to ethnic groups such as the Ukrainians, the Hungarians and the Slovaks. Weakening of ethnic identity has meant fewer pilgrims to such places.

Poor travel connections (e.g., discontinuation of train services) and lack of interest in advertising and commercializing the shrine shown by directors are additional reasons for the decrease in the number of pilgrims.

In numerous pilgrimage places, pilgrim numbers decrease because their town surroundings have changed considerably in the course of the last decade. Thus, today some pilgrim churches in Chicago, Baltimore, New York, Philadelphia, Boston and Pittsburgh no longer find themselves in what used to be the privileged residential area of the metropolis, but rather in slum areas inhabited by the impoverished social strata of the population, and they are, therefore, generally avoided by pilgrims.

The establishment of a new place of pilgrimage in the immediate vicinity can also divert the stream of pilgrims from an old place and accordingly decrease its pilgrim numbers. On the other hand, the immediate vicinity of a large shrine, as in the case of the "St. Francis Monastery" near the "National Shrine" in Washington, D.C., can also attract additional pilgrims.

Changes in the popularity and attractiveness of the saints worshipped have also an effect on the size of the pilgrim stream to a holy place. Thus, in the U.S., in the last few years, the worhship of Saint Anthony and Saint Francis of Assisi has markedly decreased while the worship of The Virgin Mary and Saint Jude Thadeus has increased, resulting in corresponding effects on the development of places of pilgrimage.

3. Types

As a rule, visitors to an American pilgrimage place are, at the same time, pilgrims pursuing religious motives. If the pilgrimage place is, however, simultaneously of historical, cultural or architectural interest or characterized by its charming location in the countryside and particular festive activities during the year, it is also visited by tourists. In Chimayo, tourists can sometimes total 30 to 40% of a number of visitors. All Spanish mission stations in California, Arizona, New Mexico and Texas are visited solely by tourists, except for regular visits to attend religious services.

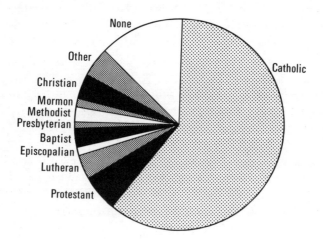

Fig. 4: Proportion of pilgrims by different denominations to "The Grotto, National Shrine of Our Sorrowful Mother" in Portland, Oregon, 1986
Source: Information (guest register) of the Shrine Office, 1987

A particular type of visitor to pilgrimage places is the participant in devotions, religious recreational activities and conventions of various types offered on shrine land. Such opportunities abound Portland, Belleville and West Haverstraw, among other places.

Along with Catholic believers an increasing number of members of other denominations are taking part in pilgrimages to Catholic places. Thus in Belleville around 35% and in Portland about 40% of all visitors are represented by non-Catholics. The faiths represented are primarily Protestant and Lutheran, but also Baptists and Methodists (Fig. 4).

4. Origin (Fig. 5 – 14)

The pilgrimage places in the U.S. are not of international importance. For this reason, they are only rarely visited by non-Americans. Thus, for example, the "Virgen de San Juan del Valle Shrine" in San Juan, TX, visited by Mexican-Americans, hardly ever attracts any pilgrims from neighboring Mexico despite its border location, since the Mexicans have enough old pilgrimage places at their disposal. On the other hand, some pilgrimage places in the Midwest and Northwest, such as the "Shrine of Our Lady of the Snows" in Belleville, Illinois, the "Shrine of Our Lady of Martyrs" in Auriesville, N.Y., and the "Our Lady of Fátima Shrine" in Youngstown, N.Y., attract a considerable influx of pilgrims from the neighboring Canadian provinces of Ontario and Québec. The "National Shrine of Our Lady of Czestochowa" in Doylestown, PA, is visited by numerous pilgrims of Polish origin from Canada and Mexico; some even come from the mother country Poland when they visit relatives and friends in the United States.

The "National Shrine of the Immaculate Conception" in Washington, D.C. financially controlled by the American Bishops, is of great national importance. It is visited by pilgrims from all dioceses that often engage a pilgrim representative responsible for organizing trips to Washington.

The ethnically orientated shrines attract pilgrims from all States in the U.S. — if only from a particular ethnic group. Thus, as already mentioned, Poles visit Doylestown, Mexico-Americans visit San Juan, and Cubans visit Miami.

Some other pilgrimage places are of great supraregional importance. For example, the Shrine in Belleville, Illinois attracts pilgrims from more than ten States within a radius of 500 miles. Slightly less important are the "National Sanctuary of our Sorrwoful Mother" in Portland, visited by pilgrims from the whole North-West, and the "Shrine of Our Lady of Martyrs" in Auriesville/N.Y. whose catchment area extends only to the whole of the Northeast.

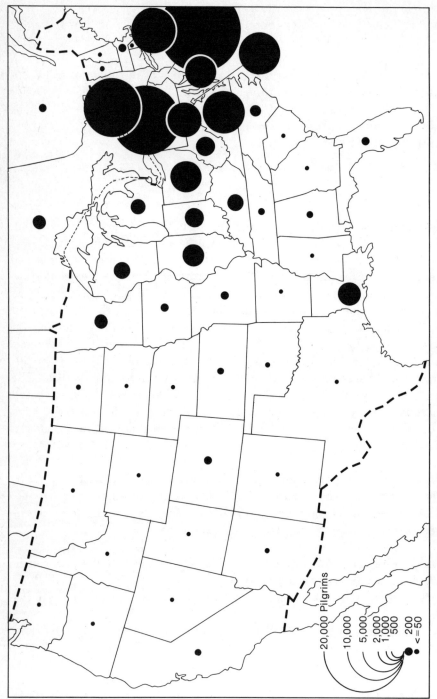

Fig. 5: Origin and number of registered pilgrims to the "National Shrine of the Immaculate Conception",
Washington, D.C., 1988
Source: Information of the Shrine Office, 1989

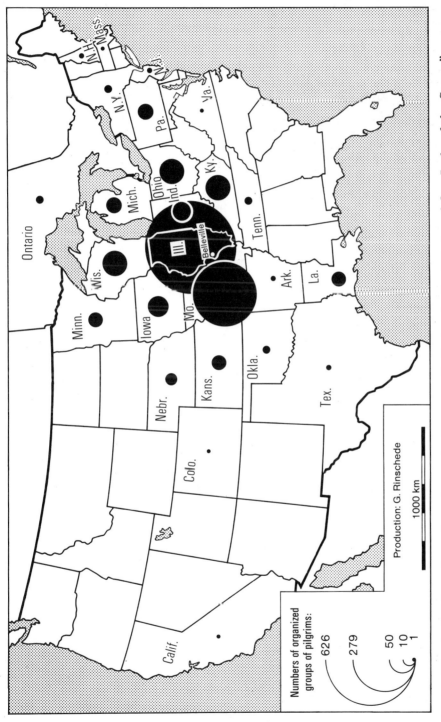

Fig. 6: Origin and number of organized groups of pilgrims to the "Shrine of Our Lady of the Snows",
Belleville, Illinois, 1986

Source: Information of the Shrine Office, 1987

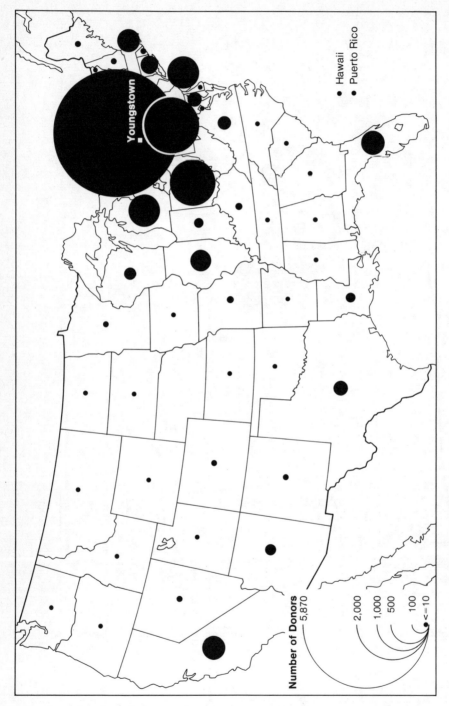

Fig. 7: Origin and number of donors to the "Our Lady of Fátima Shrine", Youngstown, New York, 1986
Source: Information of the Shrine Office, 1987

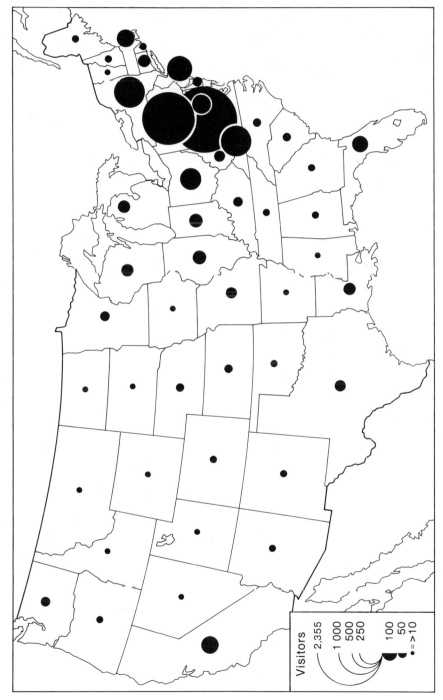

Fig. 8: Origin and number of visitors to the "National Shrine of Saint Elisabeth Ann Seton", Emmitsburg, MD, 1986
Source: Information (guest register) of the Shrine Office, 1987

78

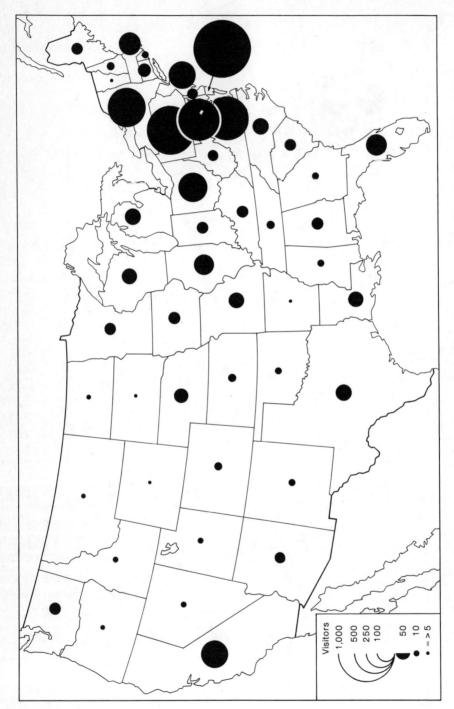

Fig. 9: Origin and number of visitors to the St.-Francis-Monastery in Washington, D.C., 1986
Source: Information (guest register) of the Shrine Office, 1987

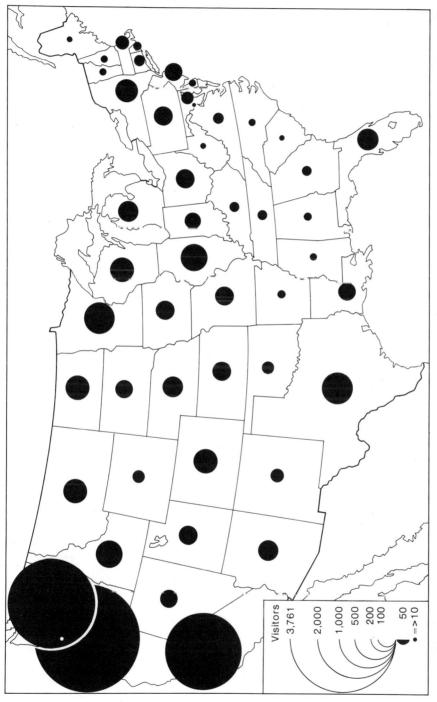

Fig. 10: Origin and number of visitors to "The Grotto, National Sanctuary of Our Sorrowful Mother", Portland, Oregon, 1986

Source: Information (guest register) of the Shrine Office, 1987

Visitors
3,761
2,000
1,000
500
200
100
50
• = >10

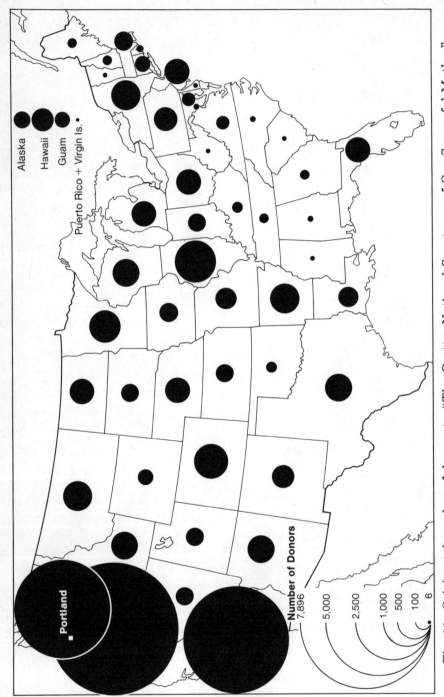

Fig. 11: Origin and number of donors to "The Grotto, National Sanctuary of Our Sorrowful Mother", Portland, Oregon, 1986

Source: Information (mailing list of donors) from the Shrine Office, 1987

The remaining pilgrimage places possess only regional importance. Their main catchment area extends only from their own state to neighboring states.

Urban areas constitute the most important sources of pilgrims in the Midwest, the Northeast and in New England. Disregarding the fact that high population density is to be found here, the following reasons explain this phenomenon:

- During weekends, numerous city inhabitants are drawn to the countryside or to the suburbs, where most of the pilgrimage places are also located.

- Above all, however, the largest part of the Catholic population lives in big cities of these regions, having immigrated at the time of industrialisation and found jobs there. They are primarily of Polish, Czech,

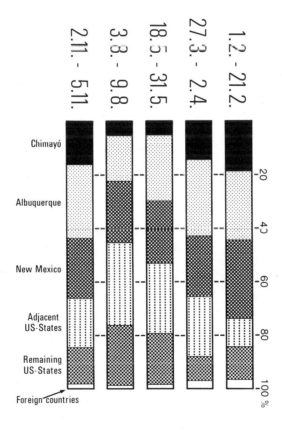

Fig. 12: Origin of visitors, in percent, to the "Sanctuary of Christ of Chimayo", New Mexico, 1987
Source: Information (guest register) of the Shrine Office, 1987/88

Hungarian, and Italian origin needed at that time as workers in industrial firms.

- The most recent, primarily Catholic, influx of immigrants from Cuba, Mexico, Puerto Rico, Haiti, the Philippines and South Korea also settled in cities.

With regard to those pilgrims coming from many parts of the U.S., especially from Florida, to the "Shrine of Our Lady of Charity" in Miami, one peculiarity connected with the deep roots of the Exile-Cubans in their native land is evident. In order to maintain the informal network of relationships and friendships that existed in Cuba, Bishop Ramon, the Director of the Shrine, keeps a computerized list of Cubans, arranged by municipality (The Confraternity of Our Lady of Charity) and forms municipality teams to call and summon each one of these 126 groups to periodic events at the shrine (Fig. 13). Three times a week and 126 times a year, pilgrimages by groups representing the 126 municipalities of Cuba — their home country — take place. In a similar manner, the Shrine invites each one of the six provinces to a Romeria, a festive occasion including a picnic lunch and a rosary procession around the shrine. Fig. 14 shows the origin of all members of the Confraternity that once lived in the six provinces of Cuba. In 1987, 35,000 members belonged to this Confraternity. The entire community is invited on September 8, the feast day of "Our Lady of Charity", when tens of thousands meet at a Miami stadium. The month of October is reserved for pilgrimages from various Latin American countries, as well as from Canada and Spain.

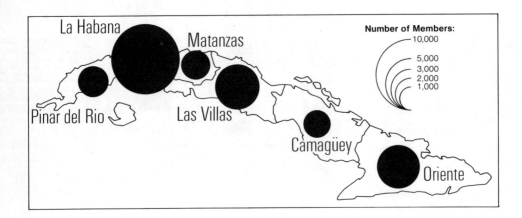

Fig. 13: Home origin of the members of the "Society of Our Lady of Charity" in Miami, 1980 (Exiled-Cubans)
Source: Information of the Shrine Office, 1987

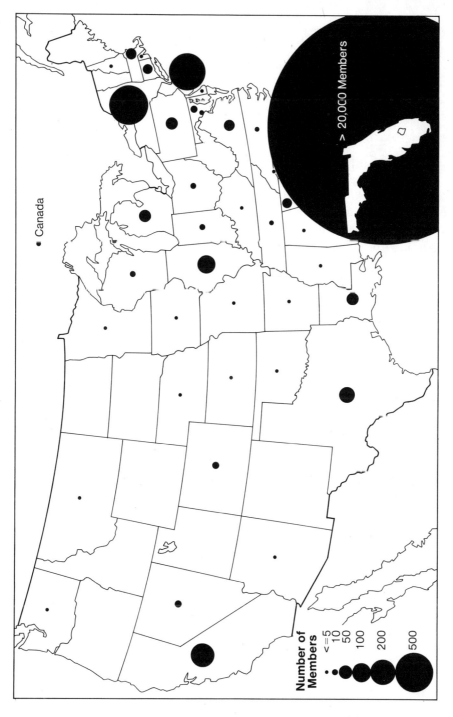

Fig. 14: Origin of members of the "Society of Our Lady of Charity", Miami, 1980
Source: Information of the Shrine Office, 1987

5. Seasonality (Fig. 15 – 20)

All pilgrimage places are open year round, with the exception of the "Open air shrines" such as, for example, in Auriesville, N.Y. and in Eureka, Missouri closing during the winter for climatic reasons. However, even among most of the shrines open all year, the pilgrim stream is generally characterized by a strong seasonality. The pilgrim year can be divided into the following two phases:

- The time of low pilgrim traffic from November to March (low season) and
- the high season from April/May to October.

In general, there is a trend at many pilgrimage places for the low season to become more important and for the high season to become longer. This is due partly to the increase in free time during the year, but also to the shorter working week with long weekends allowing short trips.

The high season lasting from April to October reaches its first high point in May and its second in September/October. During the vacation months of July/August, only some pilgrimage places register a particular peak as a result of strong tourist influx. As a rule, these summer months are of minor importance, because during this time organized pilgrimages decrease substantially.

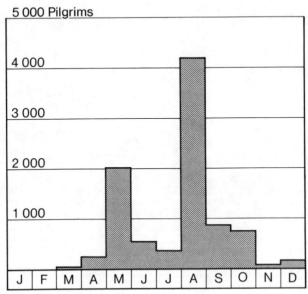

Fig. 15: Number of organized groups of pilgrims to the "Shrine of Our Lady of Consolation", Carey, Ohio, 1986
Source: Information of the Shrine Office, 1987

Weekends and, especially, Sundays are of particular importance during the week. Feast days are characterized by a strong influx of pilgrims: Palm Sunday, Easter, Whitsun, Mother's Day, various feasts of the Virgin Mary in Fátima (13th of each month from May to October). Particular festivities and events during Advent and Christmas time ("Way of Lights") have created a third and now most important season in Belleville, Illinois. However, in contrast to spring, summer and autumn seasons, at this time the overwhelming majority of pilgrims come from the adjacent areas.

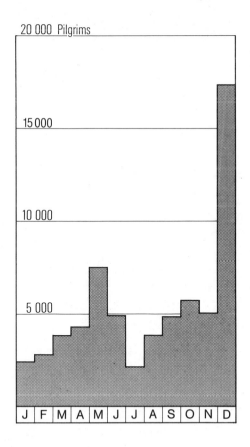

Fig. 16: Number of organized groups of pilgrims to the "Shrine of Our Lady of the Snows", Belleville, Illinois, 1986
Source: Information of the Shrine Office, 1987

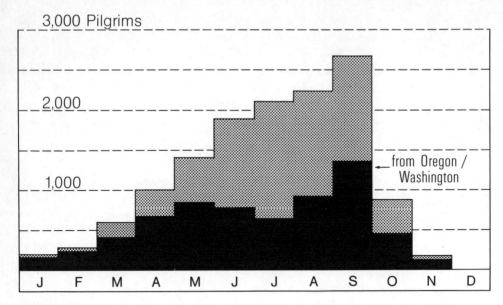

Fig. 17: Number of pilgrims to "The Grotto, National Shrine of Our
Sorrowful Mother", Portland, Oregon, 1986
Source: Information (guest register) of the Shrine Office, 1987

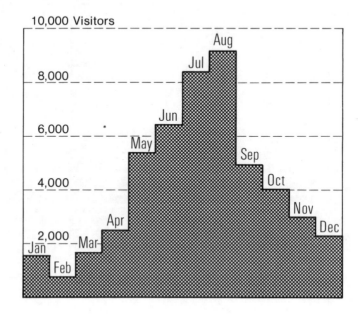

Fig. 18: Number of visitors to the "Sanctuary of Christ of Chimayo",
New Mexico, 1987
Source: Information (guest register) of the Shrine Office, 1987/88

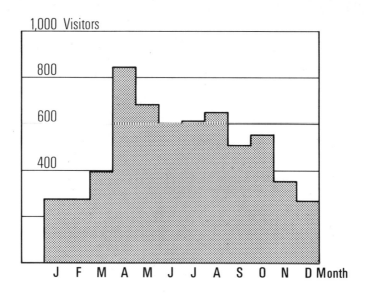

Fig. 19: Number of visitors to the "St. Francis Monastery of the Holy
Sepulchre", Washington, D.C., 1986
Source: Information (guest register) of the Shrine Office, 1987

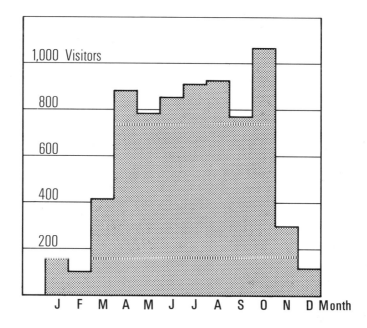

Fig. 20: Number of visitors to the "National Shrine of Saint Elisabeth Ann
Seton", Emmitsburg, MD, 1987
Source: Information (guest register) of the Shrine Office, 1988

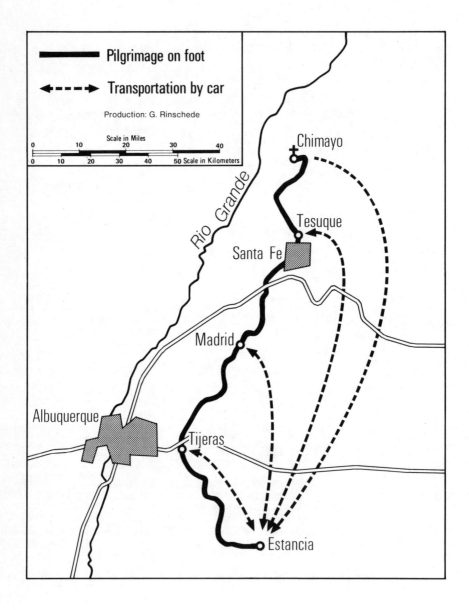

Fig. 21: Foot pilgrimage to the "Sanctuary of Christ of Chimayo", N. M. 1987
Source: Author's investigation, 1987

It can be claimed that year round pilgrimage places exist in the South and Southwest due to the mild climatic conditions. Thus, the pilgrim numbers in San Juan, Texas and Chimayo, N.M. are distributed more or less equally among all the seasons. In Miami (Cuban shrine), pilgrim groups of exiled Cubans come from the 126 communities of Cubans, according to a set plan, regardless of season, three days a week, so that the pilgrim numbers are equally distributed throughout the year. Added to this are the "Romerias" (feast days) of single provinces, also held at regular intervals during the year.

6. Means of Transportation and Forms of Organizations

Since the Catholic places of pilgrimage in the U.S. are very recent compared to European or Asian ones, and since the degree of motorization and the living standards of the population were already very high at the time of the establishment of pilgrimage places, the pilgrimage by foot could not develop as a tradition. It has never played an important role in the course of the young history of pilgrimages in the U.S.

Today, foot pilgrimage is still customary only in Chimayo, N.M., probably the oldest catholic pilgrimage place in the U.S. It has a long tradition here, because the pilgrimage place could not be reached by car until 1963, but people had made pilgrimages there for several generations. At that time, the pilgrimage was made on foot, horseback or donkey. Walking tours from the immediate surrounding start the evening prior to mass. Pilgrims walk through the whole night, covering 40 to 50 km, and arriving the next morning in time for the first Mass in Chimayo.

Some foot pilgrims cover distances of nearly 200 km to the pilgrimage place. These are primarily youth groups and women's groups (Society of Guadalupe, Legion of Mary, etc.) Priests from the diocese, together with the bishop and groups of demonstrators on annual peace marches come from all directions and cover about 40 km daily. It is, however, significant that generally only the distance to the pilgrimage place is covered on foot. The exhausted pilgrims are transported by relatives by bus or car at the end of their foot march and pilgrimage day back to their home town.

Foot pilgrims unable to find free accommodations for the night cover the whole pilgrim march in stages (Fig. 21). Thus, some pilgrims cover the distance to Chimayo from the Indian reservation South and West of Albuquerque in 4 to 5 day marches of 40 to 50 km each. At the end of the day, the group is picked up by relatives with cars or trucks and taken back to the starting point of the new day march the next morning, so that there are no accommodation costs. At the final destination, pilgrims are, as usual, picked up by car, so that in all only the vowed distance is covered on foot.

Pilgrims traveling by train are rare in the U.S. Some pilgrimage places existing since the beginning of the century or earlier, such as, for example, Auriesville, N.Y., Carey, Ohio and Starkenburgh, Missouri, were still visited after World War II until about 1955 by many pilgrims arriving by special train, where direct train connections to pilgrimage places existed. The pilgrims were greeted by the shrine-priests at the train station and led in a festive procession to the first service in the pilgrim church. These train services have now been discontinued.

Apart from a few exceptions, pilgrims nowadays reach the holy places by road, traveling either by bus or car. During the last decades, transport by bus has lost importance due to the increase in general motorization, so that, depending on the composition of the pilgrims, only up to 40% of all pilgrims reach the pilgrimage place by bus.

Among the groups chartering buses, church groups on a diocese or parish level are the most common. Diocesan groups are assembled in large numbers only for the National Shrine in Washington, since every diocese, as already mentioned, has a representative for the National Shrine and single dioceses in the U.S. have a certain responsibility and connection to the National Shrine.

In the views of pilgrimage place directors, parish groups are underrepresented, even if — like "The Grotto" in Portland in the Northwest — particular efforts are exerted by pilgrimage places to activate individual parish communities to undertake pilgrimages beyond the Marian year. To some extent, pilgrimage places are in competition with parish communities as a result of the heavy visitor's traffic on weekends and Sundays. For this reason, the "Our Lady of Charity Shrine" in Miami, for example, led by Bishop Ramon, does not allow any organized pilgrimages on Sundays.

School groups, particularly private Catholic schools, are strongly represented at pilgrimage places at special times. Various organizations and associations (Youth groups, Knights of Columbus, Senior Citizens, and women's groups, among others) as well as travel agencies and travel companies organize most groups.

Families from ethnic minorities are primarily found among the visitors who drive privately to the pilgrimage places, using this mode of transport for economic reasons or because of the wide freedom of movement it provides.

In the season lasting from March until October, schoolbuses generally visit the shrine primarily in April and May; private cars arrive mainly during the vacation from July to September; in autumn special school groups as well as various organizations and Senior Citizens return in buses and private cars.

7. Ethnicity of Pilgrims

Even today, pilgrim streams and pilgrimage places in the U.S. are, to a higher degree than one would suppose, composed of different ethnic groups. Only very few pilgrimage places, (e.g. Northwest: "The Grotto", Portland, in Colorado: "Mother Cabrini Shrine", Golden, and in Maryland, N.Y.: "National Shrine of Saint Elizabeth Ann Seton", Emmitsburgh and Manhattan) were established without any connection to ethnic groups and are, to this day, not visited by any significant percentage of ethnic pilgrim groups.

Around 10% of all pilgrimage places are visited exclusively by one specific ethnic group only. That ethnic group also founded the pilgrimage place and took a considerable part in the development of the shrine from the beginning. These are:

- "Sanctuary of Christ of Chimayo", N.M.: Indians and Mexican Americans.

- "Our Lady of Charity Shrine", Miami, FL: Exiled-Cubans.

- "National Shrine of Our Lady of Czestochowa", Doylestown, PA: Poles.

- "Our Lady of Poch, Mariapoch", Welshfield-Burton, OH: Hungarians.

- "The Ukrainian Catholic Shrine", Washington, D.C.: Ukrainians.

- "Holy Dormition Shrine", Sloatsburg, New York: Ukrainians.

Thus, the stream of visitors to the pilgrimage place of Chimayo in northern New Mexico is practically exclusively composed of Indians and Mexican Americans, aside from tourists, who have become more numerous since the construction of the access road in 1963, and who can reach it easily since the building of the "High Road of Taos". The Indians belong to the Pueblos and own 29 pueblos in the Rio Grande Valley. Even before the first contacts with Whites, the present pilgrimage place was worshipped by the Indians of the surrounding region as a holy place. Later, inhabitants of Chimayo brought the worship of the holy cross of Esquipulas in Guatemala to what is now New Mexico and combined the Indian pilgrimage place with a Christian holy place, nowadays worshipping "Christo de Esquipulas". The present pilgrim church in Chimayo was built to honor him between 1813 and 1816.

The "Virgen de San Juan del Valle Shrine" in San Juan, Rio Grande Valley, South Texas is visited exclusively by Mexican Americans. This is demonstrated by the fact that all services are held in Spanish. The Madonna worshipped here is a replica of the one in San Juan de los Lagos in Jalisco — the second largest Mexican pilgrimage place. The pilgrims had already developed their first connections to the pilgrimage place in South Texas in their old home country of Mexico. The stream of pilgrims to San Juan increases yearly due to the great distance to the original shrine in Jalisco, Mexico as well as due to a lack of passports.

A large part of the Mexican pilgrims belong to undocumented or illegal Mexicans who have been entering Texas, New Mexico, Arizona and California in tens of thousands every year since 1964 as a consequence of the restriction of legal entrance. The shrine offers these people the possiblility of taking part in a service, at a reasonable distance from their homes, within the family circle but still relatively anonymously.

The "Shrine of Our Lady of Charity" (Ermita de la Caridad) in Miami serves exclusively as pilgrimage place for the Hispanic population. Since there is a replica of the "Nuestra Señora de la Caridad" from Havanna, Cuba, it is visited primarily by Cubans in exile and also, however, by some other Hispanics from Mid and South America.

800,000 Cuban refugees arrived since 1959 and settled mainly in Miami. The Cuban refugees practically represent all levels of society, due to the various immigration periods and motives and thus form a cross-section of Cuba. The emigre Cubans came to the USA in the following migratory stages:

- The first stream consisted of "cronies of dictator Batista", who fled with their funds right at the beginning of the unrest/disorders (248,000).

- "Mostly small farmers whose lands were expropriated by the Castro government" came after the Cuban missile crisis (297,318).

- Between 1971 and 1979 only relatively few arrived via Spain and Mexico (38,903).

- The new immigrants after 1980 are called Children of the Revolution. They differ from earlier immigrants because they grew up under the communist system (126,000).

The "National Shrine of Our Lady of Czestochowa" is a pilgrimage place primarily for Polish Americans comprise more than 80% of the pilgrims. Polish immigrants left their native country, forced by political and social reasons, rather than religious ones, like many immigrants from the Netherlands, Germany, England, France and Switzerland. During the second half of the 19th century, Polish immigrants from German-controlled territories came first, and then Russian and Austrian Poles as well. After World War II, many political immigrants came, some of whom had taken part in anti-communist activities against the Russians. In the 70's a smaller influx of Poles came via South America and Africa. Most Poles arrived via New York and settled in the urban regions of the Northeast, Midwest and Midatlantic, where they very soon established parish churches. In 1960, there were 760 such Polish parishes, eight alone in Philadelphia, located south of Doylestown; the "National Shrine of Our Lady of Czestochowa" represents an important central pilgrimage place.

Other nationalities and ethnic groups are also represented among the pilgrims at the American Czestochowa. Following the Poles, the Haitians form the most important group since they, as blacks, chose the Black Madonna as their special patron saint. On particular feast and commemoration days Lithuanians, Germans, Italians and Filipinos also come to this place of pilgrimage.

Nearly all other pilgrimage sites display a strong ethnic component in their facilities and in their pilgrim numbers. Thus, the places in Washington, D.C., Belleville, Illinois, Youngstown, N.Y., Stirling, N.Y., Haverstraw, N. Y., Euclid, Ohio and others are visited mostly by a varyingly large proportion of ethnic pilgrim groups. As a rule, particular feast and commemoration days are reserved for the various groups. To be precise, these are the old immigrant groups from Western, Southern and Eastern Europe (Italians, Portuguese, Germans, Poles, Irish, Czechs, Yugoslavs, Ukrainians, Hungarians, etc.) as well as the more recent immigrant groups from Latin America (Hispanics) (Mexicans, Cubans, Haitians, Puerto Ricans, Jamaicans, Dominican Republicans, etc.) and from Asia (Vietnamese, Koreans, Filipinos, Lebanese, Assyrians, etc.) (Fig. 22).

Not only at the pilgrimage places of the Southwest does one encounter Mexican Americans and other Hispanics, but in the Midwest and the East as well. They are employed as seasonal workers or as resident workers in fields or factories of large fruit companies.

In the last few years, the number of Filipinos at pilgrimage sites has increased by leaps and bounds. Many of them are fellow exiles of Ferdinand Marcos settling in the States. Filipino immigrants can also be found at the pilgrimage places in Ohio and New York near the Canadian border (such as "Our Lady of the Snows", Belleville, Illinois and "Our Lady of Consolation" in Carey, Ohio) who have in the meantime been able to immigrate and become Canadian citizens as nurses in training or as doctors. In 1988, the American Filipinos held their first National Conference of American Filipinos within the framework of a pilgrimage to the "Shrine of Our Lady of the Snows", at which over 10,000 participants were expected.

94

After April 1975 — the time of the collapse of the South Vietnamese Republic — many Vietnamese arrived in the U.S., appearing soon after their arrival as pilgrims at the well-known holy places.

A particularly interesting ethnic pilgrim group at the "Shrine of Our Lady of Consolation" in Carey, Ohio, visited annually by 10 to 15% ethnic pilgrims, primarily Italians, Poles and Mexicans, is formed by Assyrians, who, as Eastern Catholics with Chaldean rites, have established themselves foremost in Michigan and have a parish there. They fled during the Kurdo-Iraq war of the 1970's and the Iraq-Iran war. Thus, on the 14th and 15th of August, 3,000 pilgrims from Southfield alone (near Detroit, Michigan) travel to Carey, OH because, among other reasons, according to them, they must cover nearly exactly the same distance to the place of pilgrimage as they would in Iraq from their home town to their religious center in Bagdad.

In conclusion, it can be established that pilgrims from older European immigrant groups continue to lose importance, with the exception of the Poles, and that pilgrims from more recent immigrant groups, primarily from the crisis

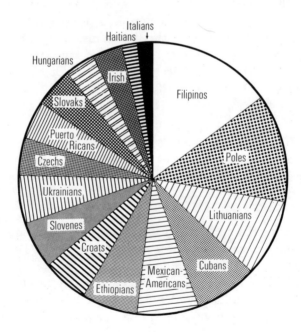

Fig. 22: Number of ethnic pilgrims to the "National Shrine of the Immaculate Conception", Washington, D.C., 1986 (estimated)
Source: Information of the Shrine Office, 1987

centers of Asia and Latin-America, are increasing rapidly. Regional concentration of ethnic pilgrimages is, in addition to certain locations in the Southwest and Southeast visited by Hispanics, at pilgrimage sites in the urbanized Midwest, Northeast and Middle Atlantic, where most new immigrants have found shelter.

III. Pilgrimage Places

The pilgrimage places in the U.S. differ considerably from pilgrimage sites in the old world. There are important differences in structure and function, as well as in origin, age, size, location, and relationship to the environment, although these are partly gradual.

1. Emergence and Establishment of Pilgrimage Places

In Europe, pilgrimage places emerged mainly because apparitions took place or miracles occured at that particular site and the place assumed church-historical relevance to give thanks for deliverance from some evil (see NOLAN 1988). These reasons for emergence play only a minor role in the U.S. Much more typical are those places for which a religious object (picture, statue, grotto, etc.) and its inherent rites were transferred from another place in Europe, and Middle America.

The Santuario de Chimayo, where a cross from Esquipulas, Guatemala was found, is one of the very rare shrines at which miraculous events occured before their erection. However, miracles are still said to occur there because of the "miraculous mud", already known of before the Spanish era.

Some shrines owe their origins to occurrences in the life of a saint or the church-historical development of a region. Disregarding most of the Spanish missions, primarily in California, as mainly touristic places, the "Mission San Xavier del Bac" on the Papago Indian Reservation in Tucson still possibly remains as a pilgrimage place with a church-historical background. It is still a functioning parish church, like many old mission stations, but does, however, receive some pilgrim groups during the year from the surroundings of Tucson, due in no small measure to the erection of additional cult places, such as, for example, a Lourdes grotto (1908).

Well-known pilgrimage places are also those shrines at which North American saints and martyrs are worshipped. Worth mentioning here are:

- The "Shrine of North American Martyrs" in Auriesville, N.Y. where, in 1642 and 1646, three missionary Jesuits were murdered by Mohawk Indians.

- The "National Shrine of Blessed Kateri Tekakwitha" in Fonda, N.Y., where a christianized Indian girl fell victim to the Indians.

- The "Mother Cabrini Shrine" in Golden, CO, dedicated to the first American citizen saint who died in 1917.

- The "National Shrine of Saint Elizabeth Ann Seton" in Emmitsburgh, Maryland who died and was buried here in 1921 and later canonized.

- The "National Shrine of John Neumann" in Philadelphia, PA who was canonized as a bishop in 1977.

- The "Shrine of the Blessed Philippine Duchesne" Mount City, KS.

In contrast, about half the pilgrimage places in the U.S. were established through the adoption of religious objects and their corresponding rites from the Old World and Middle America. As many as 60 shrines of the Virgin Mary, 14 shrines of Jesus Christ, 12 of Saint Anna and Saint Joseph and 28 shrines of additional saints of the Old World (St. Theresa 6, St. Francis 3, St. Jude 3 and others 16) were thus consecrated. Among the replicas of Old World pilgrimage shrines are notably:

- Lourdes Grottos (9)

- Fátima Shrines (4)

- Guadalupe Madonnas (2)

- Lady of San Juan de los Lagos (1)

- Shrine of Our Lady of Czestochowa (2)

- Shrine of Our Lady of La Salette (2)

- Shrine of Our Lady of Mariapoch (2)

- Shrine of Our Lady of Levocha (1)

- Shrine of the Miraculous Medal (2)

- Infant of Prague Shrine (1).

These replicas occupy a central function in the pilgrimage place and gave the whole site its name. The Lourdes Grottos, Fátima Shrines and statues of other saints erected only later as an addition to numerous pilgrimage places are not counted here.

Compared with Catholic pilgrimage places in Europe and in Latin America, whose beginnings partly go back to the early Christian times and the Middle Ages, i.e., in the first three centuries of the Latin-American colonization history, the places in the U.S. are of much more recent date.

The oldest pilgrimage sites originated, in some way, through the early missionary activity. Thus, the mission stations "San Xavier del Bac" in Tucson (1692) and "Nombre de Dios, Our Lady of La Leche" in St Augustine, FL (1620) reach back to the 17th century. The shrines "Christo de Chimayo" (1844) and "North American Martyrs Shrine" in Auriesville (1885) can be attributed to this period. Over two-thirds of shrines began, however, in the 20th century: the first shrines with Lourdes Grottos were built after 1908, the 50th anniversary of the apparition in Lourdes, and the first Fátima shrines were built after World War II, primarily in the sixties.

In the second half of the nineteenth century, a series of pilgrimage places evolved and are today mostly basilicas in large city centers, such as the "Basilica of Our Lady of Sorrows" in Chicago, the "Basilica of Our Lady of Perpetual Help" in Boston, "Nuestra Señora de la Conquistadora" in Santa Fé, the "Franciscan Monastery of the Holy Sepulchre" in Washington, D.C., and others. During the same period, cults of veneration started in the Midwest which were transferred from Western Europe to the New World by settlers and their clergy, like the "Shrine of Our Lady of Sorrows" in Rhineland, Missouri, the "Shrine of Our Lady of Consolation" in Carey, Ohio, the "Sorrowful Mother Shrine" in Bellevue, Ohio, and others. The "North American Martyrs Shrine" in Auriesville, New York also belongs to this period.

During the world economic crisis, the "Shrines of St. Jude Thaddeus" in Chicago and Orleans came into existence when the "Patron of Hopeless and Difficult Cases" was in particular demand.

The emergence of Polish, Hungarian, Bohemian and Ukrainian pilgrimage places occurred during the 1930s, but also the 1950s, although, at that time, only very few of these ethnic groups were able to migrate to the United States. The beginning of the Mexican "Virgen de San Juan del Valle Shrine" in San Juan, Texas also falls into this same period.

Apart from the Cuban "Shrine of Our Lady of Charity" in Miami, which was established in 1973, no additional truly ethnic pilgrimage places were founded during the 60s, 70s or 80s. Typical for this period are the Fátima shrines (Putnam, CT, Boston, MA, Washington, N.J. and others) the first of which came into being after the 50th anniversary of the appearance of Mary in 1917.

In addition, numerous shrines have come into existence like "Our Lady of the Snows" in Belleville, IL, the "Carmelite Spiritual Center" in Darien, IL, and the 80s, the "Shrine of Our Lady of Peace" in Santa Clara, CA, still under construction, and the "Mary, Queen of the Universe Shrine" in Orlando, FL, both of which were founded by parishes. In Santa Clara, a 120 foot high statue, visible from afar, was erected because, in the opinion of the founder, American Catholics need a pilgrimage place particularly on the West Coast. In Orlando, where 50 million tourists visit Walt Disney World, a large place of worship was needed for the spiritual care of tourists. As a result, the "Mary, Queen of the Universe Shrine" serves as religious antithesis to the nearby Epcot Center and to Cape Kennedy, which represent the technical side of the Universe.

The "National Shrine of the Immaculate Conception" in Washington, D.C., begun in 1926 and finished only in 1959, counts among the shrines established during this period, resulting from a particular wish to worship the Virgin Mary.

2. Worship Rites at Pilgrimage Places

Among the pilgrimage places of the Old World, the Marian worship cults are the most strongly represented. It is therefore not surprising that this preference has continued in the New World. In over 50% of all pilgrimage places in the U.S., worship of the Virgin Mary is of central importance and frequently also contained in the name. The second most important subject of devotion is Christ, whose worship as a cult figure amounts to more than 10% of the pilgrimage sites.

Saints assume a central function in pilgrimage places in the U.S. to a far higher degree than in Europe and other continents. The members of the holy family (St. Joseph or even St. Anne) can be mentioned in the first place, as well as St. Theresa, St. Francis and St. Jude. Especially St. Jude Thaddeus enjoys particular affection as the patron of the hopeless, as the saint of the miracles, or the saint for difficult and apparently impossible cases. American saints such as St. Francis Cabrini, St. John Neumann, and the three "North American Martyrs", St. Kateria Tekakwitha, St. Elisabeth Ann Seton and St. Philippine Duchesne, hold a small proportion of worship of saints at places of pilgrimage.

Changes in the population structure in the surroundings of the pilgrimage place due to mobility or to integration of immigrant ethnic groups into American society, together with a switch of religious interests and needs have led to the ascent and decline and to a difference in the religious objects for worship, religious observance and other activities, partly also as counter-reaction by the shrine administration.

This process can be followed in statu nascendi at a number of ethnic shrines whose founding ethnic groups are gradually losing importance. This is the case, for example, in the Hungarian "Shrine of the Weeping Madonna of Mariapoch" in Welchfield, Ohio, established by Hungarian priests and a religious order in 1956 after the Hungarian uprising, when over 200,000 Hungarians fled to the West. Visited exclusively by Hungarian immigrants from Ohio and the rest of the Midwest until 15 years ago, it soon had to open to English-speaking pilgrims as well. Statues and shrines were erected: Shrine of Our Lady of Fátima (1958), Station of the Sorrowful Mother (1959), St. Ann's Shrine (1967), Our Lady of Lourdes Statue (1969), Calvary Cross (1970) and the Statue of St. Anthony (1971). The building of further statues is not yet finished. The Polish shrine "Black Madonna of Czestochowa" in Eureka, MO has been provided with numerous grottos and statues since 1938.

The same is true for "The Grotto — The Sanctuary of Our Sorrowful Mother" in Portland, OR, where the "Shrine of Christ Carrying his Cross" (1931), St. Philip (1927), Sacred Heart Shrine (1951), Stations of the Cross (1940), The Calvary Scene (1951) and the Resurrection Shrine (1980) were erected.

The "National Shrine of Our Lady of Lourdes" in Euclid, OH shows a strong ethnic component in its pilgrim structure and has been equipped during the years with statues of National Saints aimed at particular ethnic groups such as, for example, St. Anthony of Padua for the Italians, St. Patrick for the Irish and the Infant of Prague for the Bohemians and Slovaks, besides its existing statues of St. Theresa, St. Anna, St. Jude, Our Lady of Fátima, Sacred Heart and Blessed Mother suited to all pilgrims.

The "Our Lady of Fátima Shrine", begun in 1956 in Youngstown, N.Y., in the meantime, has been enriched by 112 different lifesize statues, of which 20 alone represent Mary, 7 Jesus Christ while the other 85 represent saints from every race, nationality and walk of life.

The "National Shrine of the Immaculate Conception" in Washington, D.C. was founded particularly for the worship of Mary as the patroness of American Catholics. In addition to Mary, a total of 148 different saints from all over the world are worshipped with various statues, relief-statues, bas-reliefs, mosaics, paintings, glass windows, etc. Founded by religious orders and layman associations from various ethnic groups, the national pilgrim church displays the history of Catholicism in the U.S. and provides a mirror image of various population groups.

100

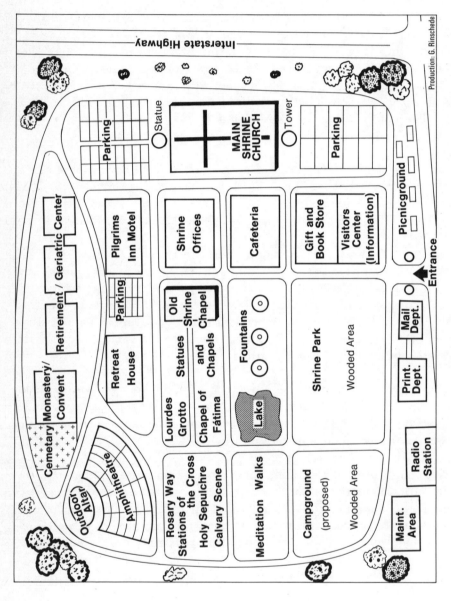

Fig. 23: Model of a Catholic pilgrimage place in the United States
Source: Author's investigation 1986 – 1989

3. Size, Structure and Facilities of Pilgrimage Places

a) Size

The size of a pilgrimage place in the U.S. ranges from fractions of an acre, as in the case of the "International Shrine of St. Jude" in the center of New Orleans and the "Shrine of Our Lady of Charity" in Miami, to several hundred acres, as in the case of the "Shrine of Our Lady of the Snows" on the outskirts of the town of Belleville, Illinois (ca. 200 acres), the "National Shrine of Our Lady of Czestochowa" (240 acres) and the "Marian Shrine" in West Haverstraw, N.Y. (250 acres).

Pilgrimage places of so large an area are, of course, possible only in rural regions at an appropriate distance from large population centers. Thus, in the Hudson Valley, for example, north of New York City, many pilgrimage places were established immediatedly after the world economy crisis, when rich bankers and business men from New York sold their properties (country homes and farms) to religious institutions or religious orders which at that time had enough money available and did not need to pay sales tax. "Graymoor", N.Y. and the "Shrine of Our Lady of Perpetual Help" in Uniontown, PA are examples.

The sanctuary itself can be the size of a small chapel or a parish church or possess a cathedral, as is the case with the "National Shrine of Our Lady of Victory" in Lackawanna, N.Y. and the "National Shrine of the Immaculate Conception" in Washington, D.C., which has the 7th largest church in the world. The size of the saints' images worshipped in these churches — primarily images of Mary — extend from decimetres, as in the case of Santo Niño and Senior Santiago de Chimayo in Chimayo, N.M. and "Our Lady of Consolation" in Carey, Ohio, to the monumental statues such as "Our Lady of the Rockies", erected on a 8,500 feet high mountain near Butte, MT and visible from afar, or "Our Lady of Peace" in Santa Clara, CA (both 90 feet high).

b) Structure and Facilities (Fig. 23)

The structure and facilities of a pilgrimage place are determined by the surface area available, the location and time of foundation and, last but not least, by the number and needs of the pilgrims. Smaller pilgrimage sites with a very small regional catchment area often limit themselves to a sanctuary, a few additional statues and, among other things, possibly even another worship cult in the form of a Lourdes Grotto. Toilet facilities and a small religious article shop are often also available for the convenience of pilgrims. Medium and large sized pilgrimage places have much more extensive structures at their disposals; they will be described here in detail.

All facilities at a pilgrimage place can be ordered into the following categories:

- Religious Sites

- Information Facilities

- Religious Article Shops and Book Stores

- Room and Board Facilities

- Public Relation Facilities (Radio Station and Mail Department)

- Educational and Recreational Facilities

- Other Facilities

Religious Sites

The most important part of every pilgrimage site and its center of concentration center are the religious places, which, as a rule, also represent the starting point of all other facilities.

The sanctuary, usually represented by a shrine church, is in the center. It can, as already mentioned, be the size of a small chapel, which was the historical starting point of the pilgrimage place, a minor basilica, such as "Our Lady of Consolation" in Carey, Ohio, or a major basilica or cathedral, such as in Washington, D.C. On the shrine land in Belleville, Illinois, now only an outdoor church, an underground basilica will be built shortly similar to and in imitation of the subterranean basilica of Pius X in Lourdes.

This main shrine church is often not the only church or place of worship on the pilgrimage site. There is often also an old church, the old original shrine church, as in the "Our Lady of Fátima Shrine" in Youngstown, N.Y., the "National Shrine of Our Lady of Czestochowa" in Doylestown, PA and many more. As a rule, it became too small a few years after the foundation of the pilgrimage place and was replaced by a larger church because of the increase in pilgrim numbers. The original shrine church is often still a functional parish church, as, for example, in San Juan, Texas, where the original replica of "Our Lady of San Juan, Jalisco", Mexico was worshipped.

A series of chapels which serve particular worship rites are usually joined to these shrine churches in almost all pilgrimage places. They can be found in the main church, in side chapels or as crypt churches in the basement, as in the National Shrine in Washington, D.C. or outside on shrine site. There are some replicas of the original "capelinha" of Fátima among these outdoor chapels, as in Youngstown, N.Y. or Washington, N.J.

In very few pilgrimage places, the outdoor church represents a kind of open air altar, the only large place of assembly, allowing all pilgrims to take part in services on the important pilgrimage days. Thus the outdoor altar combined with an amphitheater in Belleville seats more then 6,200 and allows a total of 20,000 worshippers to observe devotions at the outdoor altar. In general, however, outdoor altars have only a complementary function for special events and liturgies.

Where enough space is available and where the site suggests it, grottos provided with seats and used for services are also constructed such as on the shrine land in San Antonio/Texas, Portland/Oregon, Tucson/Arizona, etc. In most pilgrimage places of the Midwest and Northeast, which, in contrast to the strongly Spanish influenced places of the South and Southwest, are multiethnic, replicas of Lourdes grottoes, are one of the first religious items an existing pilgrimage place would use for expansion.

A number of outdoor statues, similar to the above-mentioned chapels and grottos were only added in the course of time, count among the religious places. They are often part of Rosary Ways/Rosary Gardens of the Joyful or Glorious Mysteries or of the Outdoor Way of the Cross, the Calvary Scene, or the Holy Sepulchre. Many other lifesize statues have been added. Thus, as already mentioned, 112 different statues of Christ, Mary and other saints were erected in the space of 30 years in Youngstown, N.Y. alone; they give the pilgrimage place a particular character.

Special attention must be paid to overdimensional crosses and larger than life size statues which are between 9 and 90 feet in size and usually visible from afar on raised locations. The largest statue was erected on a 2500 m peak near Butte, Montana in 1985, others can be seen in West Haverstraw, N.Y. (46 foot), in Altadena, CA (32 foot), in Golden, CO (22 foot) and in Carey, OH (18 foot).

Only very recent pilgrimage places, such as the "Virgen de San Juan del Valle Shrine" (Mex.) in Texas, the "Shrine of Our Lady of Charity" (Cub.) in Miami or the "National Shrine of Our Lady of Czestochowa" (Pol.) in Doylestown, PA, supported by only one ethnic group and hardly visited by other ethnic groups, do not have any, or only very few, additional shrines (i.e., pictures, statues and grottes) besides their main cult objects.

Monasteries and convents situated in the immediate neighborhood on shrine land are to be counted among the religious sites of a pilgrimage place. While European pilgrimage places like Lourdes and Fátima have attracted numerous religious orders over the years, this is not the case in the U.S. On the contrary, here the establishment of the pilgrimage place itself proceeds from the religious orders, who, according to some calculations, still administer about 80% of places. The adjoining convent or monastery buildings house the shrine offices for managing the shrine.

Information Facilities

Information facilities are available to varying degrees at pilgrimage places. Audiovisual or multisensory presentations, lectures and tours are offered to pilgrims; senior citizens are taken around by tour trains in cases of long distances between single locations, such as in Belleville or West Haverstraw. In places like Auriesville, N.Y., Emmitsburgh, MD, Golden, CO and soon also Orlando, FL, small museums can be visited to illustrate the works of the saints and martyrs worshipped at that place. At other pilgrimage places, such as Euclid, OH and Belleville, IL, smaller information and visitor centers are available and visited, as a rule, by pilgrims immediatedly upon arrival.

Religious Article Shops and Book Stores

Further information can be found in religious article shops and special book stores available at every pilgrimage place. The shrine book stores are often the most important religious book stores in the whole federal state, such as for example the one at "The Grotto — Our Lady of the Snows" in Portland. For this reason numerous non-pilgrims also like to go there in order to obtain religious literature.

The religious article shops offer religious literature, postcards, pictures and priests' clothing, as well as bottle openers, chocolate bars, letter openers, coffee mugs, pens, coloring books, pot holders, plates and saucers. Most of these items bear readily identifyable symbols of the shrines.

Food and Hotel Facilities

The boarding and accommodation facilities, offered in practically every pilgrimage place in varying forms of intensity and quality, are another important part of a pilgrimage place. Since pilgrims stay on shrine land for several hours and up to a day, they must be provided with food, because other restaurants and grocery stores are often too far away.

In larger pilgrimage places restaurants, cafeterias and snackbars are open at all hours at the pilgrims' convenience. In medium sized and small places visited by pilgrim groups at particular times, reservations must be made. Sometimes, as at the shrine in Doylestown, it is possible to prepare one's own food and drink. If there is enough space on the land, as is the case with all the more recent pilgrimage places situated at the edge of cities, picnic grounds are available and, in some cases, picnic tables are set up. On the new, not yet fully developed land of the Blue Army Shrine in Washington, N.J., which is far away from the town supply centers, so-called outdoor food concession trucks can be found on important pilgrimage days (13th of every month from May to October, at weekends and with larger groups also by reservation).

Accommodation facilities are made available to pilgrims in some larger pilgrimage places located very far from the next town or from a tourist center. Thus, the shrines in Belleville, IL, in San Juan, TX, and the older shrine in Carey, OH have, respectively, a Pilgrim's Inn Motel and a Pilgrims House at their disposal, run, similar to restaurants, by layman associations or by religious orders. Since pilgrims are more mobile than at the turn of the century, they spend less time at the pilgrimage place than in the past, and undertake touristic activities alongside the religious ones in the immediate and more distant surroundings of the shrine; therefore, some old pilgrims houses without modern comforts lose their guests. On the other hand, others attract tourist groups as well and offer the possibility of cheap overnight accommodations from which to visit neighboring pilgrimage places or tourist attractions in a sort of star-shaped hub-tour, such as in Belleville.

The possibility of camping on shrine land in a tent area was until recently only offered in American Czestochowa in Doylestown. Construction of a campground in Belleville, on a newly acquired piece of land at the edge of the shrine, is under discussion; this would make cheap overnight accommodation in tents, caravans and mobile homes possible.

Public Relations Facilities (Fig. 24 – 25)

In order to fulfill their manifold duties, pilgrimage places also attempt to come into contact with people outside the shrine through modern media. So far, no place has its own television station, but the shrines in Belleville and New Orleans, managed by the Oblates, have their own radio stations.

One of the two radio stations in Belleville has been transmitting since 1967 as a non-religious station (WMRY-FM 101), a commercial program aimed, above all, at the St. Louis metropolitan area. WMRY also makes possible the radio information service with its special programming for the blind and physically handicapped. It is a non-profit, non-commercial and non-sectarian closed-circuit radio station and provides up-to-date information, continuing educational and motivational programs.

The "International Shrine of St. Jude" radio station, also run by the Oblates in New Orleans, broadcasts Sunday programs through 11 different radio transmitters ranging between Houston, Texas in the West, Florida in the East and Alexandria/Louisiana, in the North. At the time of solemn novenas in spring, summer and autumn, these program are broadcast daily. During this time, a Sunday television program is broadcast in New Orleans itself.

The Oblate shrine in San Juan, Texas also transmits short religious radio programs in Spanish to 10 different local radio stations between El Paso in the West and San Antonio and Houston in the North, as well as stations in Berlin, Wisconsin and Caldwell, Idaho, in order to be received by all the Mexican itinerant workers during harvest time.

There are special facilities for printing and sending letters in almost all shrines. The "Blue Army Shrine" in Washington, N.J. and the "Our Lady of Fátima Shrine" in Youngstown, N.Y. publish periodicals such as the "North American Voice of Fátima".

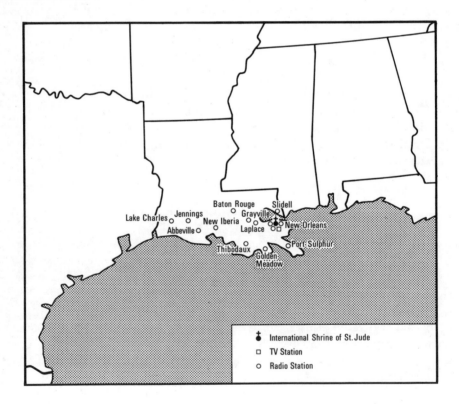

Fig. 24: Radio stations with religious broadcasts from the "International
Shrine of St. Jude", New Orleans, Louisiana, 1987
Source: Information of the Shrine Office, 1986/87

Fig. 25: Radio stations with religious broadcasts from the "Virgen de San Juan del Valle Shrine",
San Juan, Texas, 1987

Source: Information of the Shrine Office, 1986/87

Educational and Recreational Facilities

Educational and "some kind" of recreational facilities, also situated on the pilgrimage sites, are closely connected with other facilities. So-called renewal centers and retreat houses on all large pilgrimage places accommodate religious orders, priests and nuns, parish groups, married couples and young people for days of recollection, weekend retreats, and retreat camps. There is sometimes a special youth center with corresponding recreational facilities, such as in West Haverstraw, N.Y.

Some pilgrimage places, like those in Belleville/Ill., San Juan, TX, and Youngstown/N.Y. also have facilities for the special care of the needy, such as retirement centers, nursing homes or geriatric centers for elderly retired people. In Graymoor, N.Y. there is even an shelter for the homeless, developed into a rehabilitation clinic for alcohol and drug abusers in the 60s.

Walks (often memorial walks) in well-designed shrines parks and open courtyards equipped with religious statues, chapels, Way of the Cross and Rosary Way figures as well as fountains and reflecting ponds serve the recreation and meditation of shrine visitors. Examples of this are in Carey, OH, Stirling, N.Y., Washington, N.J., West Haverstraw, N.Y., etc. A "performance place" in Doylestown, PA shows Polish pilgrim folkloric performances as entertainment.

Other Facilities

Every shrine requires adequate parking facilities for pilgrims arriving by bus and car; these are easily available for recently built pilgrimage places at the edge of a town or in the countryside. The lack of parking facilities at shrines in urban areas or even in old town centers has affected the size of the pilgrim influx. Particular maintenance areas for the care of shrine and park land are necessary.

All pilgrimage places founded and managed by religious orders have a cemetery on their land. The cemetery at the "National Shrine of Our Lady of Czestochowa" in Doylestown, PA is of a special kind. The idea was to unite the mortal remains of those Poles who cherished a special devotion to Our Lady of Czestochowa at this American Czestochowa shrine that became a center of religious and cultural life for Polish Americans over the years. In the cemetery, a small section is reserved for Pauline Monks and secular priests of the shrine. Volunteers have their own section next to the religious section. Another section is reserved for special benefactors of the shrine who have given financial aid or made other contributions to the shrine. Honored Poles who contributed to Polish culture, literature, music, art and science, or those who are recognized as national heroes are buried in a larger section. There is also a large section called the "Polish Arlington" provided for Polish veterans of World Wars I and II. These simple graves are marked with the white Polish military cross. The general section is mostly occupied by Poles from Pennsylvania and the surrounding states of New York, New Jersey, Delaware, Maryland, etc. Some also come from Arizona, California and Florida where they spent their retirement. They all wanted to be buried on what is considered native soil near their Madonna.

4. Location of Pilgrimage Places

In their short history the locational factors for Catholic pilgrimage places have undergone certain changes. Besides the new places with Indian origins, such as Chimayo for example, the first pilgrimage places of the 19th century were situated primarily in the centers of large cities. These were large churches, basilicas and cathedrals, as well as smaller chapels, such as in Albuquerque, Chicago, New Orleans, Baltimore, Boston, Detroit, New York, Philadelphia, Lackawanna, etc. They were the annual destination of thousands of pilgrims from the immediate and more distant surroundings. Some parishes and churches, however, also developed earlier pilgrimage places in country surroundings such as Starkenburg–Rhineland, MO and Carey, OH closely imitating European worship rites.

Apart from a few exceptions, such as the "Shrine of Our Lady of Charity" in Miami, almost all pilgrimage places founded in the last decades are situated outside big towns, on their outskirts or in rural areas, where enough building land was available at reasonable prices. This is the case of Doylestown, Belleville, Youngstown, etc. The consideration of placing pilgrimage sites in more pleasant surroundings closer to nature to attract and make comfortable, urban pilgrims certainly also played a part.

Some of the pilgrimage places located on the outskirts of cities in the first half of this century have since been caught up by the expansion of the cities. This is the case in Portland, Euclid, Cleveland, Washington, D.C. and New York City.

Access has always been of primary importance for the development of pilgrim numbers and consequently the development of the pilgrimage place itself. After numerous rail connections to many pilgrimage places were discontinued, road access to pilgrimage sites played an increasingly important part. Thus, the really large pilgrimage places, such as San Juan, TX, Belleville, IL and Orlando, FL are located within easy access to interstate highways.

Pilgrimage places always have to be visible from afar, too. They are fleetingly noticed by passing traffic on interstate highways and indicated at exits, so they can be easily found. Churches, monumental crosses and statues erected on hills and provided with high towers aim at a similar effect.

The proximity to large tourist attractions has proved to be particularly advantageous. Thus, the positive development of the "Our Lady of the Snows" shrine in Belleville can certainly only be understood by considering the city of St. Louis situated opposite on the west bank, which attracts large tourist streams every year. The "Way of Lights", an annual light show with religious and Christmas motifs started 8 years ago on shrine land, was nominated the First Top Event of the year in 1986. The importance of the pilgrimage place in Chimayo, N.M. has increased for pilgrims and tourists, when the adjacent High Road to Taos was finished and the holy place became a historical landmark in 1970. The location of the "Our Lady of Fátima Shrine" in Youngstown, N.Y., just a few miles north of the Niagara Falls, has doubtlessly attracted additional pilgrims and contributed to the rapid rise of the shrine.

These experiences seem to have been taken into account in establishing a pilgrimage place in Orlando, Florida. A church was needed a few miles from Disney World and the Epcot center for the Catholic proportion of the approximately 50 million tourists per year. The pilgrimage place "Mary, Queen of the Universe" was designed not to become the most important attraction in Orlando, but to represent, through its offerings, a religious antithesis to the world of pleasure and technology and to help some tourists to gain peace and contemplation for a few hours during their journey.

5. Administration of Pilgrimage Places

Religious orders are by far the most important representatives and administrators of Catholic pilgrimage places in the U.S. As explained earlier, they also played an important role in their foundation. Religious orders seem to be particularly suited because of their organizational abilities and possibilities. The following orders of priests in this context are:

- Franciscan Friars of the Atonement   (S.A.)
- Franciscans Fathers   (O.F.M.)
- Conventual Franciscans   (O.F.M.CONV.)
- Jesuit Fathers and Brothers   (S.J.)
- The Missionaries of Our Lady of LaSalette   (M.S.)
- Oblates of Mary Immaculate   (O.M.I.)
- Salesians of St. John Bosco   (S.D.B.)
- Servants of Mary   (O.S.M.)

- Pauline Fathers   (O.S.P.)
- Barnabite Fathers   (C.R.S.P.)
- Missionary Servants of the Most Holy Trinity   (S.T.)

Religious orders of women are generally a minority in the administration of pilgrimage places. However, the following play a role:

- Sisters of Charity of St. Vincent De Paul   (S.C.)
- Daughters of Divine Charity   (F.D.C.)
- Missionary Sisters of the Sacred Heart (Golden)   (M.S.C.)
- The Blue Army

Parishes only manage smaller pilgrimage places. Since they lacked the means for investment, in certain circumstances dioceses assisted them. All U.S. dioceses have the sole responsibility for the "National Shrine of the Immaculate Conception" in Washington, D.C.

While smaller pilgrimage places are run only by a couple of priests and a few additional helpers, the largest pilgrimage places employ up to 100 people; retreat centers etc. employ up to 200 people. Priests are in the minority with 3 to 8 people; this number was twice as high 20 years ago. Alongside them are some brothers and sisters who officiate at the services or work in the office, gift shops, pilgrims inn or restaurant.

Lay staff, often up to half of the total staff, is responsible for maintenance, housekeeping and security, as well as for jobs in the restaurant, cafeteria, motel, shop, retirement house, radio station and mail department.

The largest part of the work force consists of volunteers, usually retired people, housewives or other helpers, who assist without payment during their spare time. They often belong to particular Catholic lay organizations such as the Rosary Guild, Reparation Society, Knights of Columbus.

6. Functions and Duties of Pilgrimage Places

Pilgrimage places originate as answers to religious needs of pilgrims, even if they are planned and constructed by religious orders. The shrine personnel have the duty to satisfy these needs for personal prayer and meditation as well as for collective participation in liturgical feasts. The ministries of the shrine provide a spiritual, cultural and hospitable environment where visitors can nurture their religious and personal beliefs through closeness to God and nature. In this respect, pilgrimage places in the U.S. are first and foremost religious and devotional sites dedicated to Christ, Mary, or other Holy Persons in the history of the Catholic church.

Pilgrimage places in the U.S. are, far more than in Europe or South America, ecumenical platforms of spiritual enrichment, especially because they are predominantly situated in non-Catholic environments. Thus many pilgrimage places are visited by religiously motivated followers of another faith or simple tourists as well as by Catholic pilgrims, and are treasured by them as a place of solitude, peace and prayer.

The retreat, renewal and educational centers at pilgrimage places, open on visitors for a longer time than for normal pilgrimage, serve primarily "to provide a secluded, peaceful retreat, where the human spirit can more readily realize the presence of God in prayer and nature".

In order to fulfill their manifold duties, pilgrimage places need financial support mostly obtained through fundraising, as well as through church subsidies. Possibilities are provided by various collections, sale of devotional articles and books, commercial radio stations and, above all, the donations of numerous believers. In order to get as many donations as possible, around 100,000 letters soliciting donations are sent out several times a year. Various organizations, foundations, banks and business people are personally called as part of a campaign. Older people are visited, so that they may remember the pilgrimage place in their wills.

Some holy places visited by pilgrims in the U.S. have taken on the duty of supporting religious orders in their pastoral and missionary activities through their large income possibilities. Therefore, religious orders most represented in the U.S. by numerous pilgrimage places, are those who distinguish themselves through active foreign missionary activity. Among them are: The Oblate Fathers (O.M.I.), the Franciscan (O.F.M.), Maryknoll (M.M.), the Conventual Franciscans (O.F.M. Conv.), the Jesuits (S.J.) and others.

The "Franciscan Monastery" in Washington, D.C., whose church and monastery land is equipped with replicas of the principal shrines and chapels of the Holy Land, performs a special gerrice, is a religious mecca for thousands of pilgrims of all faiths. Besides the Commissariat's purpose of training Franciscan missionary priests and brothers for work in the Holy Land, it has the task of raising funds to support the charitable works of the Franciscan Custody of the Holy Land. The sphere of the custody's activity comprises Jordan, Syria, Israel, Egypt, Lebanon, and the Islands of Cyprus and Rhodes.

7. Pilgrimage Places and Their Surroundings

Pilgrimage places and their surroundings are subject, all over the world, to reciprocal influences. On the whole, particular growth impulses for population, settlement, and economic structure of the town or country surroundings emanate from the pilgrimage place and its pilgrims. On the other hand, the social and cultural surroundings of the pilgrimage place naturally also influence the development and expansion of pilgrimage sites and the size of their pilgrim streams. In the U.S. the influence of pilgrimage places on the environment is not yet marked, due, among other things, to the smaller size of pilgrimage places. On the other hand, very strong effects on the pilgrimage place are caused by the socio-economic change in its surrounding area.

The influence of the pilgrimage place on the population and settlement structure of its surrounding area cannot, in my opinion, be clearly established for any place. The influence on the economic structure is also limited, even when in some cases 100 or more staff are employed. This is partly caused by the fact that pilgrimage places in the U.S. are relatively self-sufficient, with incomes from gift shops, book stores, motels, restaurants, snackbars, etc. A few religious article shops and a snack-restaurant have been set up by residents only in the small pilgrimage place of Chimayo in New Mexico.

The influence exerted by the surrounding area on the pilgrimage place is of much greater importance. Corresponding natural surroundings (National Parks, National Forests, good views) and attractive cities within reach have a positive effect on pilgrim numbers and on the development of the pilgrimage place. As already mentioned above, these effects are being taken into account in the planning of new pilgrimage places.

On the other hand, the negative influence of the surroundings cannot be overlooked. Thus, some pilgrimage places built in smart residential areas find themselves in a run-down environment within a few decades.

For example, the "International Shrine of St. Jude" in New Orleans was, in its fluctuating history, first surrounded by French population groups (1827), then by Italians (1873) and Hispanics (1921), and now finds itself in a predominantly poor black environment.

Similarly, the "National Shrine of Our Sorrowful Mother" in Chicago attracted a large number of pilgrims annually during the 30s, 40s and 50s. But in the late 1950's and early 1960's, the largely Irish and Italian middle class white population was replaced gradually by predominantly Catholic Spanish-speaking people, and in the 1960's by an economically poorer class of predominantly non-Catholic Blacks. Since that time, more and more homes and apartment buildings were abandoned, vandalized, and razed. This had a negative impact on the annual stream of pilgrims, so that today only very few groups of pilgrims are coming to the shrine.

The town environment of the "National Shrine of St. John Neumann" in the North Fifth Street, as well as the surroundings of the "National Shrine of the Miraculous Medal" in the Germantown area of Philadelphia, have undergone fundamental changes in the last decades. Pilgrim groups hardly dare venture in these high crime areas now. Only when a few parking spaces were made available on shrine land did this unattractive situation improve slightly.

The surrounding area of the "Virgen de San Juan del Valle Shrine" in Texas on the Southern border has also developed negatively. The influence on the shrine is, however, not so marked, due to a few schools in its immediate vicinity and favorable travel connections with the Interstate Highway that make a quick arrival and departure possible.

The pilgrim flow decreased noticeably even at the "National Shrine of the Immaculate Conception" in Washington, D.C. at the time of unrest in the black districts to the South, because no one wanted to drive through these areas and also (because some) of the unrest reached the edge of the shrine land. Similar situations can be described in many pilgrimage places in Baltimore, Boston, Buffalo, Chicago, and other places.

Due to the decreasing and practically exhausted pilgrim streams, some of these once important pilgrimage places have reverted to normal churches and others changed into so-called correspondence shrines or mail shrines. The Shrines of St. Jude, the patron of difficult and hopeless cases, in Chicago and New Orleans have undergone this development. Both came into existence in 1929 shortly before the Depression. The reason for their establishment was the need for a religious expression for people who were suffering financially, such as the laborers of steelmills that were drastically cutting back their work forces. Since the majority of interested people cannot attend novena services at the shrine, the St. Jude shrine officials in Chicago distribute literature to devotees throughout the whole country. They also place advertisements in Catholic church journals to offer their assistance to the needy.

8. Types of Pilgrimage Places (Synopsis)

Pilgrimage places in the U.S. can be typified according to the above comments by the following aspects:

- Age and origin

- Worship rites

- Type, location and size

- Catchment area and number of pilgrims

- Founders and administrators

- Ethnicity

- Seasonality

The following types can be distinguished in detail:

- **According to Age and Origin**

    - Church-historical shrines originated in the 17th, 18th and 19th centuries, i.e., the mission stations in Tucson, N.M. and Augustine, Florida

    - Shrines devoted to American saints, i.e., in Emmitsburgh, Maryland

    - Shrines which replicate European or Spanish-American shrines comprising form two third of all shrines, some of them were only established in the 20th Century.

- **According to Worship Rites**

    - Marian shrines (50%)

    - Christian shrines (10%)

    - Shrines of single saints of the old and new world

    - Conglomerate shrines combining the worship of various cults.

- **According to Type, Size and Facilities**

    - Single chapels, churches or cathedrals, usually situated in the center of a city and belonging to the earlier shrines in the U.S. (indoor shrines)

    - Shrines, situated at the edge of the city, at least at the time of their origin and foundation, possessing a large area and therefore equipped with numerous additional facilities. Some of them also have a lot of church land at their disposal (outdoor shrines).

- **According to Catchment Area and Number of Pilgrims**

    - Shrines of a national catchment area and from 100,000 to over a million pilgrims, such as Washington, D.C. and Belleville, IL.

    - Regional shrines with 10,000 to 100,000 pilgrims annually, such as Portland, OR and Chimayo, N.M.

- Local shrines often situated in large cities with less than 10,000 pilgrims per year, such as the Lourdes Grotto in San Antonio
- Correspondence shrines, which contact believers by letter or through radio and television program, such as in New Orleans and Chicago.

- **According to Founders and Representatives**

  - Shrines founded and managed by religious orders, which is the case in by far the largest number of pilgrimage places
  - Smaller shrines run by local parishes.

- **According to Ethnicity**

  - Shrines founded by a single ethnic group usually shortly after immigration at the end of the 19th century or in the 20th century and nearly exclusively visited by that ethnic group
  - Shrines visited by various ethnic groups
  - Shrines without ethnic elements in the composition of pilgrims.

- **According to Seasonality**

  - Seasonal shrines open only during the summer season and located in the North of the U.S.
  - Shrines open all year round with differently marked seasons, e.g., in Texas, New Mexico, Louisiana, Florida.

Based on the foregoing it may be suggested that the typical pilgrimage place in the U.S. has the following characteristics:

- It is a Marian pilgrimage place,

- has an increasingly ecumenical character,

- situated in the Midwest of the States,

- established in the 20th century,

- founded by a religious order,

- located, at least in the beginning, at the edge of a large city,

- possesses a large area with abundant facilities,

- has a regional catchment area,

- is visited by 10,000 to 100,000 pilgrims during the summer season with a strong ethnic affiliation,

- and has no, or hardly any recognizable effect on the settlement and economic development of its immediate surroundings.

IV. Spatial Aspects of pilgrim activities

For many pilgrims who regularly visit a pilgrimage place at particular time intervals, the holy place is the only destination. The area of a pilgrimage place is, for a large proportion of organized pilgrimages, part of a pilgrim tour lasting several days or weeks. As a rule, the area of the holy place represents the main incentive and motivation; tourist activities also often take up a large space.

So far, three activity spaces of pilgrim sites can be distinguished; they overlap and are not mutually exclusive:

- The activity space of the pilgrimage place itself,

- the activity space of pilgrims on pilgrimage tours and

- the activity space of pilgrim tourists.

1. Activities at the Pilgrimage Place

As a rule, pilgrims remain on shrine land only for one day, i.e., for about 5 to 8 hours. The pilgrims arriving at the pilgrimage place after a journey which can be many hours long, are sometimes led in a festive procession to the center of the site, today as it was in the times of special pilgrim trains, such as in Carey, OH. The pilgrim day often begins with a visit to the visitors center or a tour of the shrine land. Late morning mass is often attended after confession. This is followed by a collective lunch in the restaurant or cafeteria or a picnic on shrine land. Only in very rare cases is the shrine left in order to partake of refreshments or meals in the immediate vicinity. In this case, as in Chimayo, the influence of pilgrims on religious article shops and the refreshment business is immediately apparent.

After lunch, the religious article shop is usually visited, where religious souvenirs are bought for family and friends. Later everyone meets again for collective prayer (devotion, benediction, or meditation) in the church or chapel; the Rosary Garden and The Holy Cross Way are also visited. Around the pilgrim group begins its journey home or its search for a motel in the vicinity of the shrine.

On pilgrim land the pilgrims naturallyl visit the actual religious center first of all, i.e., the chapel or church with the holy relics, the saint or Christ figure, but the visitors center as well, as shown by the example of the "National Shrine of Saint Elizabeth Ann Seton" in Emmitsburgh (52,000 annual visitors). About half of these (25,000) also visit the slide presentation in the visitors center. Considerably fewer (ca. 15,000) also visit other places connected with the life of the saint revered (cemetery, Stone House, the convent and other parts of shrine land (Fig. 26).

2. Activity Space of Pilgrims on Pilgrimage Tours

Since the distance between the home location and the pilgrimage place can be considerable, pilgrims also visit other religious places when possible. This is, however, only conditionally possible in the West of the U.S., for example in Portland, Oregon, where some monasteries and convents (Mt. Angel Abbey, The Cisterian [Trappist] Abbey at Lafayette) can be reached in less than an hour from the main destination, the Sanctuary of Our Sorrowful Mother.

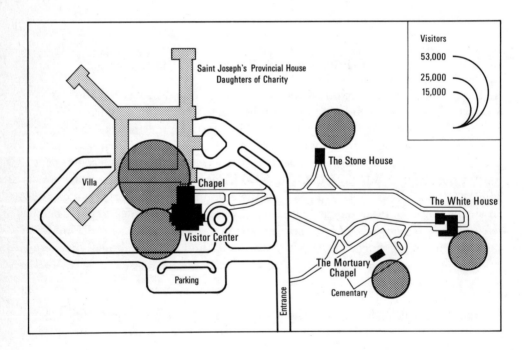

Fig. 26: Activity space and number of visitors to different places of the "National Shrine of Saint Elizabeth Ann Seton", Emmitsburg, MD, 1986
Source: Information of the Shrine Office, 1988

Due to the large number of pilgrimage places and the shorter distances between them, pilgrim tours can be found more often in the Eastern U.S. Thus, pilgrim groups from Florida to Louisiana visit a few pilgrimage places on their way to Canadian places in Québec, mostly in the Northeast and Midatlantic states such as the "Seton Shrine" in Emmitsburgh, MD and Manhattan, New York City, as well as the "National Shrine of Our Lady of Czestochowa" in Doylestown, PA, "The Shrine of North American Martyrs" in Auriesville, N.Y. and others.

Pilgrim groups visiting the "Shrine of Our Lady of the Snows" in Belleville, IL and spending the night on shrine land also include a tour of the holy places in Eureka, MO ("Black Madonna of Czestochowa") and Perryville, MO ("Shrine of the Miraculous Medal").

Pilgrim groups coming from the North and Northeast to visit the "National Shrine of the Immaculate Conception" also visit the "National Shrine of St. John Neumann" and the "National Shrine of the Miraculous Medal", both in Philadelphia, PA, as well as the "Seton Shrine" in Emmitsburgh, MD, the "National Shrine of Our Lady of Czestochowa" in Doylestown, PA and, of course, the "Franciscan Monastery" in Washington, D.C.

Pilgrims from New York City and Boston undertake regular tours of Canadian pilgrimage centers of "St.-Joseph-Oratoire" in Montreal, "Cap-de-la-Madeleine" and "St.-Anne-de-Beaupré". From there, the journey sometimes also continues via the Martyr's Shrine in Midland, Ontario to the Our Lady of Fátima Shrine in Youngstown, N.Y. and finally to the "National Shrine of Blessed Kateri Tekakwitha" in Fonda, N.Y. and the "Shrine of the North American Martyrs" in Auriesville, N.Y. (Fig. 27).

3. Activities of Pilgrim Tourists

Tourist destinations directly along the way to and from the pilgrimage place are visited even more often than additional pilgrimage places. As already mentioned above (see III, 4), the most important pilgrimage places are in the immediate vicinity of large tourist attractions. Thus, starting from various pilgrimage places, pilgrim groups visit the following places and sights, among others, often on the same day, although usually a special day is set aside in the program:

- National Shrine of the Immaculate Conception in Washington, D.C.

    - White House
    - U S Capitol

- Smithonian Institution (Museums)
- Library of Congress
- Arlington National Cemetery
- Washington Cathedral

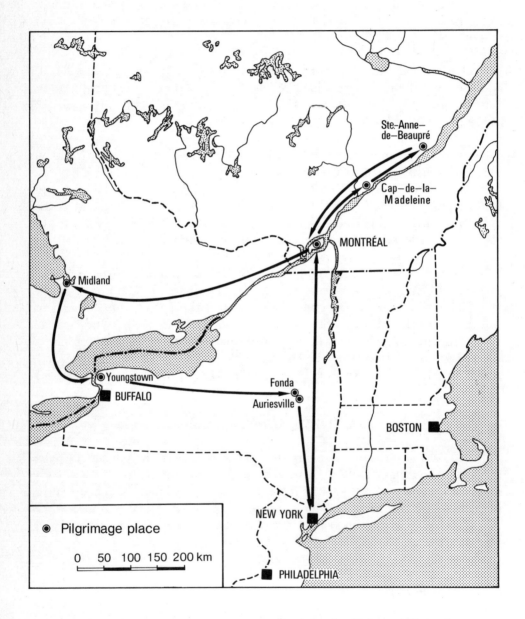

Fig. 27: Pilgrimage tour to sanctuaries in the U.S. and Canada
Source: Author's investigation, 1987 – 89

- Shrine of Our Lady of the Snows, Belleville, IL
  (The shrine office organizes and arranges so-called hub-tours for pilgrims departing from shrine land):

  - Cathedral Tour (St. Louis): Old Cathedral, New Cathedral, Union Station, Gateway Arch.
  - Old Courthouse Tour (St. Louis): Old Courthouse, Grant's Farm, Italian Restaurant.
  - Lincoln Tour: Springfield, Illinois (Lincoln Home, Lincoln Monument, Lincoln's New Salem).
  - French History Tour: Fort des Chartres, etc., French Churches, French town.
  - Pilgrimage Tour (Missouri: Eureka, Perryville).

- The Sanctuary of Our Sorrowful Mother, Portland, OR

  - Multnomah Falls
  - Timberline Lodge
  - Bonneville Fish Hatchery
  - Bonneville Power Station
  - Cannon Beach/Seaside/Astoria (Pacific Ocean)
  - Mount St. Helens
  - Columbia River George
  - Pittock Mansion, Portland
  - Oregon City

- St. Elizabeth Ann Seton Shrine, Emmitsburgh, MD

  - Washington, D.C.
  - Gettysburg National Cemetery, Gettysburg National Military Park, etc.

- Our Lady of Fátima Shrine, Youngstown, N.Y.

  - Niagara Falls
  - Fort Niagara

- Graymoor, Garrison, N.Y.

  - West Point — US Military Academy
  - Sleepy Hollow, Tarrytown

- Mary, Queen of the Universe, Orlando, FL

  - Disney World/Epcot Center
  - J F Kennedy Space Center

- Sanctuary of Christ of Chimayo, N.M.

  - Santa Fe
  - Los Alamos
  - Taos
  - Pueblos (Taos, etc.)

- Virgen de San Juan del Valle Shrine, San Juan, TX

  - Rio Grande Valley
  - Padre Island National Seashore

These few examples show that the pilgrimages are not purely spiritual activities in the U.S. They are cultural, family and group orientated activities certainly also including varying degrees of recreation and tourism.

V. Future Development of the Pilgrim Phenomenon in the U.S.

Religious pilgrimage is a very recent phenomenon in the U.S. and has experienced an expansion in the last few decades, due to the increasing motorization of the American society. Various factors, such as increase in piety, spare time and touristic activities, shift of religious activities from daily or weekly services with a local catchment area to more periodical and episodical activities with regional and international catchment areas forecast the further generation of immigrants product of loosened family ties, takes a particularly active part in leisure activities, searching new social contacts and fields of activity in the religious sphere as well.

The foundation, development and expansion of new pilgrimage places will occur in areas with favorable travel connections and in peaceful surroundings close to nature. Preferred locations for pilgrimage places are recreational areas near large agglomerations and major tourist centers, where numerous believers also need religious support.

Since the pilgrim phenomenon in the U.S. is closely connected with different ethnic groups, a change in the ethnic pilgrim structure due to new immigration waves will influence the nature of pilgrim streams. Middle and East European ethnic groups will lose importance, and Latin-American, Eastern and Southern Asiatic groups will come to the forefront.

Summary

There are at present 126 pilgrimage places in the U.S. They are found in the Southwest, South and Southeast, but also in the Midwest and Northeast, where a certain concentration of catholics is noted. This regional distribution of pilgrimage sites is closely connected with historical and present influxes of immigrants into the U.S., such as the Spaniards and Mexicans in the Southwest, the French in Louisiana, the Spaniards and Cubans in Florida, as well as the Germans, French, Poles, Italians, Hungarians, Czechs, Ukrainians, etc. in the Midwest and Northeast.

The pilgrimage places are visited by more than 7 million pilgrims annually, who, as a rule, come from adjacent states. In the states with mild winter climate, the pilgrimage places are open year round. However, even there, the pilgrim stream is characterized by a strong seasonality. Nearly all pilgrims arrive at the holy places by car or bus, the latter are usually chartered by diocesan and parish groups, Catholic schools, and other religious groups. Ethnic groups from Latin-America (Mexicans, Cubans, Haitians, Jamaicans, etc.) and Asia (Vietnamese, Koreans, Filipinos, Lebanese, Syrians, etc.) take part in particularly rapidly increasing numbers.

Some pilgrimage places owe their origins to events in the life of Americans saints or to American church history. More than half were established by assuming religious worship rites (particularly Marian cults) from Europe and Latin-America.

The religious place (sanctuary), usually consisting of a chapel or church, is the center of all pilgrimage sites. Completely developed places also have information centers and book stores, cafeterias, restaurants and motels. Some also manage devotional houses, retirement homes and geriatric centers as well as numerous facilities for leisure activities.

Religious orders are by far the most important founders and administrators of pilgrimage places in the U.S. They can realize their pastoral, missionary and social aims more easily through the generous financial donations of pilgrims.

Large pilgrimage places are characterized by particularly convenient travel connections. The proximity to major tourist attractions has also proved advantageous for the development of pilgrim numbers. The influence of pilgrimage places on the population, settlement and economic structure of the surrounding area cannot be determined in the U.S., partly because the pilgrimage places are relatively self-supporting through religious article shops, restaurants, and accommodation. The influence of the environment on pilgrimage places is considerable: positive influences result from tourist activities, negative ones from slum city areas in their immediate neighborhood.

For many pilgrims, the holy place is the only destination that will be visited regularly at particular time intervals. Their activities and activity space are limited to the various facilities at the pilgrimage place. For a large number of organized pilgrim groups, the visit to a pilgrimage place is part of a tour, during which several sites will be visited in the Northeast and Midwest of the U.S. in particular during a short time. Pilgrim tourists also visit tourist destinations along the way to or from the pilgrimage place, or in its immediate vicinity. Thus pilgrimage in the U.S., as everywhere, does not only have religious and social motives, but touristic aspects as well.

Zusammenfassung:
Katholische Pilgerstätten in den USA

Ziel dieser Studie ist es, erste Forschungsergebnisse bezüglich des kaum bekannten, aber doch weit verbreiteten Pilgerphänomens in den USA zu vermitteln. In den USA gibt es zur Zeit 126 Pilgerstätten. Sie sind in allen Kulturregionen verbreitet, besonders aber in Konzentrationsgebieten der Katholiken anzutreffen u. zw. im Südwesten, Süden und Südosten, vor allem aber im Mittleren Westen und Nordosten. Sie werden alljährlich von über 7 Millionen Pilgern aufgesucht.

Einige Pilgerstätten sind von großer nationaler Bedeutung, zu denen Pilger aus fast allen Bundesstaaten gelangen. Allein 6 Pilgerstätten erhalten pro Jahr zwischen $1/2$ – über 1 Mill. Besucher. Die meisten Stätten besitzen jedoch nur einen überregionalen, regionalen und z. T. auch einen lokalen Einzugsbereich. Wichtigstes Herkunftsgebiet sind die großen Städte, in denen sich auch der größte Teil der katholischen Bevölkerung konzentriert.

Der Pilgerstrom ist abgesehen von den wintermilden Klimaregionen des Südens, Südostens und Südwestens durch eine starke Saisonalität gekennzeichnet, durch eine Hochsaison von April – Oktober und eine Nebensaison im Winter. Nahezu alle Pilger erreichen die heilige Stätte mit dem Bus und PKW. Fußpilgerreise und Eisenbahntransport sind heute bedeutungslos. Die Pilgerströme sind überwiegend aus verschiedenen ethnischen Gruppen zusammengesetzt. Je nach Lage der Pilgerstätte sind mit unterschiedlich großen Anteilen ältere

Einwanderergruppen aus West-, Süd- und Ostmitteleuropa und neuere Einwanderungsgruppen aus Lateinamerika und Asien beteiligt.

Die Pilgerstätten verdanken ihren Ursprung nur in geringem Maße Ereignissen im Leben eines Heiligen oder der kirchengeschichtlichen Entwicklung Nordamerikas. Der weitaus überwiegende Teil ist entstanden, indem man religiöse Objekte und Kulte aus der Alten Welt und Mittelamerika übernahm. Ihre Flächengröße schwankt zwischen wenigen Ar und mehreren Hektar. Die Ausstattung besteht u. a. aus religiösen Stätten (Kirchen, Kapellen, Grotten, Kreuzwegen, Statuen etc.), Informationseinrichtungen, Devotionalienläden, Restaurants- und Beherbergungsstätten, Fortbildungs-, Erholungs- und Kommunikationseinrichtungen.

Die meisten Pilgerstätten befinden sich heute in ländlichen Gebieten oder am Rand großer Städte und bekannter touristischer Attraktionen in verkehrsgünstiger Lage. Sie werden in der Regel von Ordensgemeinschaften geführt und sollen die Gläubigen seelsorgerisch betreuen aber auch genügend finanzielle Mittel für die seelsorgerischen, missionarischen und sozialen Aktivitäten bereitstellen.

Der Einfluß der Pilgerstätte auf die Umgebung (Bevölkerung, Siedlung und Wirtschaft) ist in den USA nur wenig erkennbar, da die Stätten relativ autark sind. Größer sind die Einflüsse der Umgebung (attraktive Touristenzentren oder Slumviertel) auf die Anzahl der Pilger.

Der Aktionsraum der Pilger beschränkt sich nicht nur auf die verschiedenen Einrichtungen an der Pilgerstätte selbst, sondern schließt auch noch andere religiöse Einrichtungen in der Umgebung, vor allem aber auch touristische Zentren ein, die häufig auf einer Rundreise aufgesucht werden. So hat die Pilgerreise in den USA sowie überall nicht nur religiöse und soziale sondern auch touristische Aspekte.

Bibliography

GRACIDA, R. H. (1984): Shrines and Pilgrimages in the U.S.A., Practical Pastoral Experiences. III World Congress, Pastoral Care of Tourism, October 9 – 12, Vatican City, p. 1 – 23.

NATIONAL CONFERENCE OF CATHOLIC BISHOPS (NCCB, 1986): Proceedings, First National Meeting, Directors of Shrines/Places of Pilgrimage, Diocesan Directors of Pilgrimage. Washington, D.C.

NOLAN, M. L. (1987): Christian Pilgrimage in the Old and New Worlds: A Comparative Perspective. Paper presented at the "AAG Annual Meeting, Portland 1987".

NOLAN, M. L. (1987): Roman Catholic Pilgrimage in the New World. In: Eliade, M. (ed.), The Encyclopedia of Religion, Vol. 11, New York, p. 332 – 335.

PRESTON, J. (1986): Pilgrimage in America: An Address to the Catholic Shrine Directors of the United States. In: Proceedings, First National Meeting, Directors of Shrines, Places of Pilgrimage, Diocesan Directors of Pilgrimage, Washington, D.C., p. 1 – 10.

THORNTON, F. B. (1954): Catholic Shrines in the United States and Canada. New York.

A List of Catholic Pilgrimage Places
in the U. S.
(April 1989)

ALABAMA

• Cathedral of the Immaculate Conception, 400 Government Street, P. O. Box 1966, Mobile, AL 36633

ARIZONA

• Shrine of St. Joseph of the Mountains, Route 89, Yarnell, AZ

• Mission San Xavier del Bac, R. R. 11, Box 645, Tucson, AZ 85746

CALIFORNIA

• Sanctuary of Our Lady of Guadelupe, 7th and T sts., Res., 711 T st., Sacramento, CA

• Grotto of Our Lady of Lourdes, St. Elisabeth's Church, 1849 N. Lake ave., Altaneda, CA 91001

• Shrine of Our Lady of Peace, 2800 Mission College Boulevard, Santa Clara, CA 95051

COLORADO

• Mother Cabrini Shrine, Route 8, Box 75, Highway 40, Rt. 3, Golden, CO 80401

CONNECTICUT

• Lourdes in Litchfield, P. O. Box 667, Litchfield, CT 06759

DISTRICT OF COLUMBIA

• Franciscan Monastery of the Holy Sepulchre, Commissariat of the Holy Land, 1400 Quincy Street, N.E., Washington, D.C. 20017

• The Ukrainian Catholic National Shrine of the Holy Family, 4250 Harewood Road, N.E., Washington, D.C. 20017

- National Shrine of the Immaculate Conception, Fourth & Michigan Avenue, N. E., Washington, D.C. 20017

FLORIDA

- Shrine of Our Lady of Charity, P. O. Box 330555, 3609 South Miami Avenue, Miami, FL 33133

- Shrine of Our Lady of LaLeche, and Mission of Nombre De Dios, P. O. Box 3845, 27 Ocean Avenue, St. Augustine, FL 32085

- Mary, Queen of the Universe Catholic Shrine, P. O. Box 16891, Orlando, FL 32819

ILLINOIS

- Shrine of Our Lady of the Snows, 9500 West Illinois, Route 15, Belleville, IL 62223

- Basilica of Our Lady of Sorrows, 3121 West Jackson Boulevard, Chicago, IL 60612

- National Shrine of St. Jude, Our Lady of Guadalupe Church, 3200 East 91st Street, Chicago, IL 60617

- Dominican Shrine of St. Jude Thaddaus, 1909 South Ashland Avenue, Chicago, IL 60608

- Shrine of St. Maximilan Kolbe, Marytown, 1600 West Park Avenue, Libertyville, IL 60048

- Aylesford: Carmelite Spiritual Center, I-55 & Cass Avenue, North, Box 65, Darien, IL 60559

INDIANA

- Monte Cassino Shrine dedicated to the Virgin Mary, St. Meinrad, IN 47577

IOWA

- Grotto of the Redemption West Bend, IA 50597

KANSAS

- Shrine of the Blessed Philippine Duchesne, Sacred Heart Church, Mound City, KS 66056

KENTUCKY

- Our Lady of Guadalupe Shrine, 614 East Main Street, P. O. Box 168, Carlisle, KY 40311

- Shrine of St. Ann, St. Ann Church, 1274 Parkway, Covington, KY 41001

- Shrine of the Little Flower, St. Therese Church, 11 Temple Place, Southgate, KY 41071

- Grotto of Our Lady of Lourdes, St. Aloysius' Church, Bakewell and 7th sts., Covington, KY 41001

- Kentucky Mountain Apostolate Shrine, Mother of Good Counsel Mission Center, 329 Poplar st., Hazard, 41701

LOUISIANA

- Grotto of Our Lady of Lourdes, St. Michael, the Archangel Church, Convent, LA 70723

- Shrine of St. John Berchmans, Convent of the Sacred Heart, Grand Couteau, LA 70541

- St. Ann Shrine, 4920 Loveland, Metairie, LA 70002

- National Shrine of St. Ann, 2117 Ursulines Avenue, New Orleans, LA 70119

- Our Lady of Prompt Succor, National Shrine Church, 2705 State Street, New Orleans, LA 70118

- Shrine of St. Jude Thaddeus, 411 Rampart Street, New Orleans, LA 70112

- St. Roch Chapel in the old German cemetery, 1725 St. Roch ave., New Orleans, LA 70117

MARYLAND

- National Shrine, Grotto of Lourdes, Emmitsburg, MD 21727

- National Shrine of Elizabeth Ann Seton, 333 South Seton Avenue, Emmitsburg, MD 21727

MASSACHUSETTS

- Shrine of Our Lady of LaSalette, Immaculate Heart of Mary Province, 947 Park Street, Attleboro, MA 02703

- St. Antony Shrine, 100 Arch st., P. O. Box 2278, Boston, MA 02107

- St. Clement's, Archdiocesan Eucharistic Shrine, 1105 Boylston Street, Boston, MA 02215

- Stella Maris Oratory, 259 Northern ave., Boston, MA 02127

- Madonna Queen National Shrine, 111 Orient Avenue, East Boston, MA 02128

- St. Anne's Church and Shrine, 818 Middle Street, Fall River, MA

- St. Anne's & St. Patrick's, 16 Church Street, Fiskdale, MA 01518

- Our Lady of Fátima Shrine, 101 Summer Street, Holliston, MA 01746

- National Shrine of Our Lady of LaSalette, Topsfield Road, Ipswich, MA 01938

- Shrine of the Divine Mercy, Eden Hill, Stockbridge, MA 01262

MICHIGAN

- Assumption Grotto Shrine, 13770 Gratiot ave., Detroit, MI 48205

- Sainte-Anne-de-Detroit, 1000 Sts. Anne st., Detroit, MI 48216

- The Cross in the Woods at the Catholic Shrine, 7078 M-68, Indian River, MI 49749

- St. Mary of Mt. Carmel Shrine, 260 St. Mary pkwy., Manistee, MI 49660

- Our Lady of the Woods Shrine, P. O. Box 203, Mio, MI 48647

- St. Joseph's Church, 400 South Boulevard, West Pontiac, MI 48053

MINNESOTA

- Assumption Chapel, 715 N. 1st st., Cold Spring, MN 56320

- National Shrine of St. Odilia, Onamia, MN 56 359

- Schoenstatt on the Lake, Rt 4, Box 157, Sleepy Eye, MN 56085

MISSOURI

- Shrine of the Immaculate Heart of Mary, 1900 Grand Avenue, Carthage, MO 64836

- Black Madonna Shrine and Grottos (Czestochowa), R. R. 3, Box 39, Eureka, MO 63025
- Shrine of the Miraculous Medal, Church of the Assumption, Perryville, MO 63775
- Shrine of Our Lady of Sorrows, Starkenburg Road, Rhineland, MO 65069
- Shrine of the Blessed Philippine R. Duchesne, St. Charles, MO

MONTANA

- St. Mary's Mission, P. O. Box 228, Stevensville, Montana 59870

NEBRASKA

- The Children's Shrine, Boys Town, Nebr. 68010

NEW HAMPSHIRE

- Shrine of Our Lady of Grace, Route 3, Colebrook, NH 03576
- Shrine of Our Lady of LaSalette, P. O. Box 420, Enfield, NH 03748

NEW JERSEY

- The Sanctuary of Mary, R. R. 1, Box 106, Branchville, NJ 07826
- Mariapoch Shrine, Matawan, NJ
- Rosary Shrine, Monastery of Our Lady of the Rosary, Morris and Springfield Ave., Summit, NJ 07901
- Shrine of St. Joseph's, 1050 Long Hill Road, Stirling, NJ 07980
- Shrine of the Immaculate Heart of Mary, Mt. View Road, Washington, NJ 07882

NEW MEXICO

- Sanctuary of Christ of Chimayo, Route 64, Chimayo, NM 87522
- Holy Tortilla Shrine, Lake Arthur, NM

- Nuestra Señora de la Conquistadora, St. Francis Cathedral, P. O. Box 2127, Santa Fe, NM 87504

- Our Lady of Lourdes, San Juan Pueblo P. O., San Juan, NM 87566

NEW YORK

- National Shrine of the Motherhood of St. Ann, St. Ann's Church, 110 East 12th Street, New York, NY

- Chapel St. Francis X Cabrini, 701 Fort Washington Avenue, New York, NY 10040

- Shrine of Our Lady of Martyrs, Auriesville, NY 12016

- St. Elizabeth Seton Shrine, 16 Barclay Street, New York, NY 10007

- Shrine of Our Lady of the Island, Eastport-Manor Road, Box 31, Eastport, NY 11941

- National Shrine of Blessed Kateri Tekakwitha, Box 627, Fonda, NY 12068

- "Graymoor" (St. Paul Friary), Pilgrimage Department, Garrison, NY 10524

- Our Lady of Fátima Shrine, Swan Road, Youngstown, NY 14174

- National Shrine of Our Lady of Victory, 780 Ridge Road, Lackawanna, NY 14218

- Lourdes Grotto, Immaculate Conception, U. S. Route 20, New Lebanon, NY 12125

- Shrine of the Holy Infant of Jesus, 3452 Niagara Falls blvd., North Nonawanda, NY 14120

- Holy Dormition Shrine, Table Rock, Sloatsburg, NY 10974

- Marian Shrine and Don Bosco Retreat Center, West Haverstraw, NY 10993

OHIO

- Shrine of Our Lady of Levocha, 1160 Broadway, Bedford, OH 44146

- Sorrowful Mother Shrine, 4106 State Route 269, Bellevue, OH 44811

- Shrine of Our Lady of Consolation, 315 W. Clay st., Carey, OH 43316

- Holy Cross Monastery, 1055 St. Paul Place, Cincinnati, OH 45860

- Our Lady of Czestochowa, 12215 Granger Road, Cleveland, OH 44125

- Our Lady, Queen of the Holy Rosary, 6618 Pearl Road, Cleveland, OH 44130

- National Shrine of Our Lady of Lourdes, 21320 Euclid Avenue, Cleveland, OH 44117

- Our Lady of Fátima Shrine, St. Joseph Church, 905 South 5th Street, Ironton, OH 45638

- Sisters of the Precious Blood, Shrine of the Holy Relics, 2291 St. John Road, Maria Stein, OH 45860

- Our Lady of Mariapoch, Mumford Road, off Route 422, Welchfield-Burton, OH

OKLAHOMA

- National Shrine of the Infant Jesus of Prague, 4th and Broadway sts., Box 488, Prague, OK 74864

OREGON

- The Grotto, National Sanctuary of Our Sorrowful Mother, P. O. Box 20008, Portland OR 97220

PENNSYLVANIA

- National Shrine of Our Lady of Guadalupe, 501 Ridge ave, Allentown, PA 18102

- National Shrine of Our Lady of Czestochowa, P. O. Box 151, Doylestown, PA 18901

- Shrine of the Sacred Heart, 1 Church Place, Harleigh, PA 18225

- Prince Gallitzin Chapel House, Route 53, Loretto, PA 15940

- Grotto of Our Lady, Provincial Motherhouse of the Sisters of St. Basil the Great, 710 Fox Chase Road, Philadelphia, PA 19111

- National Shrine of the Miraculous Medal, 500 East Chelton Avenue, Germantown, Philadelphia

- National Shrine of St. John Neumann, 1019 North Fifth Street, Philadelphia, PA 19123

- St. Anthony's Chapel, 1700 Harpster Street, Pittsburgh, PA 15212

- Holy Dormition Monastery, P. O. Box 70, Sybertsville, PA 18251

- The Shrine of Our Lady of Perpetual Help, Mount St. Macrinca, 510 West Main Street, P. O. Box 878, Uniontown, PA 15401

RHODE ISLAND

- St. Therese of the Child Jesus, Douglas Pike, 7 Dion dr., R 4, Nasonville, RI 02830

TEXAS

- Shrine of the True Cross, 300 Pine dr., P. O. Box 687, Dickinson, TX 77539

- Lourdes Shrine of the Southwest, San Antonio, TX

- Our Lady of Czestochowa, Grotto Shrine and Convent, 138 Beethoven str., San Antonio, TX 78210

- Virgen de San Juan del Valle Shrine, P. O. Box 747, San Juan, TX 78589

VERMONT

- St. Anne's Shrine, Fathers of Society of St. Edmund, Isle La Motte, Burlington, VT 05463

WASHINGTON

- Holy Cross, Ahtanum Mission, 5315 Tieton dr., Yakima, Washington 98908

WISCONSIN

- Shrine Chapel to the Poor Little Man of Assisi, Portiuncula Shrine, St. Agnes Catholic Community, 106 2nd ave. E, Ashland, WI 54806

- Dickeyville Shrine, Dickeyville WI

- Our Lady of Holy Hill National Shrine, Route 167, Hubertus, WI 53033

- Schoenstatt Heights, 3601 Hwy BB, Madison, WI 53716

- Archdiocesan Marian Shrine, 217 N. 68th st., Wauwatosa, Milwaukee, WI 53213

- Schoenstatt Shrine, Holy Cross Parish, 5424 W Bluemond Road, Milwaukee, WI 53208

- Chapel of Our Lady of Good Help, New Franken, WI

- Shrine of Our Lady of LaSalette, P., O. Box 777, Twin Lakes, WI 53181

- Schoenstatt Shrine, West 284 N. 698 Cherry Lane, Waukesha, WI 53186

Gregory E. Faiers and Carolyn V. Prorok

Pilgrimage to a "National" American Shrine: "Our Lady of Consolation" in Carey, Ohio

I. Introduction

Our Lady of Consolation, enshrined at the Basilica named for her in Carey, Ohio, has attracted pilgrims for over a century. Miracles, especially related to healing and weather events, have been attributed to Our Lady by pilgrims since 1875. The annual celebration on the Feast of the Assumption in August, according to basilica officials, is the most important event of the year, attracting the largest number of pilgrims to the site. Pilgrims come to Carey from across the United States, as well as from Canada.

Pilgrimage behavior is intrinsically geographic in that humans travel in specific ways to consecrated places. Travel to sacred sites is common in the European, Catholic tradition (NOLAN 1983, 422; TURNER and TURNER 1982, 145) and immigrants carried this tradition to the United States. The shrine at Carey, Ohio is only one such transference of European, Catholic tradition.

The main purpose of this paper is to explain the historical transformation of the shrine from a small parish church to a sacred site that attracts thousands of pilgrims, as well as to place the pilgrimage to Carey within a national and regional context by examining the spatial distribution of the origin of pilgrims presently making the journey to pay homage to Our Lady of Consolation.

II. Historic Transformation of the Carey Shrine Site

According to pilgrims, Mary the Consoler performs miracles. Most commonly, she grants favors to her devotees and especially cures those who come to her with ailments, whether mild or severe. Many crutches and prosthesis equipment left at the shrine by devotees attest to the miracles performed here.

Although belief in miracles was important to the site's development as a sacred place, the establishment of a shrine to Our Lady of Consolation was not due to the performance of miracles at this site. Instead, the shrine was established due to the spriritual and social needs of the small Luxembourgan, Catholic community in the area (JEFFREY 1979, 5).

NOLAN (1987, 4) notes that establishment of Christian shrines in Europe, North America, and Latin America follow a predictable pattern. The Carey shrine was originally established by what Nolan would call devotional acts, that is, acts not related to miracles and unusual events. On the other hand, the growing sacredness of the Carey site has been due to subsequent unusual events, or from the devotees' perspective, miracles.

1. History of the Shrine

In 1873 Father Joseph Peter Gloden, a priest from Luxembourg, took over the small Catholic congregations at Frenchtown and nearby Carey, Ohio. The congregation at Carey had been in the process of building a small chapel for worship, to be dedicated to St. Edward, but which had not been completed when Gloden arrived. Father Gloden assisted the people in the completion of the chapel. Due to his inspiration, the congregation decided instead to dedicate it to Mary, Consoler of the Afflicted, and the patron of the Duchy of Luxembourg. To complete the consecration of this chapel in honor of Mary, Father Gloden commissioned a replica of the statue of Mary the Consoler in Luxembourg in order that it be enshrined at Carey. A Frenchtown parishoner returned with the statue in 1875 and May 24, 1875 was designated as the day in which the Frenchtown parishoners would take Mary in procession to be presented to the parishoners in Carey (JEFFREY 1979, 6).

NOLAN's (1987, 4) typology of shrine origination also includes the spontaneous miracle as an event around which shrine formation may occur. Such spontaneous events have occurred at Carey. From the time of the Frenchtown to Carey procession, to the present, devotees of Mary have attributed miracles to her, and it is devotees' behavior, based upon their belief in these miracles, that has transformed Carey from a local parish chapel into a 'National' shrine.

2. The Sacred Events

ELIADE (1959, 26) explains that every sacred space implies, "a hierophany, an irruption of the sacred that results in detaching a territory from the surrounding cosmic milieu and making it qualitatively different." The first hierophanic event that set the Carey church apart and made it "qualitatively different" in

Eliade's terms, was the set of circumstances surrounding the procession from Frenchtown in May of 1875. Father Gloden (JEFFREY 1979, 8 – 9) recounts the event,

> On the 23rd, towards evening, a heavy storm, accompanied by a very strong wind and thundering and lightening arose in the West and swept over the country with violence. After the storm had abated, a heavy and lasting rain set in. It simply poured down during the whole night, and on the 24th in the morning it was still raining heavily whilst we were saying our Masses. Nevertheless the people hastened to the church, and at the appointed time, formed into procession, all with their expanded umbrellas. For a moment I had decided not to let the procession proceed, but considering that the people would be sorely disappointed, I allowed the procession to start, but at the same time I ordered a man of my congregation, Mr. John Nicholas Weinimout, who had imported the statue, to come right close to the church door with his covered surrey with the intention of placing the statue inside the surrey to protect it against the rain. But behold, as soon as the statue was brought out of the church the sun pierced the clouds and was shining on the whole line of the procession all the way to about a mile from Carey, while it was continually thundering and lightning on both sides of us. When we came to within a mile from the village of Carey, the clouds from both sides clashed together right in front of the procession, and it seemed impossible for us to reach the church before the rain would pour down upon us. At this point we saw a procession conducted by the Revs. Rudolf of Clyde, Jung of Findlay, Reichlien of Cleveland and Brashcler of Upper Sandusky, coming from Carey to meet us and escort us to the church. Again I called Mr. Weinimout to come with his surrey right into the procession behind the clergy, so that at the first drop of rain, we could place the statue under cover into the surrey. When we reached the Village Carey, an immense crowd of spectators awaited us there. The streets, the houses, the windows (sic) even the very roofs were filled with people, and although Carey had always been known as very bigoted, yet not an insult, not a word of reproach was heard. On the contrary, all stood there silent and by far the greater part of them uncovered their heads as we were passing by. At last we reached the church. Father Rudolph and myself took the canopy with the statue from the shoulders of the young ladies who were carrying it, and entered the church with it. Scarcely had we entered the church with the statue, when all of a sudden the rain poured down like a cloudburst and hardly anyone found time to enter the church or seek shelter elsewhere to escape the rain. After the sa-

cred image had been placed upon the altar on the throne prepared for it, Father Rudolph, assisted by Father Bihn, deacon and Father Theobald Schoch, C.P.P.S. as subdeacon, celebrated a Solemn High Mass, at which sermons were preached both in English and German. This remarkable occurence (sic) made a deep impression upon Protestants as well as Catholics, and from this time on, people began to come to Carey from all sides, far and near to implore the help of Our Lady of Consolation in all kinds of afflictions.

A number of miracles occurred in the eyes of believers during the procession of the statue of Our Lady, all of which affirmed this place as sacred to them, and which paved the way for devotees to establish what ELIADE (1959, 25 – 27) calls a window or door to heaven, that is, a place where people can symbolically commune with the supernatural because of the extraordinary context of that place.

The first miracle was that of the parting of clouds and the shining of the sun on the procession. This is a common motif among miracles related to Christian shrine formation (for example, TEXAS 1988, A7). A few pilgrims would argue that the specific weather phenomenon in question is within the realm of naturally occurring events. In fact, it is not uncommon to have thunderstorms occurring in close proximity to each other with clear or mostly clear skies in between. Such occurrences are most likely during the summer months with convective or air mass thunderstorms. Frontal thunderstorms tend to develop in solid lines, but when a mid-latitude cyclone is occluding, the air becomes very unstable with storms, and conditions can rapidly change from clear to cloudy, or vice versa. From descriptions of the meteorological events in Carey, that is, heavy rain the previous night followed by a quiet period and then the subsequent storms, it is quite likely that an occluding mid-latitude cyclone was tracking just north of Ohio, and during the day of the 25th a line of storms was generated in the west-southwesterly flow on the backside of this system. The miracle, then, is not that storms can occur in such a fashion, but that they coincided with an important spiritual occasion. It is this coincidence that takes on sacred significance for the believer.

The second miracle was the reception of the procession in Carey. The procession was welcomed by a town that had been, on the part of the parishoners, perceived to be bigoted and unsympathetic to Catholic practices. Carey is located in Wyandot County, Ohio, where the population in 1870 was over 93% Protestant (WALKER 1872). In fact, Father Gloden had at first hesitated to take Mary in procession because he feared it might offend the large Protestant population of Carey (JEFFREY 1979, 8).

The third miraculous event was the return of the downpour after the statue was taken into the chapel. It is interesting to note that the continued rain did not spare the devotees. Although it would have still been perceived to be a miracle if the storm had simply stopped when the procession began, the miracle took on greater significance when the rain returned immediately upon the entrance of the statue into the safety of the chapel.

Finally, the fourth miracle was the "deep impression" the meteorological miracle had made upon the Protestant population; a population that could have taken offense to the procession in the first place.

The devotees probably did not see the "miracle" as a series of separate events, but instead as one integrated experience that legitimized expression of their faith within an unsympathetic social milieu. TUAN (1984, 9) argues that the significance of a place arises out of symbolic acts. The procession was such a symbolic act, and that act was legitimized by unusual events. Once legitimized, the shrine could then take on the role and function of a window to the heavens. Within a few years of the procession, not surprisingly, reports by devotees of healing miracles began to spread. Also, meteorological events continued to occur, which were perceived to be signs from Our Lady. As these reports spread the number of visitors to the shrine increased and so did the incidence of healing events. Once this synergistic process was in place, even poor management of the shrine, which occurred in the 1880s (JEFFREY 1979, 11), could not prevent this place from maintaining its status as extra-ordinary; a place imbued with sacred significance. By the time of World War II, Our Lady of Consolation was attracting as many as 40,000 pilgrims to celebrate the Feast of the Assumption in August (JEFFREY 1979, 35). Some pilgrims claim that it has never rained on a procession and, to this day, pilgrims feel that the processions are always going to be rain-free. So, regardless of the weather forecast, devotees believe the processions will be able to proceed without interruption from atmospheric elements.

III. Source Region of Pilgrims

In order to gain further insight into the distribution of pilgrims, the registry at the Basilica and Shrine of Our Lady of Consolation was utilized. All entries from June 16th to August 14th, 1988 were examined to determine the origin of the pilgrims. Since the summer months are the time of year when Americans tend to be more mobile, and despite this non-random sample, this information should provide a reasonable estimate of the distance which people will travel to make this pilgrimage.

Over the study period, 1,275 entries were made in the register. Of these entries, 1,208, or nearly 95% were from the United States (Table 1). The data, although representing pilgrims from outside the United States, indicates that this shrine has not reached the point of international recognition, as have such famous shrines at Fátima in Portugal or Lourdes in France. All of the Canadian pilgrims came from Ontario, which is in close proximity to the shrine. In fact, many of them were from Windsor, Canada, a city within easy driving distance. Expectedly, most of the entries from outside of the United States and Canada were made by people making the pilgrimage from predominantly Catholic countries, and many of them were visiting American relatives according to informants.

Within the United States and Canada, the majority of pilgrims traveled from states or provinces adjacent to Ohio (Table 2). A total of 1,194 pilgrims, or 94% of the sample, were from Ohio, Michigan, Indiana, Kentucky, West Virginia, Pennsylvania, and Ontario. Many of these pilgrims journeyed to Carey specifically to pay homage or fulfill a vow to Our Lady, while others may have been passing through Carey, and knowing of the shrine, stopped to show their respect. Those individuals from Florida and Arizona most likely were retirees returning to midwestern and northeastern states for a summer visit (BOHLAND & TREPS 1982), while the pilgrims from Texas may have been migrant workers who pass through the midwest and northeast during the summer months

Table 1: Country of origin for pilgrims to "Our Lady of Consolation"

Country	# of pilgrims	% of Total
United States	1,208	94.7
Canada	49	3.8
Chile	4	.3
Philippines	4	.3
Italy	2	.1
Poland	2	.1
Germany*	1	–
Japan	1	–
Mexico	1	–
New Guinea	1	–
Scotland	1	–
Venezuela	1	–
TOTAL	1,275	100.0

* FRG/GDR not indicated

Source: Shrine registry, summer 1988

Table 2: Origin of Pilgrims by State or Province in North America

State or Province	# of Pilgrims	% of Total
Ohio	760	59.6
Michigan	218	17.1
Indiana	78	6.1
Pennsylvania	74	5.8
Ontario	49	3.8
Florida	22	1.7
Texas	11	.9
Illinois	9	.7
New York	5	.4
Kentucky	4	.3
West Virginia	4	.3
Iowa	3	.2
Massachusetts	3	.2
New Jersey	3	.2
Arizona	2	.1
North Carolina	2	.1
South Carolina	2	.1
California	1	–
Connecticut	1	–
Maryland	1	–
Missouri	1	–
Nevada	1	–
Rhode Island	1	–
Tennessee	1	–
Virginia	1	–
TOTAL	1,257	98.6

Source: Shrine registry, summer 1988

144

(SOSNICK 1978, 286). On the other hand, pilgrims from the other states may be tourists who combine their spiritual quest with recreational travel.

The data reflect the strong regional character of the shrine in terms of the pilgrims it attracts. Spatial distribution of pilgrims in the lower Great Lakes region is largely centered around three primary clusters. These clusters are first, Toledo/Detroit/Windsor; second, Youngstown/Akron/Canton; and third Columbus (Figure 1). Secondary clusters are found at Fort Wayne, Cincinnati, Cleveland, and Erie. Pilgrims from the Carey area appear to be small in number, which may or may not be due to local population patterns in terms of religious adherence, visitors not signing the register because they do not perceive themselves to be pilgrims due to short distance travelled, or to lack of interest in the shrine by the area residents. Very few pilgrims originate south and east of a Cincinnati-Columbus-Pittsburgh line.

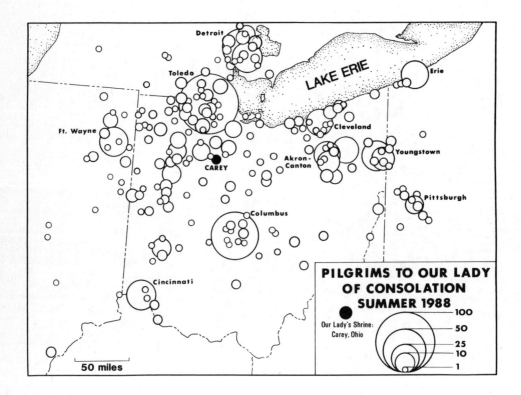

Fig. 1: Pilgrims to "Our Lady of Consolation", summer 1988
Source: Shrine registry, summer 1986

Several factors may be presented as reasons for the clusters just described. Proximity to the shrine, which presumes reasonable traveling distance for group buses and private cars, is probably a major factor in the distribution of pilgrim origins. Secondly, although the clusters are within easy driving distance, they are far enough away from Carey to constitute, for the pilgrims, a journey in the sense that pilgrims must make a special effort to visit the shrine. Generally speaking, a pilgrimage requires that the person make a special effort to visit the sacred site (BHARDWAJ & RINSCHEDE 1988, 14). Moreover, pilgrimage places usually are perceived by the pilgrim as being in a remote area, a characteristic that lends a more sacred quality to the shrine (SOPHER 1967, 26 – 27, 52). Due to the rural setting of the shrine of Our Lady of Consolation, urban Americans may perceive Carey to be "remote". Finally, the pilgrim origin clusters reflect the distribution of large Catholic populations in the northeast and midwest. Because many of America's Catholics are descended from immigrants of Italian, Polish, Irish, Lebanese, Chaldean, and other such Catholic, ethnic origins, and since many ethnic groups settled in America's urban, industrial centers (WARD 1971, 51 – 56), it is not surprising that so many of Our Lady's devotees hail from the large and medium sized urban centers around the shrine. It is also interesting to note that the majority of people living in the Carey area are members of Protestant denominations, and therefore would be less likely to visit the shrine. Thus, a combination of proximity to the shrine, the need to 'journey' in order to reach Carey, and the distribution of Catholics in urban areas surrounding the shrine site, may all contribute to an explanation of the pilgrim origin clusters.

IV. Conclusion

From a geographical perspective the shrine at Carey, Ohio cannot be characterized as a national shrine. As revealed by the shrine's registry, the majority of pilgrims hail from the lower Great Lakes area, and only minimally from locations outside of this region. The data reveal what would seem to be a regional pilgrimage shrine. Church officials at the Basilica, however, consider the shrine to be a national one. Signs leading to the shrine site indicate that the visitor is approaching a "national" shrine, and pilgrims interviewed at the site refer to its "national" character. The Conference of Bishops must approve the designation of "national" to a shrine and so explanations for such a designation, in face of the present facts, is that the shrine at one time may have attracted more pilgrims from across the nation than it does today, and it represents the nationally recognized replica of the original shrine of Our Lady of Consolation in Luxembourg.

In conclusion, the shrine of Our Lady of Consolation, located in Carey, Ohio, represents an extraordinary place in the eyes of believers. The geographically regional, rather than perceptually national status, does not diminish the site's sacred qualities, nor does it impair a devotee's quest for a spiritual experience. Our Lady of Consolation's status as a national shrine may be in question, but the window to heaven that the symbolizes for devotees is not.

Summary

Our Lady of Consolation, a Marian shrine founded in Carey, Ohio in 1875, has received pilgrims offering special devotions for over a century. The site is associated with many miracles according to devotees, which enhance the shrine's sacred quality. Such miracles are generally related to weather and healing events. Although the shrine has a "national" designation, data reveal that such a designation is not based upon the geographic origins of pilgrims visiting Carey, since most of them are from the lower Great Lakes region of the United States and Canada.

Zusammenfassung:

Pilgerfahrt zu einem "nationalen" amerikanischen Heiligtum: Our Lady of Consolation in Carey, Ohio

"Our Lady of Consolation", ein Marienheiligtum, das 1875 in Carey, Ohio, gegründet wurde, empfängt seit über einem Jahrhundert Pilger, die ihm eine besondere Verehrung entgegenbringen. Die Stätte wird mit vielen Wundern in Verbindung gebracht, welche die Heiligkeit des Ortes erhöhen. Solche Wunder stehen in der Regel im Zusammenhang mit bestimmten Witterungsereignissen und mit Heilungen. Obwohl die Pilgerstätte als "national" gekennzeichnet wird, zeigen die Daten, daß diese Bezeichnung sich nicht auf den Einzugsbereich der Pilger bezieht, die Carey besuchen, da die meisten von ihnen aus dem Gebiet der Großen Seen in den Vereinigten Staaten und in Kanada stammen.

Acknowledgement

The authors would like to thank Deborah Faiers and the cartographic services of Slippery Rock University for preparing the map.

Bibliography

BOHLAND, J. R. & Lexa TREPS (1982): County Patterns of Elderly Migration in the United States. — In: Warnes, Geographical Perspectives on the Elderly, John Wiley & Sons, Chichester, England: 139 – 158.

ELIADE, M. (1959): The Sacred and the Profane: The Nature of Religion. Trans. by W. R. Trask, Harcourt, Brace and Company, New York: reprint edition (1961): Harper and Row, New York.

JEFFREY, Bro. (1979): A History of the Basilica and National Shrine of Our Lady. Basilica and Shrine of Our Lady of Consolation, Carey, Ohio.

NOLAN, M. L. (1983): Irish Pilgrimage: The Different Tradition, Annals of the Association of American Geographers, Vol. 73: 421 – 38.

NOLAN, M. L. (1987): Christian Pilgrimage in the Old and New Worlds: A Comparative Perspective. Paper presented at the Annual Meeting of the Association of American Geographers in Portland, Oregon.

SOPHER, D. E. (1967): Geography of Religions. Prentice-Hall, Englewood Cliffs, New Jersey.

SOSNICK, S. H. (1978): Hired Hands: Seasonal Farm Workers in the United States. McNally & Loftin, West, Santa Barbara, CA.

—— (August 16, 1988): Texas Crowd Sees 'Miracle' in Clouds. Pittsburgh Press, Pittsburgh, PA: A7.

TUAN, Y. F. (1984): In Place, Out of Place, — In: Richardson, M. R., Place: Experience and Symbol. Geoscience and Man Publications, Baton Rouge, LA.

TURNER, V. & E. TURNER (1982): Postindustrial Marian Pilgrimage, — In: Preston, J. J., Mother Worship. University of North Carolina Press, Chapel Hill: 145 – 173.

WALKER, F. A. comp. (1872): The Statistics of the Population of the United States. Washington Printing Office, Washington, D.C.

WARD, D. (1971): Cities and Immigrants: A Geography of Change in Nineteenth Century America. Oxford University Press, New York.

Paolo Giuriati, Phyllis M.G. Myers, and Martin E. Donach

Pilgrims to "Our Lady of the Snows" Belleville, Illinois in the Marian Year: 1987 – 1988

1. Introduction and Historical Background

Religious pilgrimages are not well studied even though pilgrimages and other traditional forms of devotion are a resurging phenomenon (e.g., Medjugorje). Very little is known about pilgrimages in American culture. Studies of pilgrimages as an American religious phenomenon are needed in order to understand this practice more fully. In addition, more studies are needed for comparison with the characteristics of pilgrimages to the major shrines in Europe.

We have made an exploratory study of religious pilgrimages at the "National Shrine of Our Lady ofthe Snows" in Belleville, Illinois. The research was carried out by Prof. Paolo Giuriati (director of C.R.S.R. of Padua) and Prof. Phyllis M. G. Myers (Northern Illinois University) with the aid of Martin Donach (researcher of C.R.S.R. of Padua).

Among the many Catholic shrines in America, the shrine at Belleville is relatively atypical for several reasons. It is not a simple transposition of European devotion to America (as is the case with many other shrines in the States) brought by immigrants from a Catholic country (such as Ireland, Italy, Poland, France, etc.), imitating even in the structure of the buildings, the shrines of the fatherland.[1]

On the contrary, at Belleville in 1958 began the construction of a very original and certainly the largest example of an outdoor shrine in America, dedicated to the oldest Marian devotion of the Roman Catholic Church, Our Lady of the Snows, which is tied to the fourth century A.D. Basilica of St. Mary Major in Rome. But the initial decision to build the Belleville shrine had some very significant antecedents.[2]

In 1941 the Oblates of Mary Immaculate (O.M.I.) introduced the devotion to Our Lady of the Snows to the Midwest. It had its beginnings at St. Henry's Seminary in Belleville, Illinois, not far from St. Louis, Missouri.

One of the two men who promoted the devotion to Our Lady of the Snows was Fr. Paul Schulte (O.M.I.), renowned as the "Flying priest of the Arctic". While in the Arctic on many flights helping with the Oblate mission work among the Eskimos, Fr. Schulte had a deep personal devotion to Our Lady of the Snows. A photograph of Fr. Schulte depicts the fur clad missionary carrying the Eucharist to some Eskimos who were ill. An artist friend of Fr. Schulte (J. Watson Davis of New York) painted the scene adding the image of Our Lady of the Snows in the Arctic sky above the kneeling Eskimos. It was placed by Fr. Schulte in a corner of the chapel at St. Henry's Seminary in Belleville.

In a short time Fr. Schulte and Fr. Edwin J. Guild (O.M.I.) (who at the time was the school's treasurer and director of the Missionary Association of Mary Immaculate) were able to develop the devotion to Our Lady of the Snows among the priests and the students in the Seminary, the lay people of the Missionary Association, and the inhabitants of Belleville.

After some time the number of people visiting the image of Our Lady in the Seminary chapel became too large making it necessary to construct a special chapel on the Seminary grounds. On April 2nd, 1943, a perpetual novena was started to Our Lady of the Snows. The tradition of the solemn outdoor novena was started in 1951 and has been observed annually since then on the nine days surrounding August 5th (the feast day of Our Lady of the Snows).

When the number of visitors to the little shrine began to exceed its capacity, it was necessary to find a new location for the shrine and to build new and better facilities to handle the growing number of visitors. The ideal site for the proposed "National Shrine of Our Lady of the Snows" was found on the historic bluffs overlooking the Mississippi River Valley (off IL Route 15) between Belleville and East St. Louis, Illinois. The Oblates purchased 80 acres of rolling hills in February of 1958. Work began in the same year. Fr. E.J. Guild was the guiding leader of the building activity and the first director of the shrine. He carried out this role for quite some time, and now as the director emeritus still exercises the priestly ministry in the shrine.

The first installations to be started were the Outdoor Altar and its 20,000 person capacity amphitheater, the Lourdes Grotto (which is a reproduction of the original grotto of Lourdes, France) and the Way of the Cross. The Way of the Cross was completed during the summer of 1960. The Lourdes Grotto was dedicated on May 1st, 1961 and the tenth Annual Solemn Outdoor Novena was held at the grotto. By July 1962 the Outdoor Altar, which houses several chapels and the Rosary Courts, was almost ready.

The next site to be completed in 1965 was the Annunciation Garden (with the Angelus bells and fountain and the Annunciation statuary group) a place intended mainly as a source of peace, meditation and inspiration. On the same line later years witnessed the dedication of the Ressurection Garden, the Agony Garden, the Mother's Prayer Walk, and the Father's Memorial Wall.

Between 1960 and 1963 and during Vatican II the Oblates, with the help of the Layman's Association, obtained more land in the area until the present expanse of more than 200 acres was reached. In the following years they developed several facilities and activities on the line of the "ministries for people". They were the St. Joseph's Visitors Center (information, restaurant, and book-souvenir shop), the Pilgrims Inn Motel, the Dr. Tom Dooley Center (Shrine Ministries), the Apartment Community (for persons over 62 yrs. of age), the Dammert Geriatric Center, and the WMRY Radio Station (to keep physically impared persons in the mainstream of society).

Later during the 1980's an exhibit called "The Power", originally developed for the 1982 World's Fair in Knoxville, Tennesse by the Association of Christian Denominations, was located in the Edwin J. Guild Center. The program was purchased by the Oblates and some of the images have been adapted to the specific needs of the shrine. The Power, through image, light, and sound, is intended to constitute a multi-media and multi-sensory experience, a moving presentation of the story of God and humanity for rest, renewal, and growth in faith for all religious denominations. The shrine offers it for individuals and all groups that wish to find the "true" source of power for their lives.

2. The Actual Situation

The above outline of the historical growth of the shrine of Our Lady of the Snows at Belleville constitutes the preliminary phase of the research (June–August 1987), on the basis of the data collected there and also through participant observation and informal interviews with the authorities of the shrine.

In the Information Center visitors are able to know what the shrine offers them. A set of folders, brochures, and pictures explain the activities and the facilities available to them. Samples of this material were collected in the same preliminary phase of the research. Through comparative analysis of the data from all these sources it is possible to establish some reference points on the shrine of Our Lady of the Snows at the beginning of the research.

The Belleville shrine is grounded upon some specific cultural roots: the ancient devotion of the Catholic Church for "Our Lady of the Snows", the missionary minds of the Oblates, and their particular cult of the Virgin, mainly as "Mary Immaculate". In addition, the shrine combines some specific features corresponding to the subsequent phases of its growth. A first set of components can be defined as devotional and more strictly religious in nature which prevailed until the beginnings of the 1960's. To this stage it is possible to assign the Lourdes Grotto, the Way of the Cross, the Outdoor Altar and the chapels housed there, and the Annual Solemn Novena in August. In all these elements the traditional religious devotions of the Catholic Church are evident, but their adaptation to the American culture is also clear in the spectacularity of the Outdoor Altar, the ceremonies celebrated there, as well as the setting of religious facilities in a park.

A second set of components can be found in the development of the facilities for meditation (Annunciation Garden, Agony Garden, etc.) and of the "Ministries for People" added in the mid 60's according to trends inspired by the Second Vatican Council, the tradition of the Oblates, and a further adaptation to the American culture. A third set of components is related to a more recent and progressive opening to ecumenism and today's society with all of its tensions and complexity. The Power can be viewed as the symbol of this trend.

The last set of components is connected to the spiritual influence of the founder of the shrine (Fr. Guild), who is still active in the shrine, and who behaves in some ways like a charismatic leader, reinforcing the call back to the Catholic roots and tradition and guaranteeing loyalty to them.

The above sets of components are intertwined in a complex and dynamic combination of expressive means. Color, song, and praise, an ever-widening use of mass media and visual culture shape a message destined for a variety of audiences: pilgrims, visitors, youth, handicapped, the elderly, specific ethnic groups, etc. For each of them a staff of Oblates and lay people, some of them volunteers from the audience itself (elderly and handicapped), prepare and run a number of general and specially designed activities every year.

The general message underlying all of the above can be summarized below. The National Shrine of Our Lady of the Snows aims to be:

- a place of discovery and peace

- a place where one can find oneself as a person loved by God

- a place where people are called to deepen their faith and relationship with Christ

- a place where one can look for Mary, the Mother of Christ, as a model and guide in our journey and quest

- a place of revitalization and enrichment

- a place providing an awareness of our own role as missionaries, in order to go forth on our own journey, with a desire to share a deepening faith awareness through Christian interactions for and with others.

In accordance with the message, where the sacred and the human elements are not separated from one another, the shrine itself at the time of this research project had no real sacred space separated from its surrounding environment, rather it is organized like an open space in a green setting which is always available to a very heterogeneous public.[3] All this makes Belleville atypical as a shrine. But it also makes the systematic analysis of the phenomenon by means of the usual methodology of social sciences very problematic.

Before explaining the theoretical and methodological frame of reference that was used for the research, it is useful to integrate the above information with the data of the visitors to the shrine, according to the estimates by the shrine authorities at the beginning of the research.

Of the more than 1 million visitors that come to Belleville every year approximately 65% are Catholic; 35% are not Catholic. About 500,000 cars are counted each year with an average of 2.5 persons per car, suggesting approximately 1.2 million visitors to this shrine. During 1986, 610 buses came to the shrine, each with approximately 40 visitors, meaning nearly 24,000 pilgrims, and provided 2.5% of all visitors. Visitors to Belleville come from 21 different states of the US, but the majority come from only 14 states, in a radius of about 500 miles. The buses come as parish groups or special event groups (women associations, Knights of Columbus, etc.) or groups organized by travel agencies. There tend to be three main season for the visits: May, October and December (December is the busiest month due to the "Way of Lights" at Christmas).

3. Theoretical and Methodological Frame of Reference

Even in the United States pilgrimages to shrines of the Catholic Church constitute, as in Europe, a growing mass phenomenon.[4] In Europe certain scholars have interpreted pilgrimages in modern times as a process of returning to one's roots, to an idealized past, a sort of reconquering of a lost identity.[5] But others have placed it in the perspective of a rite of passage through which one accomplishes a mobilization of individual resources within a collectivity. Within this framework, some men through a sacred event continue an individual search for a religious meaning to life through an experience of existential change (conversion) which enables them to perceive how salvation is within their reach and how it can really enter into their daily lives.[6] In a society as complex as that of the United States and in a shrine where people of different denominations, races (white, black, filipino, etc.) and ethnic groups may meet, the explanations given for pilgrimages in Europe may not be sufficient to explain the American situation. Other reasons connected with the growing tendency to discover or reinforce one's cultural roots and social identity may be envolved.

In this perspective the sanctity of the place which is visited or where people meet would constitute a pretext or a supplementary framework in order to give meaning to existence and to revitalize everyday life on a human level. But it could also, under certain circumstances yet to be verified, constitute a departure point for an experience of religious conversion, a return to the source of values, and a reconciliation with one's self and others through a communion with the "radically other".

Moving from the above theoretical premises to empirical ground, it is important to realize that in Europe the collection of data on mass-pilgrimage is still at its beginning and this is even more true in America. Two pilot studies can be quoted: the project on marian shrines carried out in Lourdes, Fátima, Medjugorje, and Loreto by the Center for Socio-Religious Research (Centro Ricerche Socio-Religiose, C.R.S.R.) of Padua with the Centro Studi Antoniani of Padua and "Il Terzo Occhio per la Cultura Populare", of Bologna Italy[7] and a project on pilgrimages to "Padre Pio" conducted by G. Scaravaglieri.[8]

The research at Our Lady of the Snows was conceived as parallel and comparable to the previous investigations at Lourdes, Medjugorje, and Fátima and the simultaneous research at Loreto.[9] One must also remember that each shrine has certain unique characteristics which must be taken into account and which do not always coincide with those of other important shrines: devotional traditions and customs, seasonal and weekly rhythms of pilgrim influx, and types of visitors and pilgrims, even with respect to their race, nationality and culture.

In the case of Belleville some other factors made field work problematic. The shrine was created only in 1958 but not due to some "supernatural" event, nor was it built on the place where a saint lived or is buried. Moreover the structure of the shrine is very complex, its visitors are very heterogeneous, and the devotion to the Virgin is no longer the main element.

For these reasons at Our Lady of the Snows the primary research issues were:

- who comes to Our Lady of the Snows;
- for what reasons;

- with what spirit and level of religious practice;

- with what general orientation towards existential values. In more detail, the following information was elicted regarding those who come for devotion to Mary;

- how the devout conceives the image of the sacred interlocutor;

- with what language (presence, prayer, action) does the dialogue take place;

- what are the contents of such a dialogue....

All these general and specific interests were to be reconstructed with the consideration that a place like Our Lady of the Snows constitutes a point of reference for the social communication of a sacred message to be proposed to the visitors and eventually assimilated by them to various degrees. The hypothesis is that coming to the shrine may constitute a real religious moment if it is perceived as an experience of the "radically other" inscribed in the visitor's life and with the function of existentially recharging the visitor in order to give meaning and substance to daily routine.

Given the complex structure of the phenomenon which is the center of this research, it seemed suitable to integrate traditional approaches with a methodology which could allow for an analysis of the phenomenon from more than one point of view and on various levels. Moreover, we are living in a society of visual communication and this kind of communication is particularly important at Belleville. Therefore, it was supposed that the use of converging methods: interviews, photographs, and collecting anthropological records can contribute to better understanding the religious dynamics and their socio-cultural influence in a country as complex as the United States.

The following activities were planned:

- preliminary collection of news from the shrine;

- questionnaires distributed to all workers at the shrine having daily contact with visitors to verify their image of the pilgrims/visitors;

- interviews, using questionnaires, with visitors at the shrine;

- recordings of conversations with pilgrims, on the pattern of the questionnaire;

- participant observation and photographs (slides) of the various components of the phenomenon and of cult behavior of the devout;

- systematic collection (and analysis) of written prayer petitions;

- checking preferences in purchasing souvenirs-religious objects.

To obtain the best results it seemed convenient to conduct the investigation in such a way as to include periods of maximum, average, and minimum influx, because they may show a different mix of visitors and their behavior. Observations were made for a whole week's cycle to record variations during the same season with respect to Sundays, Saturdays, Mondays and mid-week.

The interviews, were spread out in the most distributive manner possible according to: age groups, place of origin and other specifications (ill, accompanying someone ill, pilgrim with a group or alone, tourist, etc.) in order to capture an ample and complete variety of sources. Thus the interviews had to be somewhat programed each time.

The questionnaire was divided into four blocks:

1. individual characteristics of the interviewee

2. questions on the shrine of Our Lady of the Snows

3. questions on the devotional practices at Our Lady of the Snows

4. spiritual analysis of the interviewee.

The time in which the research was carried out practically coincided with the "Marian Year", that is the year of special devotion and prayer to Mary established by Pope John Paul II from June 7, 1987 to August 15, 1988. As the Belleville shrine is dedicated to Mary, it therefore seemed very important to conduct the research during this same period.

The research commenced in June 1987. In its preliminary phase, approximately 100 brochures and folders about Our Lady of the Snows were collected and analyzed to determine the ways in which the message of this shrine is and has been presented to the faithful, and also to develop a questionnaire. This was followed by the general study of "pilgrim experience" at Our Lady of the Snows, carried out from August 1987 through August 1988, and comprised several activities:

1. Distribution of questionnaire to all workers at the shrine to verify their perception of the pilgrims/visitors. 50 questionnaires were distributed of which 30 were completed.

2. Interviews of visitors using questionnaires (analogous to the questionnaire for the "workers"). 200 questionnaires were distributed of which 66 were completed, 40 from people in retreat groups and 26 from other visitors.

3. Participant observation and photographs (slides) of various components of the phenomenon "The Pilgrim Experience at Our Lady of the Snows"; approximately 400 slides were made.

4. Collection, and subsequent analysis of 250 written prayer petitions from pilgrims and/or devout correspondence written in May 1988 (one of the main "seasons" at the shrine).

5. Verification of the preferences of pilgrims in purchasing souvenirs. Analysis of the life histories of the visitors will be done in a subsequent phase of the study.

The following procedures were adopted for the general study:

1. The questionnaires for the shrine workers were given directly to the interested parties, priests and laymen who have contact with pilgrims. The questionnaires were distributed and collected by the shrine.

2. The pilgrims interviewed do not constitute a sample chosen according to rigorous statistical criteria because the universe fluctuates too much. Instead, representatives expressing a variety of significant human situations which, according to the local experts, constitute the visitors to Our Lady of the Snows were contacted.

3. Participant observations were recorded and photographs of devout behavior were taken as a visual documentation of the distinctive aspects of Our Lady of the Snows during maximum, average, and minimum influx of pilgrims/visitors for comparative analysis and, subsequent synthesis of the characteristics in relation to those emerging from the other avenues of investigation. Specifics of the procedure were left to researchers' discretion, always linked however to the analogous areas of interest of the questionnaire.

4. The written prayer petitions and devout correspondence collected during this period, after the deletion of personal references, were photocopied for their qualitative and quantitative analysis using a simplified grid (similar to that used at other shrines) and connected to a few key questions from the questionnaire.

5. An analysis of the purchases of pilgrims, including sacramental objects took place during the period of the interviews.

4. The Site and Pilgrim Behavior

How does the shrine appear to the average pilgrim or visitor? How does the average pilgrim/visitor behave? A comparative analysis of the visual documentation and of records of participant observation indicate the following:

1. *The Entrance:* A large cement marker stands at the entrance to the shrine. It is located in the middle of a flower bed and is well lit at night. Its message is written in a script which is not typical of billboards; neither is it solemn in tone but is rather light and airy, inviting, and yet reserved; it is precisely this element which one first notices. It is an invitation to all. It is a very simple message written large enough to be seen by those arriving by car (adapted to a motorized society).

There are no gates or walls surrounding the shrine property; one can always enter. Once on the shrine grounds, wooden signs, similar to those found in any park, greet the visitor; the lettering is simple, modern and functional. These same signs are also used throughout the shrine to provide directions and indicate the various components of the shrine. During the Marian year an additional sign was present. It had a blue stylized cross and the message "1987-1988 Marian Year. Pilgrims...with Mary...to Jesus".

The shrine grounds themselves are kept much like a typical American park with trees and lawns; the few flowers are found in neat flower beds close to some of the shrine's component parts. The roads are primarily for cars and are well lit. There are usually parking places at each component site allowing for easy access. There are also several paths through the woods for pedestrians which foster a closer contact with nature. This park-like setting is no doubt meant to relax the visitor, re-establishing his relationship with the rest of creation and showing him the beauty of God's handiwork.

2. *The Lourdes Grotto:* Here one finds a faithful smaller scale reproduction in cement of the grotto of Lourdes. Photographs of the various stages of construction are on display in the Visitors Center. In front of the grotto a small square provides benches and an altar for religious services. This little square has a low surrounding wall with an explanation of the grotto and a brief synthesis of the apparitions and message of Lourdes.

The path to the grotto has plaques with the names of the faithful who wish to be remembered here (the majority of names seem to be Irish, German, Slavic, and Italian). Visitors arriving here often read the names of donors on the plaques before moving on to the grotto. The path leads to a statue of Bernadette placed on the left side of the grotto kneeling in prayer before the Virgin. Upon entering, the visitor sees the Virgin as Bernadette sees her, creating two centers of interest.

Visitors seem to have an instant confidential rapport with the site and with the statue of Bernadette. The statue is rigid and awkward, but this does not seem to discourage people; rather these defects make her seem more human and approachable. In fact the statue often has flowers, rosaries, and scapulars in its hands, placed there by visitors who draw near and touch Bernadette; she in turn gives these offerings to the Virgin as symbols of prayer, devotion, love and thanks. While visitors must leave, Bernadette remains, kneeling before Mary, ever constant in her prayer. The children explore the sacred space of the shrine as if they were in a park (the statue is roughly their height) thus experiencing a sense of communion in a relaxed atmosphere.

Near the grotto there are votive lights and a box for offerings. Visitors frequently light these lamps before prayer. Children here are brought before the statue of the Virgin to pray.

The visitors, for the most part arrive, by car. There are many families, and youths. The people look about, pray, and read or perhaps search for the names of loved ones on the plaques but all in an atmosphere of a park, rather than a sacred space. They take pictures or videotape their experience.

On Saturday evenings there is a prayer service at the grotto. Candles are distributed at the entrance, and a priest leads the prayer. The public is comprised mostly of mature persons, especially women, all nicely dressed, with propriety and distinction. Concentration can be read in the faces of the devotees during the service. Several visitors remain in private prayer after the function.

3. The Annunciation Garden: This site presents the visitor with one of the principle mysteries of the rosary. Original in its design, it is constituted by a long path which leads to a pool. Opposite the pool there is a wall with modern statues of Mary and the Archangel Gabriel. In the pool there are four bells which are located in byzantine turrets. They play the Angelus at noon. There are also fountains; one is a simple spray pattern mimicking an "M", while two others are in the form of a lily. Children seem to establish a rapport with the water. Their parents often join them in their play at the pool's edge. The sounds and movement of the fountains attract the attention of visitors and invite them to reflect and meditate.

4. Mothers Prayer Walk: This area is located along one side of the pool of the Annunciation Garden. It is marked off by two low walls which hold bronze plaques with the names of mothers to be remembered. Closer to the pool, in the middle of a bed of roses, there is a prayer capsule with names of the mothers to be remembered on Mothers Day. Children sit in the shade on the low walls (there are no benches), and just as mothers have given so much, their walls continue to provide support in front of the Great Mother.

5. *Fathers Memorial Wall:* Just like the mothers prayer walk, this area is set aside for the remembrance of fathers. Located near the Annunciation Garden, a path leads downhill to a flat area carved in the side of the slope. A cement retaining wall with a wooden texture gently rises with the hill to well over six feet, forms a right angle and then descends. The wall has bronze plaques with the names of fathers, a stone with an etching of St. Joseph, and a prayer capsule. Next to St. Joseph there is the saying: "Father of us all, remember our fathers". St. Joseph is shown as a strong young man hard at work (characteristic of the charismatic movement), an image of how we wish our fathers were or how we would like to remember them. The angular shape of the wall is reminiscent of a shoulder or an arm holding back the hill; something we can lean on, which protects us and provides us with shelter.

A trail through the woods leads to the Lourdes Grotto at the foot of the hill. Along the way there are benches and a statue of the Sacred Heart. Visitors often sit by the statue and reflect. This wooded area lets the visitor leave the world behind (mothers and fathers) and acts like a purifying filter before one arrives at the call of Mary.

6. *The Main Shrine:* This site consists of a structure housing an outdoor altar of black marble located at the center of an amphitheater. The building is white with three large parabolic arches stretching above the roof to form an "M". At the center where the three arches meet, three circles open to the sky representing the Holy Trinity. These arches are surmounted by a bronze cross which penetrates the "M" terminating in a flame shaped dove. The symbolism of the descent of salvation which arrives to us through Mary by the power of the Holy Spirit is quite evident.

The statue of Our Lady of the Snows stands in a gold niche simulating a chalice since Mary was the first chalice to contain Christ. The parabolic shape of the niche seems to be symbolic of the concentration of divine grace on one focal point, Mary. On either side of the niche the backdrop of the Northern Lights can be seen, recreating the Arctic night. The statue itself shows the Virgin holding the Christ child on her right side and presenting him to the world. Christ is seen in a regal pose and in the act of blessing.

The back of the shrine has a bas-relief of two angels, one on either side of a lotus flower representing Mary's purity. The angels carry scrolls with the inscription "Ave Maria", the greeting of the Annunciation.

The amphitheater is in a park-like setting surrounded by trees and has umbrellas which can be used for shade on hot summer days. The crowds which gather here seem free and uninhibited. There is a sense of spontaneity in the services held here.

The building of the Main Shrine also houses Christ the King Chapel, the Rosary Courts, and the Blessed Sacrament Chapel. The entrances to these other component sites can be found at the sides and to the rear of the building.

7. *The Rosary Courts:* Two corridors, one on either side of Christ the King Chapel, contain the Joyful and the Glorious Mysteries of the Rosary. The Sorrowful Mysteries are contained in Christ the King Chapel. The images are mosaics on a gold background. Each image is separated from the next by a black marble wall. The group of the Mysteries is raised on a step. The images thus form little chapels. Visitors can light votive lights on the back wall or place them in front of the image of their choice. The number of votive lights is quite large in general, and particularly in front of the scene of the Nativity. The Presentation at the Temple and the Visitation also have numerous lights, episodes which correspond to very ancient and important liturgical feasts of the Catholic Church. Memorial plaques are placed on the walls near the entrance. Envelopes for votive light offerings and a book for prayer petitions are placed on offering boxes at the entrance.

8. *Christ the King Chapel:* The bowed back wall of the Chapel is divided into five mosaics representing the five Sorrowful Mysteries of the rosary. Each of the mosaics has an inspirational saying taken from the scriptures pertinent to the scene represented. The central scene is of Christ crowned with thorns. Through his suffering Christ proclaims himself the king of heaven.

The wooden pews are arrayed in semi-circular rows around the altar much like an amphitheater. The white ceiling above the altar is almond shaped and has a circular baldachin in the center forming the image of an eye. The exterior surface of the baldachin has a repeating thorn pattern which transforms it into a crown of thorns. Within this canopy is a gold mosaic representing the Holy Spirit in the form of a dove. Placed behind the head of the dove is an eye representing God the Father. This superimposition of the two persons of the Holy Trinity creates a vertical composition which finds its completion in the third person of the Trinity, Christ, who is present on the altar below. The mosaic has a gold background representing heaven. It was through Christ's crown of thorns that heaven was opened to mankind, and here it is through the baldachin in the shape of a crown of thorns that heaven can be seen. Outside the door is an interesting note of modern technology adapted to a sacred use: a stainless steel holy water fount, shaped much like a drinking fountain with a push button dispenser.

Not many people participate in the afternoon prayer services, but the chapel is filled to capacity for Mass in which many elderly and younger families participate. A large percentage of the crowd receives Communion during Mass.

Close to a side entrance to the chapel is an area set aside for Confession, the Reconciliation Chapel, which houses a painting of Our Lady of Guadalupe. Despite this special place, pilgrims/visitors rarely seem to go to Confession.

9. Blessed Sacrament Chapel: This site is located directly behind and below the Outdoor Altar of the main shrine. The doors to the chapel are silver plated bronze and represent themes of the Old and New Testaments. The semi-circular room is painted white except for the front wall which has a shelf of black marble supporting the tabernacle and a colorful painting of adoring angels. The low ceiling ends just short of the canopy over the tabernacle leaving a semi-circular gap. Through the gap the backdrop of the Outdoor Altar representing the Aurora Borealis can be seen. A person entering from outside expects to find a normal room, and at first that is what he sees. The gap in the ceiling is seen from an angle and is less evident. When one approaches the altar the gap grows and one has the feeling of "falling" upwards into the arctic sky as the weight of the low ceiling is removed. Hence, as we approach Christ in the form of the Blessed Sacrament, all earthly obstacles and barriers disappear, and we are transported into another realm. This chapel is reserved for meditation, and it is mostly up to the visitor to discover it; as a result, very few visitors go inside.

10. The Agony Garden: This shady grove is located off the Way of the Cross and is centered around a statue of Christ kneeling in prayer. Along the path leading to the statue, bronze plaques with the names of donors are placed low to the ground. Pilgrims, when in groups, tend to keep their distance from the statue. They are very attentive and seem to almost share in and at the same time feel responsible for Christ's suffering. Even children seem moved by the scene. Individuals, however, often place rosaries in the hands of Christ.

11. The Way of the Cross: The Stations of the Cross are realistic, three dimensional, representations of the sufferings of Christ, much more traditional than the mosaics of the Rosary Court. They are placed in protective wooden shelters with kneelers before them. The structures and kneelers are painted barn red and, like so many drops of blood, mark the path of Christ's passion. Each station has two prerecorded messages to provide devotional inspiration. The wooded area along the road is dotted with benches giving the visitor a place to pause and reflect. The half-mile road is usually travelled by car; however, those who walk can find time for meditation between each station.

12. The Resurrection Garden: This area which is placed at the end of the Way of the Cross represents the sepulcher of Christ. The structure itself is egg-shaped, symbolic of new life. It was modeled on the geode stone, a hollow stone often lined with crystals. Bits of broken glass around the opening simulate the crystals. The inside shows the empty slab of Christ's tomb, for He is risen. At the rear a burning flame can be seen, a symbol of our eternal hope in the resurrection of the dead on the last day. Within much smaller but similar shaped stones there are scenes of the post-resurrection appearances of Christ testifying to his resurrection, urging the visitor to do the same. A capsule contains the names of the departed to be remembered on the feast of All Souls Day.

Pilgrims seem to react to the originality of this presentation and to the effect of the flame reflected at the rear of the tomb. They seem very involved in this scene out of curiosity rather than devotion. They point and comment to one another; they try to figure out how the effect of the flame is achieved, or whether the flame is or is not there. This is also one of the places most frequently photographed.

13. The Power: This multi-sensory presentation represents the Divine Power present in the universe. The building itself, called the Fr. Guild Center, is a low structure inserted into a hill with flower beds at the entrance. Before entering the presentation visitors wait in a lobby where they begin to show their curiosity, while children begin to explore. A bronze book which visitors often leaf through contains the names of donors who contributed to the building of the structure.

The presentation itself is designed to revitalize the visitor. In the first room the visitor sits on steps facing a large screen and is presented with the origins of the universe. What was responsible for the beginning of the cosmos? What has given us the marvels which surround us? Who established the laws of nature? The answer comes back: God. In the face of all God's goodness man by his greed has broken the relationship with his creator. Silence then allows the visitor to reflect on this fatal error.

The visitor is then ushered into a second room. The corridor he must walk through presents a circus-like atmosphere introducing him to the "carnival" of the "human parade" which is constantly in search of new thrills and attractions. Modern technology tries to fulfill this need but pollutes and litters, destroying what little remains of paradise. This idea of destruction and failure builds until "we can't handle it anymore!". Christ is then presented as the solution.

The visitor now passes through another corridor. This time however, the corridor is shaped like a cross seemingly carved in stone and has a great light coming from the other side. The visitor upon arriving in the third room is told that he has been brought nearer to God through Jesus and has received the power, the power of God's creative love. It is here that the message of

Christ's love is expounded upon. Lastly, the visitor is reminded that he must maintain his relationship with God through prayer and is sent out to continue his journey to love, to forgive, to grow and to seek.

All this is designed to remind man of his original sin and make him see the uselessness of his attempts to find happiness on his own, using his own power. Only the power of God can fulfill his needs, he is told. A very effective presentation from both a theatrical and psychological point of view, it seems to leave the visitor inspired and highly motivated with a missionary mandate to love others.

14. The St. Joseph's Visitors Center: Here the visitor can obtain information about the shrine. From this area one can proceed to the Gift Shop, the Restaurant, or the Dr. Tom Dooley Center. An audio-visual presentation prepares the visitor for his visit; it explains the places of the shrine and shows the beauty of the natural setting, providing a general orientation. There are nearby meeting rooms, and bulletin-boards list the time tables of various gatherings and events. A replica of the statue of Our Lady of the Snows occupies a small niche on one side of the room. Comfortable chairs allow people to rest while awaiting the beginning of the slide show, the departure of the tram, or friends who are purchasing souvenirs in the Gift Shop.

15. The Gift Shop: The store offers a great variety of objects from greeting cards to liturgical vestments. There is a corner dedicated to Christmas decorations all year round. The most abundant items are pictures, holy cards, frames, statues, medals and books. Visitors purchase gifts for themselves and for those back home as a way of remembering or involving others in the message or experience of the shrine. They seem to look for items with great care and attention to detail. They also tend to purchase practical items with a religious flare, such as mugs, night-lights, and picture frames.

16. The Restaurant: Visitors can find a good meal at moderate prices and with very kind service. The restaurant usually operates at full capacity, and often there is a line to be seated. The place mats have pictures of the various sites at the shrine as well as inspirational passages; this adds to the wealth of visual stimuli found at the shrine and reminds the visitor of the places he has been and what he has felt during the day or suggests new places to visit. Many people from the Belleville area are drawn to the shrine specifically for the restaurant, making the estimates of the number of pilgrims that much more difficult.

17. The Dr. Tom Dooley Center: In the lobby of this building the visitor can find many pamphlets and brochures describing the various events and ministries the shrine offers as well as other tourist attractions in the St. Louis metropolitan area. Special events and workshops are held in the various meeting rooms. For the most part, however, the average pilgrim has very little to do with this part of the shrine.

18. The Tram: This is a sort of train which takes visitors on a tour of the shrine. It departs from the Visitors Center and finishes its trip there as well. The tram is much like any other tour tram found even in the movie studios of Hollywood. The driver serves as a guide, and makes several stops at the various points of interest. The guide's explainations are functional and provide the visitor with the historical background of the sites, but ultimately it is the site itself which creates the atmosphere or mood. People here are dressed quite informally as if on vacation rather than on a visit to a sacred place. While each group is different, the general tendency is for visitors to warm up to each other slowly during the tram tour. They begin to exchange comments on the tram and eventually take pictures for others. On the whole, however, interaction is kept to a minimum.

19. Other Components: There are several other sites at the shrine with which the pilgrim/visitor comes into contact such as the Pilgims Inn, the motel located directly across from the Visitors Center, or the radio station with the call letters WMRY. There is also an apartment community (retirement center) located on the shrine grounds, but completely removed from the area frequented by pilgrims. These are not meant as places of meditation or worship and seem to have little influence on the religious experience at the shrine.

20. Special Events: Two annual events of great importance are the feast of Our Lady of the Snows in August and the Way of Lights at Christmas. These are the moments of the greatest influx of pilgrims. The feast of Our Lady of the Snows is celebrated at the Main Shrine. Pilgrims follow the statue of Our Lady in procession. They are very involved with the moment and a solemn atmosphere reigns. At sundown the pilgrims light candles and the event takes on the air of the candle-light procession at Lourdes.

The Way of Lights, on the other hand, is meant to be seen by car. Episodes of the birth of Christ are presented in light. Trees and shrubs are lit and the cityscape of Bethlehem is recreated in lights. There are scenes of the Annunciation, the Marriage of Mary, and the Magnificat. The Nativity is at the Lourdes Grotto. Billboards read: "God made peace... through the death of His son... on the cross". There is a real stable with live animals. A brightly colored kiosk is used to collect offerings. This is a major attraction for the entire region.

5. The Average Pilgrim/Visitor

Participant observation and more importantly the comparative analysis of the visual documentaion collected at Belleville brought to light how the shrine appears to the average pilgrim or visitor and how the average pilgrim/visitor behaves. The comprehensive analysis of the questionnaires, prayer petitions, and records of preferences in purchasing souvenirs brings to light the characteristics of the average pilgrim/visitor. But before going further, it is necessary to clarify certain facts.

It has already been noted that Belleville is an atypical shrine and that the people who come here are very heterogeneous. Moreover, most of the people arrive by car or bus. Very often they are brought directly to the place of interest (for example the Main Shrine or the Lourdes Grotto), and they leave very quickly immediately following the ceremony or prayers for which they came. Visitors often arrive by car, drive through the shrine grounds looking at the various sites (they may even stop to say some prayers or to observe the stations of the cross), and may leave without ever having gotten out of their cars. In addition, the outdoor temperature is very cold in winter and very hot in summer, and this does not make it easy to meet people willing to be interviewed by means of traditional questionnaires.

Further, the Belleville shrine is very complex and it offers many points of interest. For most of the events, meetings, and performances at the shrine the public has a very tight schedule making it difficult to find the time necessary to properly fill out the questionnaire. On the other hand a short questionnaire would have meant remaining on the surface of the problems to be analyzed. In fact, the questionnaire had 63 questions, and its length was somewhat discouraging to most people.

For all the above reasons it became clear during the early stages of the general study phase that means other than the questionnaire would have to be used as well, and the results of the questionnaire would have to be considered complementary. More detailed and definitive data might come from new questionnaires prepared for additionals phases of the research and focusing on specific aspects of the Belleville phenomenon.

For this research 50 questionnaires were distributed to the shrine's "staff", ie. priests, religous functionaries, and laymen who have daily contact with pilgrims/visitors. 30 of these "staff" members (60%) responded. Another 200 questionnaires were distributed to visitors who came to the shrine for special events (spiritual retreats or meetings; their responses will be classifed under "retreat group") or simply to visit (their answers will be indicated as "others"). Altogether 66 questionnaires or 33.3% were filled out; 40 from "retreat groups" and 26 from "others" (see table 1, appendix). The questionnaires for the staff and for the visitors were the same except for some specific questions, thus their results are comparable. However, it must be remembered that the staff answered according to what they believed were the attitudes, feelings, and opinions of the pilgrims/visitors.

The general characteristics of the interviewees are given in table 1. The "staff" was mainly (76,6%) between 31 and 60 yrs. of age, more female (56.7%) than male (33.3%), mostly white (86.7%), and Catholic (80.0%). Those belonging to the "retreat groups" were mainly over 60 yrs. of age (70.0%), female (77.5%), white (87.5%), Catholic (85.0%), and many have been to the shrine more than once (65.0%). The "others" varied more in age (46.1% between 31-60 yrs., 50.0% over 60) and sex (42.3% male, 50.0% female). But like the retreat groups the "others" too were mainly white (80.8%), Catholic (84.6%), and many had been to the shrine more than once (57.7%).

The reasons for coming to Our Lady of the Snows (table 2) in order of importance are:

1. Motives of a practical nature (health of body and soul: 36.7% for the staff; 32.5% for retreat groups; and 50% for others).

2. Motives of a spiritual-ascetic nature (encounter with God and to become a better person: 33.3% for the staff; 45.0% for retreat groups; only 11.5% for others), and devotion to Mary (30.0% for the staff; 30.7% for the others).

3. Motives of a secular or non-religious nature (tourism, curiosity, accompanying other people: 36.7% for the staff; 19.2% for the others).

For many questions it was possible to give two answers.

The acts which are carried out by visitors at Our Lady (table 4) do not always have the same meaning. Those more related to the devotional and strictly religious set of components (i.e. to visit the Main Shrine, attend a prayer service or Mass at Christ the King Chapel, to visit the Lourdes Grotto) may be classified into two main related groups:

1. Asking for graces

2. Union with God/the Virgin, increase in faith.

The acts more related to meditation and discovery, as for instance a visit to the Annunciation Garden and the Angelus Bells, do not have a clear-cut significance. However, asking for graces, union with God, with the Virgin, increase in faith, expressing with greater spontaneity the feeling inside oneself are the more recurrent meanings to be found in the responses of those interviewed. Even to participate in a ministry program or a special event at the shrine evokes a combined set of feelings such as asking for graces, union with God, horizontal dialogue, and the need to exteriorize and emphasize one's feelings.

The multimedia presentation "The Power", which is the symbol of the progressive opening of the Belleville shrine to ecumenism and the tensions of today's society, is especially related to experiencing the word of God in a way that is relevant to modern- day life (63.4% for the staff; 25.0% for the retreat groups; 38.5% for others). Finally, to buy and take home religious objects means, over all, to keep some remembrance of the visit to the shrine and to hold something of that experience.

The roles given to Mary (see table 3) are also perceived differently by the three groups. For example, "Our mother in heaven" was the role indicated by 23.3% of the staff, 45.0% of the retreat groups, and 46.2% of the others. Similarly Mary's role as "Mother of God" was suggested by 50.0% of the staff, 20.0% of the retreat groups, and 19.2% of the others. And Mary is seen as a "Model for our lives" by 16.6% of the staff, 15.0% of the retreat groups, and 30.7% of the others. Only the staff attributes a 20.0% to the title of "Our Lady of the Snows".

The religiosity of the pilgrim/visitor was understood through the responses to the word religion and the meanings attributed to the sacraments (table 6). "Religion" is clearly connected directly to "faith in God" (66.7% for the staff; 42.5% for the retreat groups; 73.1% for the others). No other phrase elicited a significant response. Meanings given to Confession in decreasing order are: "recognize one's own faults before God and be pardoned by Him" (56.6% for the staff; 37.5% for the retreat groups; 57.7% for the others); "free one's conscience from the burden of sins" (50.0% for the staff; 42.5% for the retreat groups; 30.8% for the others); and "union with God and a means of sanctification" (only 6.7% for the staff; but 20.0% for the retreat group; and 42.3% for the others). The Mass and Communion are seen as: "union with God and a means of sanctification" (40.0% for the staff and the retreat groups; 46.1% for the others); "memorial of Christ's Sacrifice" (23.3% for the staff; 30.0% for the retreat groups; 57.7% for the others).

Visitor responses to the "message" of the Belleville shrine (table 5) vary among the three groups. The following are the most significant points: "discovery and peace" for the "staff" (63.3%); "deepening of faith" for the "retreat groups" (35.0%) and for the "others" (65.4%). Notice that "revitalization" and the awareness of "our role as missionaries" are very important for the staff, while the retreat groups and others assign them much less relevance.

The responses to the meaning of the Belleville shrine and its message for the world of today (table 2) converge at two points: "an invitation to find faith or an encounter with it, a stimulus to change one's life" (36.7% for the staff; 35.0% for the retreat groups; 53.8% for the others); "a stimulus to learn to be brothers and sisters, praying together and loving one another" (13.3% for the staff; 17.5% for the retreat groups; 30.8% for the others) and "a guide and foundation for peace, hope, the most important values, and the salvation of mankind" (30.0% for the staff; 5.0% for the retreat groups; 26.9% for the others).

Lastly, the influence that visiting the shrine will have on the pilgrim/visitor's life (table 2) is mainly seen on three levels: "help to pray better, to be closer to God, to become a better person" (33.3% for the staff; 45.0% for the retreat groups; 30.8% for the others); "help to find the strength to carry on in life and to find meaning in life" (36.7% for the staff; 15.0% for the retreat groups; 23.0% for the others); "help to obtain needed graces" (10.0% for the staff; 32.5% for the retreat groups; 26.9% for the others).

The data reported above represent only the most significant results of the questionnaire. But to complement these results it is useful to consider another source of written information, prayer petitions from pilgrims/visitors. These were collected during one of the main seasons of the shrine, May 1988, and subsequently analyzed. As many notes and papers as possible were collected. They were written and placed in one of several boxes located at the Lourdes Grotto or Christ the King Chapel. They can be divided into four main categories:

1. *Special intentions Form "A".* This is a combination of a list of printed petitions (peace of mind, resignation to God's will, respect for life, peace in the world, thanksgiving for a favor, health of family and friends, peace in the family, a peaceful death, vocation direction, solution of problems, the poor souls, the seminarians, the Holy Father, the Church, financial difficulties) and the pilgrim/visitor's own words. There is a box that can be checked in front of each intention. There is also space to add other special intentions. Moreover, there are several lines for the person's name and address. The intentions indicated on the forms are mentioned during the daily novena prayers at the Lourdes Grotto.

2. *Special intentions Form "B".* This form is analogous to form A except that it is shorter and has a partially different list of petitions (health of family and friends, peace in the family, a peaceful death, financial difficulties, employment, for someone who is addicted to alcohol or drugs, for someone who has lost his faith, increase of vocations).

3. Votive lights. The envelopes for offerings, placed at the Lourdes Grotto and Christ the King Chapel, allow the pilgrim/visitor to indicate their intentions when lighting the votive lamps. There are several lines for intentions as well as for the person's name and address.

4. Petitions. These are pieces of paper written by the pilgrim/visitor and placed in the same offering boxes as the above categories. At Belleville this last category is very simple in that it is not directed to some specific sacred interlocutor; it follows the model of the other three forms.

In order to analyze and compare the four catagories of petitions a simple grid was prepared. It contained, among other information, a list of petitions combining the lists from form A and form B and adding those intentions most often repeated on the written petitions (sucess at school or work, a safe journey, happy marriage, family and friends, protection and help in general, "special intention", deceased family and friends, increase in faith, other).

Considering all of the petitions it is possible to point out some of their common features. The petitioners very often do not write their name or address. There are very many more female petitioners than male, but they ask for fewer graces. In the special intentions form A and B, where many petitions are already written, the petitioner is inclined to check many of the petitions and write a few of his own. On the petitions written without forms, petitioners tend to ask for few graces. In general, the petitioners tend not to come from large cities but from middle- sized or small centers, mostly from a radius of 500 miles around the shrine. Further information can be drawn from the analysis of each category of written prayer intentions.

Seventy form A special intentions were collected (see table 7). They contain a high average number of petitions, 8 per petitioner. Only 11.4% of the petitioners (8) indicated just 1 petition while over 30% listed more than 10 intentions. Very few intentions are for oneself; 11.2% are for others; 86.25% are not specified. The most recurrent petitions, among those already printed, are "peace in the world" (7.2%); "peace of mind" (7.0%); "health of family and friends" (7.0%); "for the poor souls" (6.7%). Among those written by hand the most recurrent were "employment" (2.4%) and "for someone who has lost his faith" (2.2%).

Seventy form B special intentions were also collected (see table 8). They have a lower average number of intentions (3.9); 20.0% of the petitioners indicated 3 intentions. Once again the petitions were made mostly for others (43.6%) or were not specified. The most recurrent intentions, among those already printed, are for "health of family and friends" (15.8%); for "peace in the family" (12.5%); for "someone who has lost his faith" (11.8%); for "an increase of vocations" (9.9%). Among those written by hand, the most recurrent petitions are for "peace in the world" (2.6%); for "protection and help in general" (2.6%); for "thanksgiving for a favor" (2.2%); for a "happy marriage" (2.2%); and for "deceased family and friends" (2.2%).

Sixty votive light envelopes were collected (see table 9). They have a low average number of intentions (1.9); 48.3% of the petitioners listed only 1 intention, mainly for others (31.6%) or did not specify who the intention was for. The petitioners here are mostly worried over "health of family and friends" (21.1%) and "family and friends" in general (9.6%).

The last category of papers and notes collected is that of the petitions written by petitioners without the use of pre-printed forms. Fifty of these were collected (see table 10). They have the lowest average number of intentions, 1.7. 58.0% of the petitioners wrote only one intention and mainly for others (51.2%). There are mainly two purposes for writing petitions: "health of family and friends" (22.1%) and for "someone who has lost his faith" (11.6%).

Finally, the visitors' preferences in purchasing objects and souvenirs at the shrine's gift shop was examined.

80% of the purchases were of religious objects, 30% also included the purchase of religious books; only 20% of the purchases were of non-religious objects or books. Most of the buyers are middle aged persons.

The religious objects finding greatest favor are: rosaries, prayer cards, medals, statues and images. The rosaries are sold mostly at Christmas and, above all, in the spring when there are Baptisms, First Holy Communions, and Confirmations of children and newly converted adults. The most frequently sold large-sized statues are those of Our Lady of the Snows. The more popular statues of a smaller size are of Our Lady of the Snows, St. Joseph, St. Francis, and the Baby Jesus of Prague (this last one mostly at Christmas).

The medals that visitors buy are those representing St. Christopher, St. Jude, and St. Michael the Archangel. The most popular prayer cards are "Footprints" and the "Serenity Prayer", holy cards of the Sacred Heart of Jesus, and of the Guardian Angel.

6. Concluding Observations

Several observations can be made from the data reported above.

The Belleville shrine of Our Lady of the Snows is atypical in comparison to other traditional shrines in Europe and in the U.S.A., not only due to its structure but also due to its public. It seems that, in general, it would be improper to call a trip to the Bellville shrine a "pilgrimage" and call the visitors "pilgrims" at least in the traditional sense of these words.[10] It might be more proper to speak about going to the Belleville shrine in terms of a trip or journey to a place which is also a sacred space where people can encounter and experience a multi- dimensional message whose core is clearly but not solely religious. It follows that the people who come may be better defined as visitors, and among them three groups can be distinguished: those who come for religious reasons, for both religious and non-religious reasons, and for non-religious reasons.

At this point it might be interesting to compare the message proposed at Belleville and its impact on the average visitor. But before doing this, it is necessary to summarize some of the main features of the shrine's message and its presentation on the one hand and the main attributes of the average visitor on the other.

The message proposed at Belleville appears very complex; it is transmitted in a well structured and sophisticated way, is brought up to post-Vatican II thinking but still integrates traditional devotion, and combines a highly selected symbolism with a very realistic language which is synchronized with a mass-media culture and today's everyday problems. In the final analysis the Belleville message aims to be a practical and reliable proposal of the Gospel for modern-day society.

The average visitor to Belleville, on the other hand, whether Catholic or non-Catholic, white or of other race, appears to be a person sharing a simple day-to-day existence and mentality grounded in a plain and non-complex religiosity deeply dependent on the traditional teachings of religion. The visitor's frame of reference is not very broad; it is mainly based in that part of the middle west of the United States, where there are fewer large cities compared to the Atlantic or Pacific coasts or along the Great Lakes, and therefore, less of the social pathology associated with them, and less stimulus of their pluralism. Nevertheless, the average visitor shares in the stress of an uncertain future, and the tensions of the complex modern American society, which is highly individualistic, utilitarian, and competitive and where people feel alone and insecure and maybe implicitly wonder about their life style.

All of the above elements appear in the motives underlying the decision to go to Belleville, in what the visitor feels and asks, in the meanings given to the acts he performs at the shrine, and the role he assigns to Mary. But at Belleville he meets a message whose core is a proposal for the sharing of all our goods, and for showing consideration to every human being, even if old, handicapped, or infirm, as a person who is able not only to receive but to give something as well. And this is due to the fact that all of us come from the same love and are moving towards it by means of our good will. This love is fundamentally the Lord Our Father, Jesus Christ Our Savior, Mary Our Mother, whose lives are made manifest in many ways at Belleville. Moreover, the way in which people are welcomed and treated is itself an expression of this message.

Although the full message of Belleville may be beyond the grasp of the average visitor, this analysis suggests that something inside the visitor changes because of the visit to the shrine. The visitor becomes much less interested in practical and instrumental religious goals. Rather he becomes more concerned with his individual spiritual and ascetic improvement, with the encounter with others considered as neighbors, and the improvement of life values in general. The Belleville shrine and message are tantamount to a recharging of the visitor on an interior- existential level and serve to generate values for a contemporary society.

This research suggests that somehow the shrine at Belleville with its blend of religious, architectural, landscape, and environmental components creates an ambience in which the central message is brought out and is internalized by the visitors. The shrine is perceived by the visitors not as something foreign but as an integral part of their day-to-day life. In fact, there are many repeat visitors to this shrine. In some ways, Our Lady of the Snows opens the door to religion, especially the kind proposed by the shrine; a religion that is not alien or peripheral to contemporary man and society but is a relevant focal point, and a significant and effective frame of reference for life.

In this perspective it seems that the theoretical premises from which the research started have been proven reliable by the results of the research. That is, the trip to the sacred place can be considered as: a return to one's roots to regain a lost identity; a mobilization of individual resources through a sacred event leading to the perception that salvation is a reachable goal by means of existential change; a framework to give meaning to and revitalize everyday life on a human level.

The above three points are not mutually exclusive but rather make each other more effective through the communication of the shrine's message and through the experience of having visited the shrine. For that reason, at the semantic level there should be no difficulties in considering Belleville a shrine according to the traditional meaning of the word. Moreover, it seems that the initial hypothesis of the research has been a workable departure point, and on the basis of the data already collected, it is possible to agree with some of the statements of Scarvaglieri,[11] at least regarding the function of religion and its meaning within the framework of the shrine phenomenon:

1. Religion is not to be considered a social and cultural by-product.

2. In this context the theory of religion as both a dependent variable (Durkheim, Marx) and an independent variable (Weber, Tawney) when applied to the relationship between religion and society seems to minimalize the importance of religion.

3. It seems more accurate to consider the above relationship as an open process, in which religion plays a role of never-ending feed back so that knowledge, means, decisions, actions and goals can adjust one another in the on going process of existence.

In this third hypothesis it may be correct to apply a cybernetic theoretical model to the relationship between religion and society. But on the basis of the results of this research it is possible to suggest that the phenomenon of shrines and shrine visits today may have a cybernetic effect on religion itself both at the institutional level and at the cultural-spiritual level, and through religion, on contemporary society itself. In this light, the output of the research at Belleville is very similar to the results of the parallel studies on Lourdes, Medjugorje, and Fátima.[12]

However, to improve our knowledge in this field it is necessary to go on with the research project on contemporary shrines and to proceed from a general study phase to the specific research in shrines where studies have been started, such as for Belleville.

It seems that it will be possible to achieve this goal only if, on the methodological level, the multi-dimensional approach is not abandoned but improved. Some believe that empirical research based on questionnaires and statistics is the only scientific means to sociological knowledge. The results of the studies already completed on the shrines at Lourdes, Medjugorje, Fátima, Loreto, and Belleville seem to indicate the need for cooperation with other disciplines and the use of other means (anthropological and visual records) in addition to the traditional ones.[13]

To justify this program it is sufficient to remember that every researcher is an intermediary of knowledge. As such, his scientific integrity depends on his ability to present only what he has observed, make this understood by others, give the reasons for what was done, and do his work in such a way as to allow others to repeat the experiment and consciously change it. On the other hand, in every cognitive process, and even more so in those which are systematic and scientific, reproductions and abstractions are created. To that end, numbers/measures which can be consciously and conscientiously compared must follow.

Acknowledgment

This research was accomplished with a grant from the Religious Research Association and with the cooperation of the shrine administration and staff.

Notes

[1] P.L. HIGGINS, Pilgrimage USA, Prentice Hall, Englewood Cliffs, 1985.

[2] E.J. GUILD, Dreams Realized, Missionary Oblates, Belleville, 1988.

[3] In 1987-88 plans were already being made for the construction of a new church more in line with traditional prototypes.

[4] For the U.S.A. see P.L. HIGGINS, op. cit.; for Europe see M.L. NOLAN and S. NOLAN, Christian Pilgrimage in Modern Western Europe, Univ. of North Carolina Press, Chapel Hill and London, 1989; for pilgrimages in general see S.M. BHARDWAJ and G. RINSCHEDE (eds.) Pilgrimage in World Religions, D. Reimer Verlag, Berlin, 1988.

[5] J. REMY-L. VOYE, Pelerinage et Modernite, from "18eme C.I.S.R. Leuven-Louvain La Neuve 1985", pp. 205 – 214.

[6] W. TURNER, The Ritual Process, Aldine, New York, 1969; G. TILLY, From Mobilization to Revolution, Addison-Wesley, Reading M., 1979.

[7] P. GIURIATI, Pilgrimage and Modernity, from G.E.G. KARLSAUNE, "Supplementshefte den X Nordiske Conferansen I Religionssosiologi - Contemporary Religiosity", Universitetet I Trondheim, 1989, pp. 28 – 38.

[8] G. SCARVAGLIERI, Pelegrinaggio ed esperienza religiosa. Ricerca socio-religiosa sul santuario Santa Maria delle grazie in San Giovanni Rotondo, Ed. Padre Pio da Pietralcina, San Giovanni Rotondo (Fo), 1987.

[9] P. GIURIATI, op. cit.

[10] See for instance: V. TURNER, Drama, Fields and Metaphors. Symbolic Action in Human Society, Univ. of Chicago, 1986, pp. 166- 230; G. SCARVAGLIERI, op. cit., pp. 36 – 46.

[11] G.SCARVAGLIERI, op. cit., pp. 378 – 399.

[12] P. GIURIATI, op. cit., pp. 32 – 33.

[13] In this respect see for instance: J. COLLIER, Jr. and M. COLLIER, Visual Anthropology: Photography as a Research Method, Univ. of New Mexico Press, Albuquerque, 1986.

Summary

This study is a preliminary analysis of pilgrimages and ministry at the National Shrine of Our Lady of the Snows in Belleville, Illinois. The research at Our Lady of the Snows is the fifth in a line of previous comparable studies done at shrines in Lourdes, Fátima, Medjugorje, and Loreto, Italy. The research was accomplished through the use of a variety of methodological tools: questionnaires, socio-historic documents, photographs, prayer petitions, and participant observation. The preliminary results show that the pilgrims were mostly women, over 60, white, and Catholic. The pilgrims' reasons for visiting the shrine and their experience of the shrine had a spiritual/ascetic nature – to be closer to God and increase faith. The ministerial element of the study resulted in a comparison between the pilgrims' beliefs and behaviors and the staff's view of the pilgrims. In most cases there was remarkable agreement between what the pilgrims said and did and how the staff viewed them. Future research will involve a comparison between these results and the results of the studies in Lourdes, Fátima, Medjugorje, and Loreto.

Zusammenfassung:

Pilger zu "Our Lady of the Snows" Belleville, Illinois im Marienjahr 1987 – 1988

Diese Studie ist eine vorläufige Analyse des Pilgerphänomens auf dem "National Shrine of Our Lady of the Snows" in Belleville, Illinois. Sie ist die fünfte in einer Reihe vergleichbarer Studien, die in Lourdes, Fátima, Medjugorje und Loreto, Italien, durchgeführt wurden. Bei der Untersuchung wurden verschiedene methodische Verfahren angewandt: Fragebogenaktion und teilnehmende Beobachtung, Auswertung von sozio-historischen Dokumenten, Photographien und Fürbitten der Pilger. Die vorläufigen Ergebnisse zeigen, daß die Pilger meistens über 60 Jahre alte Frauen katholischen Bekenntnisses und weißer Hautfarbe waren. Die Gründe der Pilger, diese heilige Stätte aufzusuchen, und die Erfahrung, die sie dort machten, waren spiritueller und asketischer Natur – Gott näher zu sein und den Glauben zu stärken. Der seelsorgerische Teil der Studie führt zu einem Vergleich zwischen Glauben und Verhalten der Pilger einerseits und dem Urteil der Mitarbeiter über sie andererseits. In den meisten Fällen gab es eine bemerkenswerte Übereinstimmung zwischen dem Tun und den Aussagen der Pilger und der Art und Weise, wie sie von den Mitarbeitern eingeschätzt wurden. Weitere Untersuchungen werden diese Ergebnisse mit den Ergebnissen früherer Studien in Lourdes, Fátima, Medjugorje und Loreto vergleichen.

Appendix

Table 1 : General data

Interviews	Total: 96	Staff 30	Retreat groups 40	Others 26
Age	30 yrs. or less	16.7	–	3.8
	31 - 60 yrs.	76.6	12.5	46.1
	Over 60 yrs.	3.3	70.0	50.0
	N.R.	3.4	17.5	–
Sex	Male	33.3	2.5	42.3
	Female	56.7	77.5	50.0
	N.R.	10.0	20.	7.7
Racial or Ethnic Group	Black	6.7	–	11.5
	White	86.7	87.5	80.8
	Hispanic	–	–	3.8
	Asian	–	–	3.8
	Other	–	–	–
	N.R.	6.7	12.5	–
Denomination	Catholic	80.0	85.0	84.6
	Jewish	–	2.5	3.8
	Protestant	16.7	–	11.5
	None	–	–	–
	Other	–	–	–
	N.R.	3.3	12.5	–
Number of trips	First trip	–	–	34.6
	More than one	–	65.0	57.7
	N.R.	–	35.0	7.7

Table 2: Reasons for coming to Our Lady; its influence on people's lives; its role in today's world

Reasons	Staff	Retreat Groups	Others
1. Practical - instrumental	36.7	32.5	50.0
2. Spiritual - ascetic	33.3	45.0	11.5
3. Nostalgic - traditionalistic	3.3	–	–
4. Ecumenical - fraternal		22.5	11.5
5. Marian	30.0	7.5	30.7
6. Interior - existential	10.0	10.0	15.4
7. Philanthropic - humanitarian	–	–	–
8. Profane or semi-profane	36.7	–	19.2
9. Ex-voto	13.3	5.0	11.5
10. Celebration of the Marian yr.	–	–	3.8
11. For a ministry program	–	10.0	3.8
12. For a Feast Day Celebration	–	–	3.8
13. For other reasons	3.3	2.5	15.4
14. No response	6.7	27.5	3.8

Note: two answers were possible

Influence	Staff	Retreat Groups	Others
1. Practical - instrumental	10.0	32.5	26.9
2. Spiritual - ascetic	33.3	45.0	30.8
3. Nostalgic - traditionalistic	6.7	–	–
4. Ecumenical - fraternal	6.7	–	7.6
5. Marian	26.7	10.0	15.3
6. Interior - existential	36.7	15.0	23.0
7. Philanthropic - humanitarian	–	5.0	15.3
8. No change	–	2.5	15.3
9. Improvement of values	16.7	5.0	23.1
10. Other	3.3	–	3.8
11. No response	26.7	35.0	11.5

Note: two answers were possible

Role	Staff	Retreat Groups	Others
1. Practical - instrumental	–	15.0	3.8
2. Spiritual - ascetic	36.7	35.0	53.8
3. Nostalgic - traditionalistic	3.3	5.0	7.7
4. Ecumenical - fraternal	13.3	17.5	30.8
5. Marian	16.7	7.5	19.2
6. Interior - existential	26.7	10.0	7.7
7. Philanthropic - humanitarian	6.6	2.5	15.3
8. Profane	6.6	7.5	3.8
9. Foundation for values	30.0	5.0	26.9
10. Other	–	–	–
11. No response	23.3	42.5	15.4

Note: two answers were possible

Table 3: The role of Mary

	Staff	Retreat Groups	Others
1. "Our Mother in the heavens"	23.3	45.0	46.2
2. Dispensor of Graces	3.3	2.5	–
3. Co-redeemer	3.3	7.5	19.2
4. Role model	16.6	15.0	30.7
5. Guarantee of salvation	3.3	7.5	7.7
6. Sister - friend	10.0	7.5	19.2
7. Mother of God	50.0	20.0	19.2
8. The Immaculate Conception	10.0	5.0	3.8
9. The Queen of Peace	–	7.5	–
10. Mother of the Church	10.0	–	11.5
11. Our Lady of the Rosary	6.6	2.5	7.7
12. Our Lady of the Snows	20.0	2.5	3.8
13. No response	20.0	32.5	14.4

Note: two answers were possible

Table 4: Meanings of behaviors of pilgrims/visitors

		Retreat	
To visit the Main Shrine	Staff	Groups	Others
1. Health of body and soul	40.0	52.5	42.3
2. Vertical dialogue	36.6	32.5	50.0
3. Conformism	3.3	5.0	3.8
4. Horizontal dialogue	3.3	22.5	23.0
5. Reconciliation - purification	–	10.0	15.3
6. Exteriorization	20.0	7.5	7.7
7. Need to touch	6.7	–	7.7
8. Remembrance of Our Lady	23.3	2.5	7.7
9. Manipulation - superstition	16.7	7.5	26.9
10. Traditionalism	–	–	–
11. Personal experience	–	–	–
12. Other	6.7	–	3.8
13. No response	20.0	30.0	–

Note: two answers were possible

		Retreat	
To attend a prayer service or Mass at Christ, the King Chapel	Staff	Groups	Others
1. Health of body and soul	36.7	32.5	34.6
2. Vertical dialogue	20.0	27.5	46.2
3. Conformism	6.7	–	7.7
4. Horizontal dialogue	33.4	10.0	23.1
5. Reconciliation - purification	–	17.5	23.1
6. Exteriorization	13.3	17.5	11.5
7. Need to touch	3.3	–	3.8
8. Remembrance of Our Lady	10.0	–	–
9. Manipulation - superstition	10.0	7.5	3.8
10. Traditionalism	3.3	2.5	11.5
11. Personal experience	–	–	–
12. Other	6.7	2.5	7.6
13. No response	16.7	37.5	7.7

Note: two answers were possible

To visit the Lourdes Grotto	Staff	Retreat Groups	Others
1. Health of body and soul	20.0	30.0	34.6
2. Vertical dialogue	40.0	22.5	50.0
3. Conformism	3.3	5.0	3.8
4. Horizontal dialogue	–	7.5	11.5
5. Reconciliation - purification	3.3	7.5	3.8
6. Exteriorization	3.3	10.0	11.5
7. Need to touch	6.6	7.5	11.5
8. Remembrance of Our Lady	16.7	–	7.7
9. Manipulation - superstition	10.0	12.5	7.7
10. Traditionalism	13.4	–	–
11. Personal experience	23.3	12.5	3.8
12. Other	6.7	–	7.7
13. No response	20.0	40.0	15.4

Note: two answers were possible

To visit the Annunciation Garden and the Angelus Bells	Staff	Retreat Groups	Others
1. Health of body and soul	16.7	32.5	19.2
2. Vertical dialogue	33.4	20.0	34.6
3. Conformism	10.0	5.0	11.5
4. Horizontal dialogue	3.3	5.0	15.4
5. Reconciliation - purification	–	12.5	7.7
6. Exteriorization	16.6	5.0	23.1
7. Need to touch	16.6	12.5	3.8
8. Remembrance of Our Lady	30.0	2.5	11.5
9. Manipulation - superstition	10.0	7.5	11.5
10. Traditionalism	16.7	2.5	3.8
11. Personal experience	–	–	–
12. Other	6.7	–	19.2
13. No response	23.3	45.0	11.5

Note: two answers were possible

To participate in a ministry program or a special event at the Shrine	Staff	Retreat Groups	Others
1. Health of body and soul	33.3	27.5	23.1
2. Vertical dialogue	13.3	17.5	15.3
3. Conformism	10.0	–	3.8
4. Horizontal dialogue	20.0	12.5	23.1
5. Reconciliation - purification	–	12.5	11.5
6. Exteriorization	20.0	–	3.8
7. Need to touch	26.6	7.5	11.5
8. Remembrance of Our Lady	3.3	–	3.8
9. Manipulation - superstition	16.7	2.5	–
10. Traditionalism	3.3	2.5	3.8
11. Personal experience	–	–	–
12. Other	10.0	2.5	3.8
13. No response	20.0	55.0	42.3

Note: two answers were possible

The multi-media presentation "The Power"	Staff	Retreat Groups	Others
1. Health of body and soul	6.7	20.0	15.4
2. Vertical dialogue	6.7	12.5	15.4
3. Conformism	–	5.0	–
4. Horizontal dialogue	6.7	5.0	11.5
5. Reconciliation - purification	10.0	5.0	7.7
6. Exteriorization	3.3	12.5	15.4
7. Need to touch	–	2.5	11.5
8. Remembrance of Our Lady	13.3	10.0	7.6
9. Manipulation - superstition	40.0	20.0	15.4
10. Traditionalism	–	–	–
11. Personal experience	63.4	25.0	38.5
12. Other	6.7	2.5	11.5
13. No response	16.7	35.0	19.2

Note: two answers were possible

To buy and take home religious objects	Retreat Staff	Groups	Others
1. Health of body and soul	10.0	17.5	15.4
2. Vertical dialogue	23.3	12.5	26.9
3. Conformism	6.6	5.0	3.8
4. Horizontal dialogue	–	5.0	3.8
5. Reconciliation - purification	3.3	5.0	7.7
6. Exteriorization	3.3	5.0	15.4
7. Need to touch	–	2.5	–
8. Remembrance of Our Lady	46.7	20.0	26.9
9. Manipulation - superstition	30.0	5.0	15.3
10. Traditionalism	6.6	2.5	11.5
11. Personal experience	–	–	–
12. Other	16.7	–	19.2
13. No response	23.3	57.5	19.2

Note: two answers were possible

Table 5: The message of the Shrine – the most significant points –

	Retreat Staff	Groups	Others
1. Discovery and peace	63.3	30.0	53.8
2. To feel loved by God	43.4	30.0	49.9
3. Deepening of faith	49.9	35.0	65.4
4. Mary as model	56.7	27.5	57.7
5. Revitalization	48.9	15.0	42.2
6. Our role as missionaries	43.3	5.0	23.0
7. No response	23.3	62.5	19.2

Note: up to four answers were possible

Table 6: The religiosity of pilgrims/visitors

Meaning of the word "religion"	Staff	Retreat Groups	Others
1. A sense of justice	–	–	–
2. Meditation and prayer	10.0	12.5	–
3. Something that belongs to the past	–	2.5	–
4. Faith in God	66.7	42.5	73.1
5. Feeling close to other people	–	–	–
6. Superstition	–	2.5	–
7. Other	3.3	–	11.5
8. No response	20.0	40.0	14.4

Meaning of Confession	Staff	Retreat Groups	Others
1. Freedom from sin	50.0	42.5	30.8
2. Spiritual - ascetic	6.7	20.0	42.3
3. Conformism	3.3	–	–
4. Reintegration in the Church	–	2.5	3.8
5. Reconciliation	56.6	37.5	57.7
6. Comfort - consolation	16.6	10.0	23.1
7. Dialogue with a priest	6.7	7.5	–
8. Coming closer to Mary	–	–	7.7
9. Premise to the Eucharist	3.3	2.5	–
10. Other	–	–	3.8
11. Non-Catholic	–	–	11.5
12. No response	26.7	35.0	3.8

Meaning of the Eucharist	Staff	Retreat Groups	Others
1. Purification	10.0	20.0	7.7
2 Spiritual - ascetic	40.0	40.0	46.1
3. Conformism	13.3	–	–
4. Brotherly encounter	3.3	2.5	–
5. Memorial of Christ's sacrifice	23.3	30.0	57.7
6. Comfort - consolation	16.7	15.0	7.6
7. Individual devotion	13.3	17.5	34.6
8. Coming closer to Mary	–	5.0	3.8
9. Culmination of Confession	–	–	–
10. Other	3.3	–	3.8
11. Non-Catholic	–	–	11.5
12. No response	26.7	32.5	3.8

Note: two answers possible for the meanings
of Confession and the Eucharist

Table 7: Special intentions (Form "A")

Sex of petitioners		
Male	10	(14.3%)
Female	31	(44.3%)
Not specified	29	(41.4%)
Total	70	(100.0%)

Petitions		
1. For peace of mind*	41	(7.0%)
2. Resignation to God's will*	32	(5.5%)
3. Respect for life*	30	(5.1%)
4. Peace in the world*	42	(7.2%)
5. Thanksgiving for a favor*	35	(6.0%)
6. Health of family and friends*	41	(7.0%)
7. Peace in the family*	39	(6.7%)
8. For a peaceful death*	33	(5.6%)
9. Vocation direction*	11	(1.9%)
10. For solution of problems*	36	(6.1%)
11. For the poor souls*	41	(7.0%)
12. For the seminarians*	24	(4.1%)
13. For the Holy Father*	35	(6.0%)
14. For the Church*	30	(5.1%)
15. Financial difficulties*	31	(5.3%)
16. For employment	14	(2.4%)
17. For someone who is addicted to alcohol or drugs	4	(0.7%)
18. For someone who has lost his faith	13	(2.2%)
19. For an increase of vocations	–	–
20. Success at school - work	7	(1.2%)
21. Safe journey	6	(1.0%)
22. Happy Marriage	6	(1.0%)
23. Family and friends	7	(1.2%)
24. Protection and help in general	6	(1.0%)
25. Special intention	3	(0.5%)
26. Deceased family and friends	1	(0.2%)
27. Increase in faith	5	(0.9%)
28. Other	13	(2.2%)
TOTAL	586	(100.0%)

Note: * = petitions were already printed

Distribution of petitions

Male	112	(19.2%)
Female	240	(40.9%)
Not specified	234	(39.9%)
Total	586	(100.0%)

Average number of petitions made

In general	8
Specifically	
for oneself	0.5
for others	0.9
for oneself and others	0.1
not specified	6.9

Number of petitions made by each petitioner

petitions	persons	percent
1	8	11.4
2	2	2.9
3	5	7.1
4	6	8.6
5	8	11.4
6	4	5.7
7	3	4.3
8	4	5.7
9	1	1.4
10	2	2.9
11	3	4.3
12	3	4.3
13	1	1.4
14	5	7.1
15	1	1.4
16	6	8.6
17	2	2.9
18	–	–
19	2	2.9
20	1	1.4

187

Table 8: Special intentions (Form "B")

Sex of petitioners		
Male	–	–
Female	–	–
Not specified	70	(100%)
Total	70	(100%)

Petitions		
1. For peace of mind	4	(1.5%)
2. Resignation to God's will	1	(0.4%)
3. Respect for life	1	(0.4%)
4. Peace in the world	7	(2.6%)
5. Thanksgiving for a favor	6	(2.2%)
6. Health of family and friends*	43	(15.8%)
7. Peace in the family*	34	(12.5%)
8. For a peaceful death*	13	(4.8%)
9. Vocation direction	4	(1.5%)
10. For solution of problems	2	(0.7%)
11. For the poor souls	3	(1.1%)
12. For the seminarians	–	–
13. For the Holy Father	1	(0.4%)
14. For the Church	1	(0.4%)
15. Financial difficulties*	13	(4.8%)
16. For employment*	14	(5.1%)
17. For someone who is addicted to alcohol or drugs*	18	(6.6%)
18. For someone who has lost his faith*	32	(11.8%)
19. For an increase of vocations*	27	(9.0%)
20. Success at school - work	1	(0.4%)
21. Safe journey	2	(0.7%)
22. Happy Marriage	6	(2.2%)
23. Family and friends	2	(0.7%)
24. Protection and help in general	7	(2.6%)
25. Special intention	4	(1.5%)
26. Deceased family and friends	6	(2.2%)
27. Increase in faith	2	(0.7%)
28. Other	18	(6.6%)
TOTAL	272	(100,0%)

Note: * = petitions were already printed

Distribution of petitions by sex

Male	–	–
Female	–	–
Not specified	70	(100.0%)
Total	70	(100.0%)

Average number of petitions made

In general	3.9
Specifically	
for oneself	0.7
for others	1.7
for oneself and others	0.06
not specified	1.4

Number of petitions made by each petitioner

petitions	persons	percent
1	11	15.7
2	12	17.1
3	14	20.0
4	10	14.3
5	10	14.3
6	3	4.3
7	3	4.3

Table 9: Votive lights

Sex of petitioners		
Male	4	(6.7%)
Female	19	(31.7%)
Not specified	37	(61.6%)
Total	60	(100 %)

Petitions		
1. For peace of mind	1	(0,9%)
2. Resignation to God's will	–	–
3. Respect for life	–	–
4. Peace in the world	4	(3.6%)
5. Thanksgiving for a favor	7	(6.1%)
6. Health of family and friends	24	(21.1%)
7. Peace in the family	6	(5.3%)
8. For a peaceful death	–	–
9. Vocation direction		–
10. For solution of problems	2	(1.8%)
11. For the poor souls	–	–
12. For the seminarians	–	–
13. For the Holy Father	–	–
14. For the Church	–	–
15. Financial difficulties	5	(4.4%)
16. For employment	2	(1.8%)
17. For someone who is addicted to alcohol or drugs	4	(3.6%)
18. For someone who has lost his faith	5	(4.4%)
19. For an increase of vocations	–	–
20. Success at school - work	2	(1.8%)
21. Safe journey	4	(3.6%)
22. Happy Marriage	6	(5.3%)
23. Family and friends	11	(9.6%)
24. Protection and help in general	6	(5.3%)
25. Special intention	4	(3.6%)
26. Deceased family and friends	5	(4.4%)
27. Increase in faith	5	(4.4%)
28. Other	11	(9.6%)
TOTAL	114	(100.0%)

Distribution of petitions by sex

Male	12	(10.5%)
Female	44	(38.6%)
Not specified	58	(50.9%)
Total	114	(100.0%)

Average number of petitions made

In general	1.9
Specifically	
for oneself	0.4
for others	0.6
for oneself and others	0.08
not specified	0.8

Number of petitions made by each petitioner

petitions	persons	percent
1	29	48.3
2	11	18.3
3	11	18.3
4	6	10.1
5	3	5.0

Table 10: Petitions

Sex of petitioners:		
Male	1	(2.0%)
Female	6	(12.0%)
Not specified	43	(86.0%)
Total	50	(100.0%)

Petitions		
1. For peace of mind	2	(2.3%)
2. Resignation to God's will	–	–
3. Respect for life	–	–
4. Peace in the world	2	(2.3%)
5. Thanksgiving for a favor	2	(2.3%)
6. Health of family and friends	19	(22.1%)
7. Peace in the family	4	(4.7%)
8. For a peaceful death	3	(3.5%)
9. Vocation direction	2	(2.3%)
10. For solution of problems	1	(1.2%)
11. For the poor souls	1	(1.2%)
12. For the seminarians	–	–
13. For the Holy Father	–	–
14. For the Church	–	–
15. Financial difficulties	–	–
16. For employment	1	(1.2%)
17. For someone who is addicted to alcohol or drugs	1	(1.2%)
18. For someone who has lost his faith	10	(11.6%)
19. For an increase of vocations	–	–
20. Success at school - work	5	(5.8%)
21. Safe journey	1	(1.2%)
22. Happy Marriage	2	(2.3%)
23. Family and friends	7	(8.1%)
24. Protection and help in general	1	(1.2%)
25. Special intention	3	(3.5%)
26. Deceased family and friends	3	(3.5%)
27. Increase in faith	1	(1.2%)
28. Other	15	(17.4%)
Total	86	(100.0%)

Distribution of petitions by sex

Male	5	(5.8%)
Female	7	(8.1%)
Not specified	74	(86.1%)
Total	86	(100.0%)

Average number of petitions made

In general	1.7
Specifically	
for oneself	0.4
for others	0.9
for oneself and others	0.06
not specified	0.5

Number of petitions made by each petitioner

petitions	persons	percent
1	29	58.0
2	11	22.0
3	5	10.0
4	2	4.0
5	1	2.0
6	2	4.0

Carol Cameron

Pilgrims and Politics:
Sikh Gurdwaras in California

A. Introduction

California is a land of religious diversity. Once a singularly Catholic landscape, California now abounds in monuments to a multiplicity of religions. One of these is Sikhism, the adherents of which are the Sikhs.

The focal point and meeting place of the Sikh community, whether in the Punjab or California, is the temple or *gurdwara* (lit. meaning gateway to the guru). This cultural institution is both a religious edifice and social center. The *gurdwara* is the most prominent component of the Sikh cultural landscape, and is indicative of a population significant enough in size to support it. At present there are 18 *gurdwaras* in California (Fig. 1). They are distributed from Live Oak in the north to El Centro in the south. The oldest temple, founded in 1915, is located in Stockton and the newest center of Sikh life opened in the summer of 1987 in the small farming community of Carouthers near Fresno.

The focus of this paper is the Sikh society in California concentrating on *gurdwara* building activities. The changing role of the *gurdwara* from a center of pilgrimage to an arena of political factionalism is emphasized.

Although Sikhism's gurus discouraged pilgrimage in the Hindu tradition the sociological reality is different. Religious travel continues primarily to the place of birth and martyrdom of Sikhism's gurus in India and Pakistan. The visit to sacred centers, in California or India, although not always following the general classical definition of pilgrimage, is nevertheless *religiously motivated travel* and therefore constitutes an important geographic dimension of Sikh religious behavior.

Fig. 1: Sikh gurdwaras in California 1989
Source: Author's investigation, 1989

B. Sikh Migration and Settlement

The Sikhs have had a colorful but difficult existence in their short history, for they have experienced repeated religious persecution. Until 1984, none were better known than the events of 1947. In that year, India gained independence but at the price of the partition of its land into two countries, India and Pakistan. In northwestern India, the Punjab region and its people bore the brunt of partition. The eastern segment, about 38 percent of the old Punjab province, remained in India; the western segment, about 62 percent, went to Pakistan (Fig. 2).

Hindus and Sikhs in Pakistan migrated to India; many Moslems from India, but especially from eastern Punjab, moved to Pakistan. More than two million refugees exchanged countries travelling by foot, horseback, in carts, and by train. Many thousands of Sikhs, Moslems, and Hindus were murdered when villagers, enraged by rumors of violence, became violent themselves. It has been estimated that during this time over two million Sikhs poured into India. Those who were alloted "evacuee" land in the Punjab tended to settle again as farmers, others moved further inland. Many Sikhs went to Delhi and to other states in India. A large segment of the displaced Sikhs decided to join others who had earlier migrated to East Africa, England, Canada, and the United States.

Immigration of Sikhs to the United States became significant during the early years of the twentieth century. In fact, Sikhs were the first people of India to migrate to America in significant numbers. A few Indian businessmen, students, lecturers and swaims did come earlier, but none put down roots in America.

It is important to put the life and the activities of the early Sikh immigrants into perspective, as much of the early literature is loaded with ethnic misrepresentation and cultural prejudice of those days against "Hindus" as the Sikhs and all Indians were then called. The word "Hindu" was used by Americans to describe all people from India regardless of their religion. "East Indian" was used in the early literature to avoid confusion with "Indian", that incorrectly used word for members of the native race of America. The United States Department of Justice, Immigration and Naturalization Service records do not differentiate between immigrants from India based on either religion or state of origin.

Thus, the story of Sikh migration to the United States must be told as part of the East Indian experience. (LA BRACK 1980, 70 – 71) states:

> "Hindu, Sikh and Moslem faiths were all represented in early migrations, but the proportions are the reverse of their numbers in

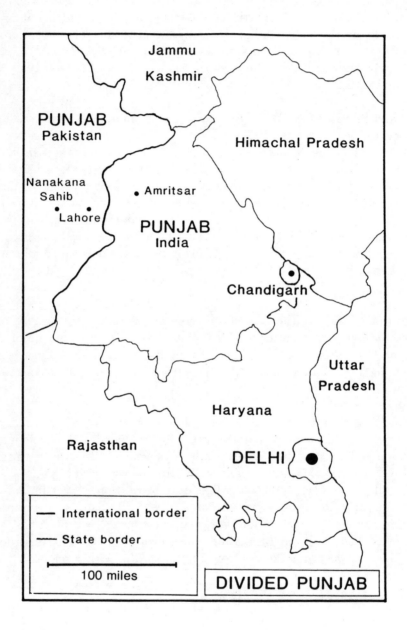

Fig. 2: Divided Punjab
Source: Adapted from Tully and Jacobs (1985): Mrs Gandhi's Last Battle

India. In India, the Hindu religion in some form is followed by 80% of populace, followers of Islam comprise some 10% and Sikhs less than 2%. Since most of the Moslems were also from the Punjab, the Sikhs and Moslems taken together make early immigration a largely Punjabi affair."

The American legislative history concerning immigration, from the Asian point of view, can be summed up simply as:

"a classic century-old instance of professed American ideals of democracy and freedom on the one hand, and the practical realities of rank prejudice and flagrant discrimination on the other" (CHANDRASEKAR 1983, 11).

C. Sikh Migration to the United States

Sikh migration to the United States and California can be divided into three phases. These phases are based primarily on changing immigration regulations and legal sanctions which either helped or hindered the development of Sikh settlement. The three phases are:

1. Initial Migration of Sikhs (1904 – 1923)

Initial migration of Sikhs and the establishment and early growth of their community was marked by popular resentment and a clamor for restrictions by labor groups. Popular newspapers and even a national magazine reported that the country was experiencing a "Hindu Invasion by a Tide of Ragheads" (COLLIERS 1910, 15; SCHEFFAUER 1910, 616 – 618; SURVEY 1910, 2 – 3). The most severe reactions to the Sikhs came from labor organizations working together with such groups as the Asiatic Exclusion League and the Native Sons of the Golden West. It is unfortunate that the East Indian immigrants arrived late in the Asian immigrant experience. They came on the heels of the massive Chinese and Japanese migrations which had attracted adverse reaction from most Americans. Thus, from the beginning, East Indians faced many legal sanctions based upon the public reaction to the "Yellow Peril" (LA BRACK 1980, 137).

Federal laws are illustrative of the initial period of Sikh immigration. They show the intent of the United States Government to enact a policy of exclusion against East Indians and other Asians.

The California Alien Land Act of 1913 was primarily aimed at the Japanese, but the East Indians were victims of its backlash. The Act prohibited the sale of California property to aliens and those not eligible for citizenship. The Federal Immigration Law of 1917 was a further attempt to discriminate against Asians. One clause imposed further restrictions on the immigration of aliens by the creation of a "Pacific Barred Zone", the natives of which were declared inadmissible to the United States. It included most of present-day China, India, Burma, Thailand, Malaysia, most of Arabia, Afghanistan, Polynesia and Indonesia (Immigration Law of 1917; CHANDRASEKHAR 1982, 18).

2. Decline in Migration Period (1923 – 1944)

Owing to the enactment of legislation, the year 1923 became a period of illegal entry by Asians into the United States. Thus, many Sikhs entered by crossing the Mexican border via other Latin American countries, such as Panama. In order to avoid local law enforcement officials, they usually concealed themselves during the day and travelled by night. Many had to shave off their beards and remove their turbans. Because of their dark skin, East Indians were taken for Mexicans (LA BRACK 1980, 58; HESS 1982, 32).

3. Rise of Migration Period (1946 to present)

In 1946, legislation was enacted to change the immigration laws and to permit Indian immigration to the United States. The quota for immigrants from India was set at 100, which applied to all persons entering from India regardless of their place of birth. Three-quarters of the quota was given to Indians born in and residents of India and their dependents. With the passage of this bill, the doors were again open for immigration.

With the enactment of the Immigration Act of 1965, the quota system was dropped. (CHANDRASEKHAR 1982, 25) listed the major provision of the Act as:

1. The natural origins quota system will be abolished as of July 1, 1968. Until that time, unused visas will go into a pool and be made available to countries with long backlogs of waiting lists.

2. The bigoted Asia-Pacific Triangle provision of the Immigration Act of 1917 is repealed immediately.

3. A ceiling of 170,000 immigrant visas for Eastern Hemisphere nations exclusive of parents, spouses and children of U.S. citizens is established on a first-come first-serve basis.

4. A ceiling of 29,000 immigrant visas annually for any one country.

Only by taking into account the various regulations that helped and/or hindered the Sikhs does the study of their immigration acquire its full significance. The Sikh case exemplifies the fact that immigrations are not random phenomena. Rather, immigration flows are consequences of specific economic, political, and ideological conditions which affect immigrant ethnic groups differentially.

D. The Emergence of the Sikh Ethnic Group in California

The Sikh community established settlement patterns early in their occupation that separated their numbers into two groups: rural and urban. This division continues and is a major characteristic of Sikh society in California.

The majority of the early Sikh pioneers were agriculturalists from the Punjab. These Sikh farmers went to work in the valleys of California, especially the fertile plain of the Central Valley. Sikhs were present in the San Joaquin and the Sacramento Valleys as early as 1907, and in the Imperial Valley of southern-most California near the United States-Mexican border in 1910 (DASS 1923, 23). Many Sikhs felt that the valleys of California resembled their ancestral home, the Punjab, in both topography and climate, and would provide job opportunities and the possibility of the eventual ownership of land. Only a small portion of the early Sikh migrants were from the educated elite combining professionals and students from throughout northern India. These Sikhs tended to migrate to the urban areas of Los Angeles and San Francisco.

JENSEN (1974) has noted that both in the Punjab and other parts of the world where Sikhs have immigrated, many persons from rural backgrounds moved into urban occupations such as policemen and truck drivers, but "little or no such diversification of occupations was to occur in the United States". Occupations such as policemen, drivers, electricians, and carpenters were not open to each successive group of Asian immigrants, becoming narrower as the anti-Asian movement grew and became institutionalized.

At the time of their arrival, Sikhs found themselves in a situation similar to the Japanese, Chinese, Koreans, and Filipinos. They found that California was not a land of golden opportunity and jobs were hard to come by. Because only agricultural positions were open to them, many Sikhs were drawn into the migrant labor cycle. The men worked in labor gangs with one person acting as spokesman and bargaining for the group's wages which ranged from US $1.00 to $1.75 per day/per man. In those early days, living conditions were poor and the men often slept in barns or in the fields. The labor gangs migrated from farm to farm and region to region as the need for workers dictated. Although the majority of Sikhs were employed as migrants, a few obtained permanent jobs on farms and ranches where crews of men were employed on a permanent basis. Such Sikhs were able to learn about California crop types, land conditions, and the labor situation in the state. During these years a few Sikhs were able to save money and move from migrant farm worker status to land lease-holders and even landowners.

HESS (1979) estimated that in the years prior to the close of legal immigration the population reached a probable height of 7000, but following the close of immigration in 1917 the population underwent a drastic reduction. HESS estimated that fewer than 1500 Sikhs remained by 1946. This reduction was due in part to the death of many of the early pioneers and the return of a significant number to their Punjab homeland. From this narrowed base, the Sikhs have increased to their present population.

Until 1946 the Sikh population could be characterized as essentially rural, concentrated directly or indirectly in agricultural activities. Sikhs in the urban areas were mostly students and businessmen, with some professionals, but this group represented only a very small percentage of the population.

After 1946 the character of the Sikh population changed. The occupational levels of many of the new immigrants was high. A majority of them were well-educated urbanites from the cities of the Punjab (LA BRACK 1980, 268). These people were attracted to the urban centers in search of university educations and professional employment. At the same time, however, the number of Sikhs immigrating to the rural areas also increased with a definite shift of the population hub northward to the Sacramento Valley. With the abolition of the quota system in 1965 not only did the population increase, but so did its social composition. Large numbers of Hindus and Moslems immigrated to California and settled primarily in the urban areas.

The 1980 census shows that 361,000 Asian Indians resided in the United States. Of that number 57,901 were distributed throughout California. This figure is second only to New York State, which has the largest Asian-Indian population in the United States. The largest concentrations of Asian Indians in California are located in the Los Angeles Metropolitan Area, the San Francisco Bay Region, the Central Valley and the Imperial-Coachella Valley. Although the exact number of Sikhs is not known, their migration has been well documented by LA BRACK. The older California gurdwaras can be found in the centers of the agricultural communities, while the newer temples, located in the urban areas of the state, follow the rural-urban migration patterns of these Asian Indians.

E. The Form and Function of the Sikh Gurdwara

The California Sikh *gurdwara*, although primarily a religious focus, is a multi-purpose facility. The temple often has several rooms, as the building serves many functions. In addition to the large meeting hall which houses the holy book, *The Adi Granth*, each temple has a library with a circulating collection of Punjabi materials that are available to everyone. Many of the larger temples have several additional rooms in which language and dance of the Punjab are regularly taught. Also found at each temple site is a kitchen and storage facilities where large quantities of food are prepared each Sunday and every holy day throughout the year. The *langar* is a significant institution within Sikhism. The community cooks and shares a meal together. This practice strikes at the very heart of an important aspect of caste, and was no doubt instituted for this reason. Sleeping rooms are also available to those in need.

To many Sikhs the trip to the *gurdwara* is not only a part of worship, but an occasion to meet and chat with friends and relatives. The *gurdwara* also acts as a link to their homeland where Punjabis gather to discuss, and argue, the latest news from India. The temple is the principal institution in the Sikh community's attempt at maintenance of its cultural traditions and it is the very heart of Sikhism and the Punjabi way of life.

All *gurdwaras* in California are pilgrimage sites both to the regionally based Sikh and the traveler from India in the sense that they are symbols of Sikhism's implantation in the United States. The temples are viewed by California Sikh society as part of a pioneering effort to establish overseas communities for perpetuation and propagation of the Sikh faith. It is only the degree to which a temple site is considered a "special place" that is important here. Among the 18 gurdwaras in California 3 hold special significance; the Stockton gurdwara because it was the first temple built in North America, and two temples in Yuba City because they are the religious, social and political centers of contemporary Sikh life in California (Fig. 1).

1. The Stockton Gurdwara

The first *gurdwara* in the United States was built in 1915 in Stockton, California. The temple functioned as a home for numerous laborers who lived near or regularly travelled through the area. To the migrant farm workers, their attendance at the *gurdwara* was a source of communication and the temple often symbolized the center of Sikh faith and life in rural California. The *gurdwara* served for many years as the primary channel of information about the Indian Independence Movement. The temple acted as a link in the underground (railroad) channels which moved Sikhs from the Mexican border to northern California in their period of illegal immigration. Prior to that time, and throughout the 1930s, the temple grounds were recruiting areas for contract laborers. Many work gangs were drawn from men staying at the temple. It was the earliest and the most important formal social institution in California for the Sikhs. The *gurdwara* served a variety of functions, but it was first and foremost a religious place (LA BRACK 1980, 245). Numerous conversations with long-time residents substantiated the fact that for thirty-one years the Stockton *gurdwara* was the only religious and social site for the Sikhs of California.

It was not until 1946 that the Sikhs of the Imperial Valley purchased and remodeled a closed Buddhist temple in El Centro and it would be another twenty-four years before a third house of worship would open its doors to the Sikhs of Yuba City (Fig. 1).

2. The Yuba City Sikh Temple

With the 1965 revision of the immigration laws under the Johnson administration the Sikh population of the north Sacramento Valley grew at a tremendous rate. Due to the fact that there was no temple in Yuba City, Sikh worshippers were forced to travel to Stockton for Sunday services. Most of each holy day would be taken in travel to and from the temple, in addition to time spent participating in religious and social activities. Many Sikhs considered this excessive expenditure of time away from their agricultural activities.

With the rapid growth in the Sikh population, it became obvious to some leaders that Yuba City should have its own temple. It was impossible for the *granthi* (reader of the Sikh holy book, Adi Granth), of the Stockton *gurdwara* to administer to the needs of the growing population. Discussions among members of the Yuba City Sikh community began focusing on plans for a local temple. This idea, however met with considerable resistance. Quite a number of local Sikhs felt that the Stockton *gurdwara* would be abandoned by the faithful and lose its historic significance. Others felt that the cost of financing such a project could be prohibitive (SINGH, ROBERT personal communication, 1983).

With the increasing population and the fact that the new arrivals tended to be more orthodox and religiously active than the older California residents, planning for a temple accelerated in 1967 and 1968. Finally, a committee was formed to secure the land and obtain appropriate financing. A local non-Sikh architect was commissioned to draw the plans and build the temple. The ground-breaking ceremony coincided with the 500th anniversary of the birthday of Guru Nanak, the founder of Sikhism.

The 18,680 square foot temple contains a very large meeting hall and adjacent dining room in size approximately that of an American basketball court. Two large kitchens are kept busy preparing Punjabi meals. The dining room is furnished with numerous long tables and chairs while the walls are lined with paintings of historic Sikh battles. In addition, the building contains several meeting rooms and a special room that houses copies of the *Adi Granth*. Several years ago an addition was built at a cost of $100,000. This annex houses a library, two classrooms, two large meeting halls, a health center, and two apartments that house the permanent *granthis* in addition to acting as homes for visiting dignitaries.

The Yuba City Sikh Center has remained a focal point for the community. Regular services are held daily in the morning and at dusk with a weekend service on Saturday night or Sunday morning. During the non-harvest season the congregation is substantial. During the harvest season, however, services are infrequent or postponed entirely.

3. The Guru Nanak Sikh Temple

Until 1965, Sikhism in California had evolved several practices which were different from the traditional ones in the Punjab. Many of the California Sikh males were clean-shaven. The practice was adopted during the years when Asians were not considered citizens of the United States. In order to avoid deportation many Sikhs shaved off their beards and removed their turbans. In this way, Sikh men were taken for Mexicans and were able to continue as agricultural laborers. In the Stockton temple chairs were introduced at one time for the "comfort of the people" and shoes were a common sight in the meeting hall. These men felt that the new practices signalled a relaxed, more liberal way of observing the faith. To them, one did not need any outward manifestations of religion. Their true feeling of being a Sikh need only be in their heart. Over the years, with little immigration of people from India, a new cultural adaption had evolved.

With the change in the immigration laws Sikh immigrants arrived, primarily from the Punjab, and a split developed between the older liberal residents and the new arrivals who practiced the more traditional orthodox worship methods. To the new arrivals, what they saw was not only wrong, but in direct conflict with Sikh ideology and they attempted to right what they considered evil. In the years following the opening of the Yuba City Sikh Temple, the growing orthodox population was successful in banning chairs and making it known that all Sikhs who wanted to participate fully in temple activities must have a beard and cover their heads at least with a cloth if not a turban. Shoes were banned in the meeting hall. Bowing to these pressures, many of the older Sikhs renewed their Khalsa vows and donned the turban and regrew their beards; others, however, refused to do so.

To the older, clean-shaven Sikh what was being practiced was *Singhism* not Sikhism. They accused the orthodox Sikhs of following more the tenets set down by GOBIND SINGH than those of GURU NANAK. The liberal Sikhs felt that the purpose for the beards and turbans was no longer valid. To the liberal Sikhs one needed only follow the tenets of peace set down by NANAK.

Such differences in religious interpretations caused a massive split in the community and violence broke out often in the *gurdwara* (SINGH ROBERT personal communication, 1983). The new arrivals, however, far outnumbered the older residents who no longer felt welcome in their own temple. With the arrival of a *granthi* from the Punjab, the orthodox point of view became institutionalized.

It was not until the late 1970s that the older, more liberal Sikhs, wanting a temple of their own, set about in search of land and finances. In 1980 the Guru Nanak Sikh Temple opened to the Sikh community of Yuba City. Services are held at the temple daily in the morning, at night and the weekend service is held early on Sunday mornings. Although the building of a second temple helped alleviate the pressure of the situation, the orthodox Sikhs far outnumber the older population and at this time the practices in the Guru Nanak Temple are consistent with orthodox Sikhism.

F. Analysis of California Temple Communities

"Wherever there are 3 Sikhs you will find 4 political philosophies". This statement, attributed to KHUSHWANT SINGH has never been more true than it is *today* in California. Although Sikh history is rife with disagreement, the society has never been more polarized. A tragedy that brought Sikhs together to fight a common cause has created a situation that is deeply affecting the immigrant ethnic group. Throughout the temples, major splits have occured in the congregations as to the methods that must be employed to bring about the perpetuation of the Sikh faith.

Following the "Blue Star Operation", by the Indian armed forces, to flush out extremists from the Golden Temple complex in 1984, the worldwide Sikh community, was, even if momentarily, brought together by the actions of the government perceived as an attack on Sikhism's holy shrine. In their frustration and anger, California Sikhs congregated at the *gurdwaras* to receive and bring comfort to one another. With the assassination of INDIRA GANDHI, some 4 months later and the ensuing "reprisal" riots in Delhi in which many innocent Sikhs were killed, the Sikh community of California became deeply divided as to how to insure the lasting qualities of Sikhism. What California Sikhs fear more than anything else is the assimilation of Sikhism into the folds of Hinduism.

During August, 1987 I travelled throughout the state of California visiting as many *gurdwaras* as possible to assess the state of mind of California Sikhs. Without exception, of the 15 *gurdwaras* visited, temple management committees were actively supporting independent sovereign status for the Punjab, to be called *Khalistan*. Speeches were given in support of the movement and money was being raised for the cause. In addition to the traditional pictures on the walls of the temples, one now finds photographs of the damaged Golden Temple complex, pictures of corpses lying along the walkways, photographs of BHINDRANWALE, now a martyr of the faith, and the assassins of INDIRA GANDHI, now considered heroes by some.

Flags, T-shirts and maps can be found at any temple advertising the cause of *Khalistan*. To many Sikhs the formation of *Khalistan* is the only way to ensure perpetuatiion of the Sikh faith. As one community leader noted, "Sikhs living abroad were not always so serious about the dream of *Khalistan*, but since the attack on the Golden Temple, people are against the Indian government. After Mrs. GANDHI's assassination and the massacre of Sikhs, people just made up their minds that government has no feeling for the Sikhs". "There are some who do not want this status," he continued, "but they are black sheep government-paid people" (BAINS 1983, 8).

Some Sikhs in California, however, hold a more modest point of view. To these Sikhs the idea of the formation of a *Khalistan* in India is totally unfeasible and they feel that Sikhs holding the more radical point of view are doing more to hurt the cause of peace in India rather than to promote it (ANAND 1987, personal communication). "It is the Sikhs in India who count," stated another community member, "and they never have asked for an independent *Khalistan*, even BHINDRANWALE, asked only for a economically autonomous state. We have to side with what the Sikhs in India want. We are nobody; we are outsiders" (SINGH 1985, 8). "*Khalistan* has always been the brainchild of the government and they've always used it as a pretext to weaken the Sikhs, ever since Partition", stated a California Sikh professor. "First, they set up the Hindus against the Sikhs, and now they are saying we are out to kill our enemies. It is the Indian government who is sponsoring all this" (KAHLON 1985, 8).

Because of this polarization of the California Sikh community. plans for several new *gurdwaras* have been cancelled. Money had been raised and plans had been drawn up for two temples in southern California, but because of the differences within the community, Sikhs holding the more moderate view withdrew funding. It is feared by many that the *Khalistanis* would use the new temples as platforms for the raising of funds for *Khalistan* rather than administering to the spiritual needs of the immigrant ethnic community.

Summary

Sikhs have been in California for more than three-quarters of a century. Settling first in the agricultural areas of California, these Asian Indian farmers became very successful even introducing new irrigation techniques to their California neighbors. Early temples appeared in the Central Valley communities for perpetuation of the faith. Following the 1965 reduction of the immigration laws, the California Sikh population increased with a substantial portion of the new arrivals settling in the urban areas of the state where temples of worship were built.

On the surface, it would appear that Sikhism is flourishing in California. The number of Sikhs is substantial and the population is growing. Sikhs are one of the most economically successful immigrant groups in recent state history. The fundamental health of the faith, however, cannot be as easily discerned.

Throughout California Sikh history, the *gurdwara* has served primarily as a place of religion congregation but in recent years the temples have become arenas of political factionalism. In this sense, they appear to be closer in recent years to the major *gurdwaras* in India where religion and politics are inseparable. Although support for the formation of *Khalistan* among California Sikhs is substantial, a very vocal minority continues to try to return California *gurdwaras* to their original religious focus.

The solution to the issue of Sikh separatism and terrorism has to come from within the Punjab. A settlement there, a reconciliation of the Sikhs with the Hindus and the reassurance that their culture and religion will survive, might put an end to a separatist movement.

But until such a settlement comes about, Sikh discontent will continue to fester. The expatriate Sikhs are becoming increasingly alienated from their homeland, and soon may witness their children and grandchildren becoming worse than alienated-indifferent.

Zusammenfassung:

Pilger und Politik: Die Gurdwaras der Sikhs in Kalifornien

Die Sikhs sind seit mehr als einem dreiviertel Jahrhundert in Kalifornien. Sie siedelten zuerst in den landwirtschaftlichen Regionen Kaliforniens, wo diese indischen Bauern sehr erfolgreich wurden und ihren kalifornischen Nachbarn sogar neue Bewässerungstechniken zeigten. Schon bald gab es in den Gemeinden des Central Valley die ersten Tempel, die der Beibehaltung des Glaubens dienten. Auf den Abbau der Einwanderungsgesetze von 1965 folgte ein Anwachsen der Sikh-Population in Kalifornien, wobei sich ein wesentlicher Anteil der Neuankömmlinge in den urbanen Regionen des Staates niederließ, in denen Tempel für den Gottesdienst errichtet wurden.

Oberflächlich betrachtet, hat es den Anschein, daß der Sikhismus in Kalifornien einen Aufschwung erlebt. Denn die Anzahl der Sikhs ist erheblich und ihre Bevölkerung wächst weiter. Die Sikhs sind eine der ökonomisch erfolgreichsten Einwanderergruppen in der neueren Geschichte des Staates. Die religiöse Situation der Sikhs entspricht jedoch nicht diesen äußeren Merkmalen und ist weit weniger positiv zu beurteilen.

In der gesamten Geschichte der kalifornischen Sikhs dienten die *Gurdwara* in erster Linie als ein Ort für die religiöse Versammlung, in den letzten Jahren jedoch wurden die Tempel auch zu Schauplätzen politischer Auseinandersetzungen. In diesem Sinne scheinen sie sich in den letzten Jahren den bedeutenderen *Gurdwaras* Indiens zu nähern, wo Religion und Politik untrennbar miteinander verbunden sind. Obwohl die kalifornischen Sikhs die Gründung eines freien Staates Kahlistans stark befürworten, versucht eine sehr lautstarke Minderheit weiterhin, die *Gurdwaras* Kaliforniens zu ihrem ursprünglichen religiösen Mittelpunkt zurückzuführen.

Die Lösung der Probleme des Separatismus und Terrorismus muß bei den Sikhs aus dem Punjab selbst kommen. Wird dort eine Einigung erreicht, nämlich eine Versöhnung der Sikhs mit den Hindus und die Zusicherung, daß ihre Kultur und ihre Religion überleben, könnte der separatistischen Bewegung ein Ende bereitet werden.

Aber bis zu dieser Einigung wird die Unzufriedenheit der Sikhs weiter gären. Die in der Fremde lebenden Sikhs werden ihrer Heimat zunehmend entfremdet, und bald werden sie vielleicht Zeugen sein dafür, daß ihre Kinder und Enkelkinder nicht nur entfremdet werden – schlimmer noch – sie werden gleichgültig.

Bibliography

ANAND, R. S. (1987): Personal Communication, August 1987. Los Angeles, California.

CENSUS BUREAU OF THE UNITED STATES (1980): 1980 Census of Population and Housing. Washington, D.C.: Department of Commerce.

CHANDRASEKHAR, S. (1982): From India to America: A Brief History of Immigration, Problems of Discrimination, Admission and Assimilation. La Jolla, CA. Population Review Publications.

COLLIERS (1910): The Hindu Invasion. Colliers. Vol. 45: March 26, p. 15.

HESS, G. R. (1961): The Hindu in America. Pacific Historical Review. Vol. 31:1. February, pp. 59 – 79.

HESS, G. (1969): The Hindu in America: Immigration and Naturalization Policies in India, 1917 – 1946. Pacific Historical Review. Vol. 38: pp. 46 – 52.

JENSEN, J. M. (1969): Apartheid: Pacific Coast Style. Pacific Historical Review. pp. 335 – 340.

JENSEN, J. M. (1976): Outcastes in a Savage Land. The East Indians of North America. Santa Barbara: Cleo Press.

KAHLON, G. K. (1983): Sikh Voices. This World. Sacramento, California.

KURTZ, C. C. (1985): The Sikhs of Yuba City, California: A Study in Ethnic Geography. M.A. Thesis. California State University, Hayward.

LA BRACK, B. W. (1975): The East Indian Experience. Unpublished bibliography of East Indians in America.

LA BRACK, B. W. (1975): Occupational Specialization Among Sikhs: the interplay of culture and economics. Syracuse, N.Y.

LA BRACK, B. W. (1976): South Asian Peasants on the Pacific Coast: East Indian Contributions to California Agriculture. Stockton, CA. University of the Pacific.

LA BRACK, B. W. (1980): The Sikhs of Northern California: A Socio-historical study. Ph.D. dissertation. Syracuse University.

SCHEFFAUER, H. (1910): The Tide of Turbans. Forum. Vol. 31, pp. 616 – 618.

SINGH, A. (1985): Sikh Voices. This World. Sacramento, California.

SINGH, R. (1983): Personal Communication, Yuba City, California.

SURVEY (1910): Hindus, the New Immigration Problem. Survey. Vol. 25, pp. 2 – 3.

Surinder M. Bhardwaj

Hindu Deities and Pilgrimage in the United States

I. Introduction

Hindus began to settle in the United States in significant numbers in the wake of liberalization of American immigration policies in 1965. The Hindu immigration was, of course, only part of the larger stream of predominantly non European immigrants. Derived from the various Indian cultural-linguistic regions of India, these immigrant Hindus have tried to partly express their distinctive regional religious ensemble including temple styles, and the worship of their prominent regional and secretarian deities. A major expression of this religious transference process has been the development of many Hindu iconic temples (temples with statues of deities), and a variety of other religious centers. These sites have acquired many characteristics of Hindu holy places in India, and some seem to have become centers of Hindu pilgrimage.

The purpose of this paper is to first describe some significant changes in the Hindu religious landscape due to the development of temples in America and, secondly, to suggest that centers with certain distinctive geographic and regional religious attributes are likely to develop into significant pilgrimage places. The study is based upon personal site visits to most of the major American Hindu temples (especially during 1986), and is closely related to earlier research on the S. V. Temple (BHARDWAJ and RAO 1988).

To some, Hindu pilgrimage in America might seem a contradiction in terms because, like most other recent immigrants to the United States (and Canada), the Hindus came here in quest of affluence, not spiritual fulfillment. Unlike some earlier European communities, escaping religious persecution or war in their native lands, Hindus from India came for higher education, and to fill the many highly desirable professional, technical, scientific, and medical vacancies in post industrial America.

For most in India, America is the land of economic opportunity, professional advancement, and limitless freedom. Whereas most Hindus in India might perceive their expatriates as having adopted the American culture to the fullest, ironically, Hindus in America seem to have developed a much "heightened sense of religiosity". Hindus who return to India after many years, are frequently shocked to find that they, the American Hindus, are the ones trying harder to teach their children Hindu epics, Hindu philosophy, and "high tech" yoga. Such accentuated religiosity among first generation expatriate communities seems to be a general phenomenon (ABRAMSON 1980, 869 – 75). The developing practice of pilgrimage among Hindu immigrants in America is only one of the religious dimensions which expresses a renewed consciousness of Hindu spiritual heritage. Hindu pilgrimage in America is, thus, not a contradiction, but rather an expression of a general human desire. Pilgrimage in America may appear to be somewhat peculiar, even discordant, behavior because America, though predominantly Christian, is generally perceived as a secular, scientific and materialistic nation.

II. Changes in the Hindu Religious Landscape

– The Variety of Hindu Temples

Hindu religious landscape, which was confined to the outwardly invisible family altars, began to change as the number of Hindus rapidly increased in the seventies. It took about a decade for the first architecturally and ritually authentic Hindu temples to emerge, but since then, virtually every major concentration of Hindus in America has started, or has already finished construction of a temple. News of such events are regularly reported in the ethnic newspapers such as *India Abroad, India Tribune, India West, Lotus*, and others. *India Abroad* regularly publishes "Date Line" column as a community service, wherein religious organizations, especially temples give out information about upcoming religious events. Consecration of a large number of Hindu temples in America, some still housed in adapted buildings, halls, and even former churches, compellingly illustrate ELIADE's idea that religious man cannot live except in an atmosphere impregnated with the sacred (ELIADE 1959, 28). The flurry of Hindu temple building activity in America is a visible expression of heightened religiosity. The Hindus seem to be in a hurry to make their adopted homeland a "sacred" place in ELIADE's terms.

Hindu temples are now found in virtually all significant clusters of Hindu population in America (Fig. 1). The monthly *Hinduism Today*, published by a white American Swami, Sivaya Subramuniyaswami, regularly provides a list of temples in the United States and Canada. The January 1989 issue of this journal lists as many as seventy five "Temple Services" in North America, including some duplications (due to separate listing of temples' society address' from that of the temple itself). This list is by no means complete but includes the more prominent ones. Although statues of the deities, or other forms of images or symbols are an integral part of the sanctums, most temples are not architecturally indentifiable as Hindu temples from the exterior. A number of concessions to local conditions have had to be made. Several temples are housed in former churches while others have sanctums within community halls. Relatively few Hindu temples are architecturally authentic.

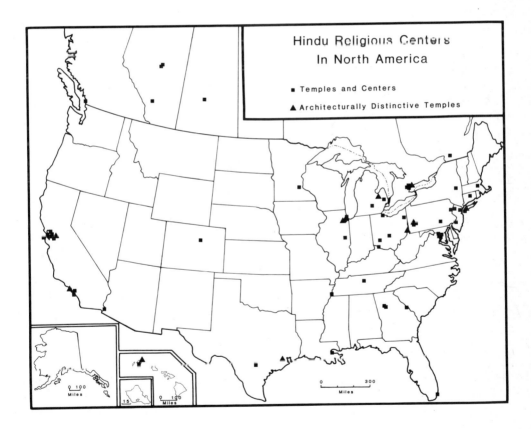

Fig. 1: Hindu religious centers in North America
Source: Author's field work, INDIA ABROAD (various issues), and
HINDUISM TODAY, January, 1989

Some of the temples have large and growing assets. For example, the Sri Venkateswara Swami (Balaji) Temple of Greater Chicago, which was established as a non profit organization only in 1983, has assets of well over two million dollars (S.V. NIVEDIKA 1986: 20). Similarly, The Hindu Temple of Greater Chicago (HTGC), founded much earlier (1977), but inaugurated only on the 4th of July 1986, had total income of almost one million dollars in 1985 (HTGC 1986). The Sri Venkateswara Temple (Pittsburgh), inaugurated a decade earlier than the above two temples, posted its assets on December 31, 1986 at over $ 2.8 million (SAPTAGIRI VANI 1987: 10). Other major temples of this type include the Ganesa Temple in Flushing (New York), the recently inaugurated Shiva Vishnu Temple at Livermore in Northern California, the Lord Venkateswara Temple in Malibu, Los Angeles, Paschima Kasi Sri Viswanatha Temple (Flint, Michigan), and the Minakshi Temple at Pearland near Houston Texas. Hindus in Canada are similarly in the process of building major (and local) temples in Toronto, Montreal, Edmonton, and Vancouver. Bengali Hindus of Toronto, for example, are constructing a Kali temple (Toronto Star 1986: L 12).

In addition to the major nonsectarian iconic temples where a variety of deities are installed (although one is normally considered a presiding deity), there is a growing number of sectarian temples and worship centers. The most influential of such places of worship are the almost exclusively Gujarati temples of Swaminarayan sect in Flushing (New York), Los Angeles, and Chicago. The predominantly Punjabi congregation centers of the Nirankari Mission are located in several cities with substantial Punjabi speaking population such as Chicago (headquarters), Toronto, and New York, but these centers should not be confused with iconic temples, since they do not believe in images for worship but do believe in a living *guru*. Although such "missions" and organizations purport to spread a universal message, their following is primarily from language bound regional communities.

The International Society for Krishna Consciousness (ISKCON) has centers of worship in many American cities from Boston to Berkeley and from the Great Lakes to the Gulf Coast (PROROK 1987, 134). Originally composed of American (predominantly white) followers of A.C. Bhaktivedanta Swami Prabhupada, the movement has gained immigrant Hindu devotees although the management remains in the hands of American leaders. Plagued with internal organizational and legal problems in the last few years (*Record Courier*, August 23, 1987: A5. CONGER 1988), after the death of its founder, the image of this movement has been tarnished. The New Vrindaban Community of the Hare Krishna movement, until recently a part of the ISKCON movement, has built an exquisite memorial at New Vrindaban, in West Virginia, to its founder Prabhupada. The most interesting aspect of the movement until recently was that "White Hindus" had been at least partly successful in forging links with the Hindus from India. This linkage is useful to followers of Prabhupada because otherwise the ISKCON movement might remain only an American phenomenon, frequently stigmatized as a cult.

The immigrant Hindus admire, even envy the devotion to Krishna of the Hare Krishna sectarians but have not allowed their own children to follow the archaic lifestyle of the White American Hindu devotees. New Vrindaban has become a great tourist attraction in the State of West Virginia for Americans, but a place of religious pilgrimage for the devotees of Prabhupada and, to a degree, for immigrant Hindus from different parts of the world.

III. Emerging Hindu Pilgrimage Places

From among the many emerging Hindu temples in America, a few have the potential to become pilgrimage centers at the national, even international, level. Others will probably remain popular, but of relatively local or regional importance. The Sri Venkateswara Temple at Pittsburgh is an outstanding example of an iconic temple that has already become a renowned pilgrimage center.

1. The Sri Venkateswara Temple (frequently referred to as the S.V. Temple), situated in the Penn Hills suburb of Pittsburgh, Pennsylvania, has already become the most renowned Hindu pilgrimage site in North America. Consecrated in 1976, the Bicentennial year of American Independence, the temple attracts pilgrims from many areas of the United States and Canada. We have examined elsewhere in some detail the donor distribution and pilgrimage pattern of the S.V. Temple (BHARDWAJ and RAO 1988). Even in the very first years of this temple's evolution pilgrims from virtually all over the United States and the adjoining metropolitan areas of Canada had started to converge here.

Pilgrims to the S.V. Temple are generated from among the Hindu population clusters of the Megalopolis communities which form the largest such concentration, and from the populous metropolitan areas of the Midwest. Relatively few pilgrims originate from the Deep South, except from its growth centers such as Atlanta, New Orleans, and the "Research Triangle" communities of North Carolina (Durham, Chapel Hill and Raleigh). Although California has a large number of Hindus, both in the San Francisco Bay area and in Southern California (MATHUR ca. 1985), they are too far away to effectively generate a large number of pilgrims. The S.V. Temple nevertheless has a widespread distribution of donors in North America, and they form its basic pilgrim field. The July-December, 1986 donor list included over 4,400 contributors from various parts of North America (Table 1). The vast majority of the S.V. Temples' pilgrims have Dravidian cultural linguistic roots. Year after year the donor

lists show a preponderance of southern Indian names as donors from all over
the United States and Canada.

2. The Sri Venkateswara Swami (Balaji) Temple of Greater Chicago (hence-
forth called Balaji Temple) and the Hindu Temple of Greater Chicago (HTGC)
are together likely to become major twin pilgrimage center for the Hindus.
Many of the reasons for these temples together becoming important places of
pilgrimage are the same as for the S.V. Temple. For example, Chicago com-
mands a superior location with respect to the population distribution of the
United States' Hindus East of the 100th meridian. The same locational attributes that have made Chicago the third largest city in the United States
make it potentially a great location for the Hindu pilgrims to converge. In
addition, the Balaji Temple has the same deity, Sri Venkateswara, the most
popular *vaisnavite* deity of the Dravidian cultural region of India. The presiding deity in the Hindu Temple of Greater Chicago is Rama, the hero of

Table 1: Sri Venkateswara Temple (Pittsburgh),
Donors by State (Top Ten)

July 1, 1986 – Dec. 31, 1986

N = 4463

State	Number	Per cent of Donors	Donation Ratio *
Pennsylvania	497	11.1	2.5
New York	461	10.4	0.6
Ohio	415	9.3	2.7
New Jersey	375	8.4	1.1
Maryland	284	6.4	1.8
Michigan	284	6.4	1.6
Illinois	261	5.8	0.6
Texas	225	5.0	0.8
California	158	3.5	0.2
Virginia	144	3.2	1.4

* Donation ratio = Percent of donors divided by
percent of Asian Indian population in the state

Source: Calculated from *Saptagiri Vani*, First Quarter, 1987.

the Hindu epic Ramayana. Thus, the two temples do not compete but rather complement each other with respect to the presiding deity. That however is not entirely true as regards donations from the Hindu community.

Although no formal pilgrim survey of the Balaji Temple, as compared to the S.V. Temple has been conducted, it can be assumed that the donor distribution is a reasonable clue to the future pilgrim field of this temple (Table 2). The October, 1986 donor list published by the Balaji Temple lists over 1900 donors representing thirty seven states. Surprisingly, no names from Canada were found in the list. Over 44 percent of the donors are from the state of Illinois alone, far ahead of New Jersey (6.2%), New York (5.6%), and Michigan (5.5%).

Table 2: Balaji (Sri Venkateswara Swami) Temple, Chicago, Donors by State (Top Ten)

As of October 1986

N = 1904

State	Number	Per cent of Donors	* Donation Ratio
Illinois	843	44.3	4.6
New Jersey	119	6.2	0.8
New York	106	5.6	0.3
Michigan	104	5.5	1.4
Wisconsin	79	4.1	4.1
California	79	4.1	0.3
Texas	68	3.6	0.6
Indiana	58	3.0	2.5
Missouri	58	3.0	2.7
Ohio	55	2.9	0.8

* Donation ratio = Percent of donors divided by percent of Asian Indian Population in the state

Source: Calculated from *Sri Venkatesa Nivedika*, October 1986

A comparison between the Balaji Temple's donation distribution (Table 2) and that of the S.V. Temple (Table 1) brings out the interesting fact that donors from the home state of each temple make up distinctly different percentages of total number of donors; the Balaji Temple is much more dependent upon its home state donors than the S.V. Temple, indicating the latter's more widespread appeal. However, this situation may change due to Chicago's geographically central position.

3. The Hindu Temple Society of Southern California has completed its Lord Venkateswara Temple (L.V. Temple). The list of donors to the L.V. Temple shows that 70% of the 693 donors are from Los Angeles SMSA. Donors from the state of California alone make up 82% of all contributors to this temple. But, at the same time, twenty six other States and the Province of British Columbia were also represented even though the location of this temple is far from central. Although the regional diversity of pilgrims from America at this temple may never match that of the S.V. or the Balaji Temple in Chicago, it will certainly increase because of the popularity of Southern California as a tourist focus.

4. The Shiva-Vishnu Temple of Livermore, California had its grand opening, *kumbhabhishekam* in July, 1986. This unique temple juxtaposes two major Hindu architectural styles, North Indian Kalinga, and South Indian Dravidian (India West 1988, 24). The temple is also the result of close cooperation between the North and the South Indian communities to have a single sacred center. Such cooperation has rarely manifested itself in the Indian homeland. However, a clear microspatial separation, as well as chromatic distinction of North and South Indian symbols is maintained; the South Indian deities are carved from black granite, and the North Indian ones from white marble. Since the San Francisco Bay area has one of the four major concentrations of the Hindu community, and is also a popular tourist focus, the attraction of this temple as a potential pilgrimage place is assured. The donor lists of this temple show only the names, thus making it difficult to identify the spatial dimensions of its pilgrim field. However, the last names of donors do indicate that the majority of them are of South Indian origin.

5. The Sri Meenakshi Temple, Pearland, near Houston, inaugurated in 1982 is one of the most interesting temples of the United States because a goddess is the presiding deity, flanked by Siva on her right and Sri Venkateswara on her left. Although the goddess is the chief deity, there was also the necessity of compromise among the donor-devotees of other deities. Thus, the temple can serve the devotees of any one of the three deities. Significantly, this temple also symbolizes the union of the three major religious traditions of India, vaisnava, saiva, and sakta. Symbolically, this temple is located in the South

of the United States, just as in the Indian homeland the Meenakshi Temple is located in southern India. This symbolism is quite evident in the inaugural volume of this temple. Prominence of the female as an autonomous deity should be of special interest to second generation, culturally American, ethnically Indian females interested in discussions about the status of the female in India. Donor lists of this temple are unfortunately not available, making it difficult to evaluate its spatial popularity.

6. Paschima Kasi Sri Viswanatha Temple at Flint, Michigan is symbolically the primary American abode of Siva, as Kasi (modern Varanasi) is the primeval Indian home. Its location, in the northern part of the United States mirrors Kasi's location in northern India. This symbolism, and the geographic location close to the populated Midwest and Canada are likely to ensure a diversity of visitors who are votaries of Siva by preference, in addition to the majority of Hindus who are characteristically syncretic. This place is also likely to be associated with the cremation symbolism of Kasi, and thus attract Hindus who wish to have funeral rites performed here, especially if they cannot conveniently go to India.

All the temples, described above as functioning or developing as pilgrimage sites, have a strong common bond, that is with the Hindu Temple Society of North America, and through it to the Tirupati temple in Andhra Pradesh in India (ALAGAPPAN 1978, 27 – 29). They have received encouragement and support from the Tirupati Temple, the wealthiest temple in India. These temples have been able to obtain trained *archaks* (ritualist priests), temple architects, *shilpis* (artisans), and management advice from the Tirupati Temple. These temples have also enjoyed encouragement and in some cases active support of some of the state governments of India, especially from Andhra Pradesh and Tamil Nadu. The statues installed in these temples were made in India by sculptors of temple images, whose skills have been passed on through generations.In some instances, the traditional silversmiths and goldsmiths who make the decorative *kavachas* (precious metal ornaments) for the deities have been brought to the US to prepare these adornments at the temple site in the traditional Indian manner. The S.V. Temple trustees even set up a small smithy for these artisans, replicating the traditional Indian style, complete with a wood- and charcoal-using furnace to smelt and forge silver.

IV. Sub-Regional and Local Temples

Temples that have relatively tenuous organizational affiliations in India, and are primarily the result of local efforts are in a class by themselves. They like their Indian counterparts are places of worship and centers of Hindu festivals, but unlike them are also centers of community activities. A majority of these temples have north Indian motifs as expressed in the deities installed, and the modes of worship. These temples are almost inevitably highly syncretic because of the diversity of the Hindu population, most of whom are likely to be from northern India.

An example of such a temple is the Sri Lakshmi Narayan Temple of the Hindu Temple Society of North Eastern Ohio. The temple is conceived to be part of the sub-regional rather than the national scene. It does not significantly compete with the already established temples, such as the S.V. Temple at Pittsburgh, but rather complements it by being a proximate religious center. Most of its donors are from the neighboring communities of Northeastern Ohio. Other examples include the Hindu Temple and Cultural Center, Fremont, California; the Hindu Temple of the Hindu Worship Society, Houston, Texas; the Hindu Society of Minnesota, Minneapolis, and many others.

The Hindu Temple of the Hindu Community Organization Inc., Dayton, Ohio, is a somewhat higher level center. Although over 80% of the donors are from Ohio (43% from Dayton alone), twenty three other States and even two provinces of Canada are represented. There is no "competition", as yet, from any other temple in the neighboring states to the South because of their relatively small Indian populations. This temple has the potential to become a regional center for the lower Midwest.

One of the most impressive examples of Hindu syncretism in North America is the Hindu-Jain Temple in Pittsburgh. Under one roof, there are in fact several individual temples; one each for Lakshmi Narayan, Krishna, Rama, Shiva, two niches for goddesses, a *havan kund* (fire oblation spot) for the Arya Samajists who perform ancient vedic *havan* (sacrifice) and a Jain temple which has the images for *digambar* and *svetambar* sects. Such a temple, without a specific presiding deity, might be unacceptable to the Hindus of southern Indian origin, but seems perfectly acceptable to the northern Indians. Non-association with a specific presiding deity might mean that Hindu worshippers at this temple will be drawn from the local surroundings rather than from distant places. In general, this temple has a primarily northern Indian ambiance and devotees, in clear contrast to the S.V. Temple only a few miles away, whose devotees are predominantly of southern Indian origin.

V. Attributes of Emergent Hindu Pilgrimage Centers in America

The temples that may ultimately become major holy places of the evolving Hindu pilgrimage circulation system, are likely to have some or all of the following attributes:

221

1. A Specific Deity Whose Temple in India Is Already a Major Pilgrimage Center

The most prominent example is Sri Venkateswara, whose temple at Tirupati is the most renowned place of pilgrimage for most of Southern India, and is gaining increasing popularity in Western and even Northern India (NAIDU 1985). Deities without strong sectarian or regional symbolism are not likely to attract adherents from distant places. A specific manifestation of Vishnu (e.g. Sri Venkateswara) whose symbolic regional identification is already well established in India, has a much better chance of attracting adherents from distant places in the adopted homeland of immigrant devotees. This is so because the immigrants from any given area of India are widely dispersed in the United States. Since this incarnation of Vishnu has both a temporal and spatial specificity, legends about his actions have a strong South Indian regional basis. This regional strength, rooted in linguistic attachment, ensures regional following, and serves even as a regional sacred emblem.

Similarly, Krishna *avatara* (incarnation) has a Hindi belt specificity because of his birth in that region. Although Krishna is worshipped in most parts of India, it is in northern India that his popularity is at a maximum. Thus, Krishna as a specific deity is more likely to be generative of a new pilgrimage place, than his root form as Vishnu. This, to some extent, explains the popularity of New Vrindaban (West Virginia) among the northern Indian Hindus of North America. It is interesting to note that many people of southern Indian origin visit New Vrindaban but they do so as tourists, whereas Hindus from northern India consider it a pilgrimage center.

When a deity is considered as a regional or supra-regional symbol, the fund raisers find it easier to raise money for the building of a temple dedicated to that deity by appealing to a particular regional or linguistic group. Attachment to regional religious symbolism also has a distinct potential for the emergence of pilgrimage sites, because an appeal can be made to the devotees irrespective of where in America they live. Since the nature of immigration of Indians has ensured a nationwide distribution of Hindus irrespective of their Indian regional origins, information about a deity symbolic of a region can spread among Hindu immigrants of that region rapidly. This process ensures widespread diffusion of the regionally symbolic deities of India. Temples with such deities are, therefore, more likely to emerge as pilgrimage places; the donors forming a nationwide distribution will sooner or later wish to visit the place.

2. A Deity Who Is Already Famous for Granting of Wishes, at Whose Temples the Concept of Wish Fulfillment, and Healing, Are Already Well Developed

Temples of autonomous goddesses such as Kali, Meenakshi, and Durga, have also the potential to become pilgrimage places because of the special wish granting reputation of these goddesses. Non autonomous female deities on the contrary (Lakshmi, Saraswati), are less likely to form the nuclei for potentially important pilgrimage sites. Autonomous deities alone, known for grace and wish fulfillment, are likely to generate significant pilgrimage sites. The Kali temple of Toronto is one such example.

Even in the affluent society of America, problems of material wellbeing abound. More important, however, are the problems of adjustment to new culture, especially of raising children in a different culture. Such problems often produce stress, but most Indians are not accustomed to seeking psychological counsel for stress-related problems. Visitation to temples serves as a culturally acceptable stress reducing behavior.

3. Favorable Geographic Location

Remoteness may be a positive attribute for many pilgrimage sites in India, because the act of pilgrimage is a symbolic break with the physical world, in the quest of spiritual merit. American Hindus, and their families may not wish to go too far away into the woods in search of the spiritual. Since spiritual and secular journeys may be combined together, as they often are, pilgrimage places with a more convenient location are likely to supersede those that are excessively isolated in less populated states, unless the place has truly unique attributes, e.g., Prabhupada's Palace of Gold in West Virginia. Relatively convenient detours from the major circulation routes across the country are conducive to the development of holy sites. Places such as the Rajarajeshwari Pitham in the Pocono Mountains, and New Goloka in the vicinity of the "Research Triangle" (North Carolina), are in this category.

4. Topography Symbolically Replicating or Evoking the Indian Scene of the Favorite Pilgrimage Site

Local site characteristics, especially topographic attributes of a holy place when found in a new holy place can act as a powerful impulse in evoking the sanctity of the "original" place. HIROSHI TANAKA, and CAROLYN PROROK have made this point in reference to Shikoku, and New Vrindaban respectively (TANAKA 1977 and 1981; PROROK 1987, 132 – 133). During the "Sahastra

Shiva-Linga Abhiseka" ceremonies in the Hindu-Jain Temple at Pittsburgh, one of the speakers on this occasion likened the confluence of the Allegheny and the Monongahela (forming the Ohio River) to the sacred *tribeni* confluence of the Ganga, the Yamuna and the invisible (mythical) Saraswati at Prayag. Thus, Pittsburgh was instantly made the holy Prayagraj of America.

The deity Tirupati in India is also called the lord of "seven hills" because of hills surrounding the Tirupati Temple. Likewise, the S.V. Temple at Pittsburgh, surrounded by the hills of Pennsylvania, evokes the feeling of sanctity of the original temple in India. It is not a mere coincidence that the News Letter of the S.V. Temple is called *Saptagiri Vani* (literally, seven hills' voice). A song in praise of the deity Sri Venkateswara of Pittsburgh refers to him literally as the Lord whose abode is Penn Hills.

Such symbolical attempts to see, in either topography or toponymy, a reflection of the sacred in India is consciously to make the newly consecrated place an actualization of the original in India. The priest (Mr. RAVI CHANDRA) of the Shiva Vishnu temple (Livermore CA, April 6, 1986) spoke to me of Springtown locality of the temple as "Vasant Puri" (literally, spring town), and the State of California to rhyme with Kapilaranya (the forest home of sage KAPILA). By the use of familiar evocative names for the adopted alien landscape features the new land becomes immediately familiar, understandable, and even holy. Uncertainty and the feeling of being an alien give way to a sense of emotional bond with the place. In short, the unfamiliar becomes intimate, and comprehensible (TUAN 1974 and 1977).

5. Uniqueness About the Place, That Has Some Symbolic Value

TANAKA (1981) has admirably articulated the spatial-symbolic dimension of pilgrimage. All individual places are unique, but a striking uniqueness with a clear symbolic value can enhance experiential feelings about a pilgrimage place. The Meenakshi temple (Pearland, Texas) is unique in that the presiding deity there is a female. This could be a powerful symbol of the significance of the divine female in Hinduism for the second generation Hindus both male and female. Similarly, the Shiva-Vishnu temple in Livermore, California is unique in bringing together two culturally different architectural symbols (northern and southern Indian) in one place. One wing of the sacred complex, beginning to be referred to as the "Hari-Hara Kshetra", is composed of the temples and deities representing the northern tradition, the other wing is architecturally southern. Even the colors of the deities are reflective of the two different traditions. This temple is an emblem of two very different traditions of Indian Hinduism, able to seek cultural accommodation, even if it has happened in a "foreign" land. This model, symbolic of Hindu unity, could become popular at local levels as well.

6. Organizational Ability

Temples that aspire to become well known, and thus become pilgrimage sites
have to be extremely well managed. The components of this management include (but are not limited to) the concept of the temple and its scope, fund
raising, building, establishment of donor network, linking the temple with
experienced and philanthropic organizations in India, and leadership in community affairs. Some of the best organizational ability has been seen in the
temples associated with the Hindu Temple Society of North America. Other
organizational linkages include the Tirupati Temple in Andhra Pradesh, Par-
martha Niketan of Hardwar in Uttar Pradesh, the Birla Trust, and Endowments Department of some state governments, and the Sankaracharya *maths*
(centers) in India.

7. Authenticity

The potential pilgrimage place has to be perceived by the devotees as authentic in its various dimensions. The temple architecture must be authentic to
evoke the feeling of athomeness. It is not sufficient to have a consecration ceremony. It must be followed by routine authentic ritual by *pujaris* (traditional
priests). The images must be made by the traditional artisans (*shilpis*), and
these images must be duly consecrated, installed and worshipped. No wonder,
every major Hindu temple in the United states and Canada has been at pains
to obtain traditional priests to perform the daily ritual in the correct form.
Whereas some modifications to suit the place are necessary, the temple must
be an authentic Hindu place. The pilgrims cannot feel a sense of belonging unless the whole landscape, soundscape and even aroma evoke sacredness. Thus,
the *sivalinga* (Shiva's stone emblem) at the Hindu-Jain Temple (Pittsburgh)
was made authentic, by bathing it in the holy waters brought all the way from
numerous sacred spots in India.

VI. Major Pilgrim Routes

The development of Hindu temples in America has begun to generate certain
popular pilgrimage routes and circuits. One of the most popular ones is from
the Vighaneswara or Ganesa Temple of Flushing (New York) to the S.V. Temple, Pittsburgh, and then to New Vrindaban in West Virginia. A second major
pilgrim route is from Montreal or Toronto to the S.V. Temple and from there
to New Vrindaban. Both these routes may include sight-seeing at Niagara
Falls. Many pilgrims, most by automobiles and some by chartered buses, who
visit the S.V. Temple, also visit the Hindu-Jain Temple. Likewise those who
visit the Hindu-Jain Temple try to visit the S.V. Temple. The pilgrims of the

Dravidian language region of India primarily visit the S.V. Temple for very specific types of worship, and for the fulfillment of vows and promises but also visit the Hindu-Jain Temple as a matter of courtesy and curiosity. Hindus of Northern Indian origin primarily visit the Hindu-Jain temple followed by a visit to the S.V. Temple.

It will not be long before a major new Hindu pilgrim circuit develops. That should be most likely from Toronto (or Montreal) to The Pschima Kashi Temple at Flint, Balaji and HTGC at Chicago, New Vrindaban, S.V. Temple at Pittsburgh, and return via Niagara Falls. A variant of this circuit could be from New York to Pittsburgh, New Vrindaban, Paschima Kashi, Balaji and HTGC. Some chartered bus tours from New York have been operational since the early 80's.

It is significant to note that major Hindu temples are now located in the cardinal directions, Ganesa and S.V. Temple in the East (New York, and Pittsburgh respectively), Paschima Kasi Sri Viswanatha Temple in the North (Flint, Michigan), Lord Venkateswara Temple, and Shiva Vishnu Hindu Temple in the West (California), and the Meenakshi Temple in the South (Pearland, Texas). The center of the country is occupied by the two big temples in Chicago (Balaji and HTGC). Thus, from the Hindu perspective the land of their adoption seems to have been sanctified and made fit for permanent residence.

These major temples in the cardinal directions could one day be looked upon as the American "char dhams" (the four sacred abodes) of the Hindu pilgrimage system that is currently evolving. This development may follow a symbolic evolutionary course somewhat similar to the Shikoku pilgrimage, which has been eloquently conceptualized by TANAKA (1981). Other temples might become part of the pilgrim circuit as the population of Hindus in the United States grows and ages, and as devotees find more time to visit sacred centers, and as more elderly relatives of the permanent resident Hindus emmigrate to the United States during the 1990's.

VII. Conclusion

Hindu pilgrimage in America, a very recent phenomenon, is evolving largely on the basis of iconic temples. Although the visiting gurus and swamis attract "pilgrims", the real centers of nascent pilgrimage in America are the temples developed primarily under the southern Indian Hindu cultural symbolics. The leadership shown by the southern Indian Hindus has its basis in the fact that temples have always played a crucial role in the life of people there (APPADU-RAI 1981) unlike the non-Dravidian people of India. Other strong regional religious traditions will probably make their mark in time for example, the

Kali tradition of Bengal, Jagganath of Orissa, Swaminarayan of Gujarat, and Ayappan of Kerala.

The development of temple based pilgrimages is tantamount to creating or recreating a religious landscape, a transference of holiness in which the Hindus can increasingly feel a sense of spiritual fulfillment as well as temporal and spatial security. For the religious Hindus the various sacred nodes and the paths leading to them are beginning to create a sacred "circulation manifold" (a term I first heard used by FRED LUKERMANN) flowing through which they can experience a feeling of insulation from the ill effects of the non-sacred realm to which they had originally migrated for entirely non-spiritual goals. Hindus have tried to reactualize their sacred landscape which they left behind. This sacred landscape, however, is being continually nourished by strong spiritual links with Indian sacred centers and religious and philanthropic organizations. Emphasis on authenticity, and the ability to put their belief into practice has meant that Hindu holy places in America will be not only of value to the immigrants but a source of vitality to the original sacred hearth in India as well. The institution of pilgrimage in Hinduism is so deep-rooted that it would be a surprise if it did not transfer to America.

Acknowledgment

I wish to thank the many dedicated individuals, members of the temple trustee boards, the *shilpis*, the *swamis*, and the priests who were kind enough to talk to me, and in some cases even provided free lodging on my visits to the various Hindu temple sites in America.

Summary

Hindu iconic temples represent a recent imprint of Hindu religious landscape in America. They are also part of the transference process of the various religious traditions of Hinduism. Pilgrimage centered upon the iconic temples is one such religious tradition which is in the process of being transferred to America. Several temples have been identified as probable centers of evolving Hindu pilgrimage in America, in addition to the few already established pilgrimage sites. These types of temples have been differentiated from the sub-regional and local centers of worship. Several attributes of the emergent pilgrimage places in America have been identified. It is proposed that the deities symbolic of strong regional identity are the ones most likely to be the focal points of pilgrimage. A preeminent deity in this category is Sri Venkateswara, symbolic of the southern Indian cultural tradition. Favorable geographic location, topographic symbolism evoking Indian sacred landscape, striking uniqueness, authenticity of religious architecture and ritual, and organizational ability to develop donor network and institutional ties with India are likely to be valuable in the evolving pilgrimage patterns. In their desire to reactualize their religious beliefs, Hindus are likely to evolve a pilgrimage circuit in America.

Zusammenfassung:

Hindu-Gottheiten und Pilgerfahrten in den USA

Die ikonischen *Tempel der Hindu* sind jüngster Bestandteil der religiösen Landschaft der Hindu in Amerika und auch Teil des Übertragungsprozesses der verschiedenen *religiösen Traditionen* des Hinduismus. Die auf die ikonischen Tempel ausgerichtete Pilgerfahrt stellt eine solche religiöse Tradition dar, die zur Zeit nach Amerika übertragen wird. Einige Tempel lassen sich als mögliche Zentren des sich zusätzlich zu den wenigen bereits anerkannten Pilgerorten herausbildenden hinduistischen Pilgerwesens in Amerika kennzeichnen. Dieser Tempel-Typ unterscheidet sich von regionalen und lokalen Kultzentren.

Die *in Amerika entstehenden Pilgerstätten* müssen bestimmte Voraussetzungen erfüllen: So wird die Behauptung aufgestellt, daß die Gottheiten, die Symbol für eine *starke regionale Identität* sind, mit größter Wahrscheinlichkeit zu Zentren der Pilgerfahrt werden. Eine herausragende Gottheit dieser Kategorie ist Sri Venkateswara, Symbol für die kulturelle Tradition Südindiens. Eine günstige geographische Lage, ein *topographischer Symbolismus*, der an eine bestimmte heilige Landschaft Indiens erinnert, eine auffallende Einzigartigkeit, die *Authentizität* von religiöser Architektur und Ritual und die *organisatorische Fähigkeit*, ein Spendennetz und institutionelle Beziehungen zu Indien zu erreichen, sind wahrscheinlich besonders wichtig für die Entstehung des Pilgerphänomens. In ihrem Wunsch, ihre religiösen Überzeugungen wiederzubeleben, werden die Hindus wahrscheinlich ein *System der Pilgerfahrten* in Amerika entwickeln.

Bibliography

ALAGAPPAN, A. (1978): Links with Andhra Pradesh. In: The Hindu Temple Society of North America, Commemorative Souvenir, n.p. 27 – 29.

BHARDWAJ, S. M. and RAO, M. (1988): "Emerging Hindu Pilgrimage in the United States: A Case Study." Geographia Religionum 4: 159 – 188.

CONGER, G. (1988): "Life and Death among the Krishnas at New Vrindaban." Beacon, Magazine of the Beacon Journal (newspaper), February 7, 1988.

ELIADE, M. (1959): The Sacred and the Profane: The Nature of Religion. Harper and Row, New York and Evanston.

INDIA WEST (newspaper), July 18, 1986.

MATHUR, R. (1985): Asian Indians in Southern California (map). Cultural Map Service, Diamond Bar (California).

NAIDU, T. S. (1985): Pilgrims and Pilgrimage: A Case Study of Tirumala Tirupati Devasthanam. In: Makhan Jha, ed. Dimensions of Pilgrimage. Inter-India Publications, New Delhi.

PROROK, C. (1987): "The Hare Krishna's Transformation of Space in West Virginia." Journal of Cultural Geography, 1987, 129 – 140.

RECORD COURIER (newspaper), August 23, 1987.

SAPTAGIRI VANI (1987): A Publication of the Sri Venkateswara Temple, Pittsburgh, Various dates.

SRI VENKATESA NIVEDIKA (1986): A Publication of the Sri Venkateswara Swami (Balaji) Temple of greater Chicago. Various dates.

TANAKA, H. (1977): "Geographic Expression of Buddhist Pilgrim Places on Shikoku Island, Japan." Canadian Geographer 21: 111 – 132.

TANAKA, H. (1981): "Evolution of Pilgrimage as a Spatial Symbolic System." Canadian Geographer, 25: 240 – 251.

TORONTO STAR (newspaper), June 28, 1986.

TUAN, Y. (1974): Topophilia: A Study of Environmental Perception, Attitudes and Values. Prentice-Hall, Englewood Cliffs.

TUAN, Y. (1977): Space and Place: The Perspective of Experience. University of Minnesota Press, Minneapolis.

J. W. Davidson, Alfred Hecht and Herbert A. Whitney

The Pilgrimage to Graceland

I. Introduction

When Elvis Presley, "The King" of rock and roll, died in August 1977, eighty thousand people gathered at the gates of his mansion called Graceland, in Memphis, Tennessee. A few thousand of the mourners were allowed a short glimpse of the body as it lay in state in the front hall of the mansion (BRIXEY and DIXON 1983, 58). The public's response to the singer's passing was unprecedented (GREGORY and GREGORY 1982, 168). People throughout the world were shocked and saddened upon hearing the news. Five months later, ten thousand Presley fans arrived in Memphis to mark his forty-third birthday (NEW YORK TIMES 1978, 16). On the first anniversary of Presley's death, nine thousand people from the United States, Canada, Europe and Japan came to Memphis (NEW YORK TIMES 1978, 64), and many more may have been discouraged from visiting because of a police strike then (NEW YORK TIMES 1978, 27). In June, 1982, Graceland was opened to the public, and during its first six months of operation, 280,000 people toured the mansion (MEMPHIS TOURIST REPORTER 1984, 8). Only five percent were from Memphis and its surrounding region (DIXON 1985). In 1988, some 640,000 visited Graceland, bringing the six and a half year total to more than three million visitors (TIME 1988).

Who was this person whose home has become a late twentieth century mecca in North America? During the mid 1950's, Elvis Presley emerged as the primary catalyst of rock'n'roll music. His energetic performances on stage, television and phonograph records captured the attention of young people in all the world. On the other hand, adults tended to see him as a bad influence on their children because of his blatant sexuality and 'Negro' vocal qualities. They were afraid that he would encourage promiscuity and racial equality. In a famous appearance on an Ed Sullivan Show in 1957, television viewers were shown only his head und upper torso, not his swiveling hips. By 1960, after a two year term in the army, he was much more subdued and was hailed by the United States Government as a model soldier. He made thirty-three feature length films but, becoming disenchanted with Hollywood, made a triumphant return in 1969 to live performing after an abscence of eight years and broke attendance records in stadiums throughout the United States. By the early 1970's, Elvis Presley had become a symbol of everything that was good about America. He was at that time probably the most photographed human in history, and could be identified throughout the world by his first name alone (LICHTER 1978; MARSH 1982). Obese during his latter years and rumored to have an addiction to prescription drugs, Elvis Presley died at the age of forty-two on the second floor of his home in Memphis.

Graceland, located on Elvis Presley Boulevard, was Elvis Presley's primary home for twenty years (Fig. 1). Elvis loved Graceland. He often said, "I feel I belong here" (GRACELAND ENTERPRISES 1982). The 13.8 acre property was originally owned by Mr. S. E. Toof, founder of a printing company in

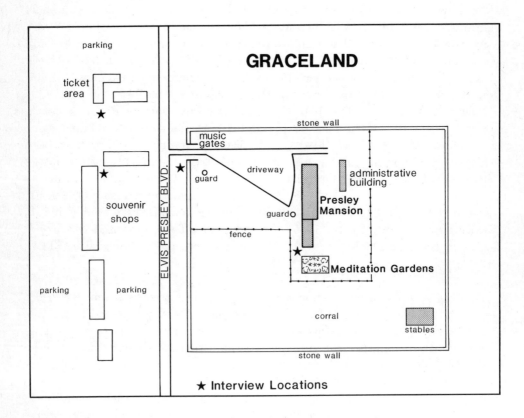

Fig. 1: Graceland in Memphis, Tennessee

Memphis, whose daughter Grace inherited the land, which was subsequently dubbed "Grace's Land" or "Graceland" by the local people. Miss Toof's niece, Ruth Brown Moore, built the twenty-three room house in 1939 with her husband, Dr. Thomas Moore. Elvis purchased Graceland in 1957 from Mrs. Moore for the sum of $ 100,000 (ROBERTS 1982, 5). He retained its original name because it reflected the home's tranquility (PRESLEY 1984). Graceland was declared an historic site by the Tennessee Historical Commission in 1982.

Elvis Presley's remains are now interred at Graceland in an area known as Meditation Gardens, where Presley had often sat in quiet contemplation (BRIXEY and DIXON 1983, 5). The singer's body was originally entombed in a mausoleum at Forest Hill Cemetery, five kilometers north of the mansion. Relocation was necessary for two reasons: Elvis fans disrupted the serenity of the graveyard by their vast numbers and by removing greenery for mementos, and the corpse was in danger of being stolen. The body of Elvis's mother, Gladys Presley, who had died in 1958 was also moved to Meditation Gardens on the same day in October 1977 (WORTH and TAMERIUS 1981, 129). In 1979, Vernon Presley passed away and was laid to rest between his wife and son. The following year, Elvis' paternal grandmother, Minnie Mae Presley, died and was also buried beside her famous grandson. Bronze plaques mark each of the graves. An eternal flame was erected at the head of Elvis' grave by several of his friends. Finally, a small marker was placed in memory of the singer's twin brother, who died at birth.

Although Presley's home and adjacent grave site are visited throughout the year by many people, devoted followers tend to congregate on the singer's birthday and on the anniversary of his death (BRIXEY 1984). What brings these people to Memphis and Graceland? What do they experience while there? To understand the importance of these pilgrimages, we need to consider human motives, beliefs, expectations, and the like. The focus of this paper is on the pilgrims' view and the satisfactions they derive from the pilgrimage.

II. Data Collection

A pilgrimage is much more than a journey to a significant site. Among other things, it may be an expression of faith, and it may offer opportunities for spiritual and bodily healing, for prestige, and for camaraderie. Accordingly, it was necessary to contact Graceland visitors directly to elicit their feelings and to observe their behaviours. The present study reports on 209 interviews conducted in Memphis over five weeks in 1984, from July 16 to August 20. The final week of interviews coincided with the Elvis International Tribute Week, when 21,000 Presley fans converged to commemorate the seventh anniversary of the singer's death. This was in addition to the normal flow of 3,000 tourists per day in the summer.

The major information was derived from open-ended questions. It was felt that too specific questions could stifle the respondents' actual feelings. The first of the three sets of questions focused on attitudes and perceptions. Respondents were asked to express any feeling they might have for Presley, to state whether various sites in Memphis related to Presley were meaningful to them, and to describe their experiences and expectations of these places. The second set of questions focused on their motivations for travel, activities and length of stay in Memphis. The final set of questions focused on demographic information. Following each session, the interviewer recorded a brief description of the respondent. Interviews ranged in length from a few minutes to half an hour, depending on the participant's interest in Presley and Graceland. Each day interviews were held in one of three locations: the front gate of Graceland, a location within yards of the Presley mansion and grave, or in front of one of the souvenir shops across the street (Fig. 1). Altering the locations of the interviews did not influence the range of answers. Which visitors to approach was determined primarily by a random number table.

Also, special interviews were arranged with four former associates of Elvis, with the operations manager of Graceland Enterprises which runs the tours, and with six of the seven people identified as having moved to Memphis because they wanted to be where Elvis had lived and died.

Additional information on the importance of Graceland was obtained by observing and recording visitor behaviour. For fifteen minutes prior to every random interview, overt behaviour of visitors was recorded. Visitors' reactions on tours were also unobtrusively observed and recorded. Every second ot third day, Meditation Gardens was visited from 6:30 to 7:45 A.M., when, before the daily tours commenced, people were allowed in. Again, unobtrusive observations of behaviour were noted and recorded after the visitation period. No visitor was approached for an interview during that time lest it affect the behaviour of the person involved or others.

III. Findings

The 209 visitors randomly selected for interview comprised two major different groups, subsequently called "tourists" and "pilgrims". The division was made on the basis of the primary destination for their journey, of the meaning of Elvis, of the inportance placed on visiting Graceland and, to a lesser extent, of the length of stay in Memphis. By far the largest proportion were tourists (85%). The smaller but more interesting remaining 31 visitors were called "transient pilgrims" to distinguish them from the seven "immigrant pilgrims" who had moved permanently to Memphis because of attachment to Elvis. In what follows, feelings and behaviour of transient and immigrant pilgrims will be contrasted and compared with each other as well as with tourists, and with the interviewed associates of Elvis when appropriate.

First, however, we turn to where the whole group of Graceland visitors came from. Although people came from around the globe, some areas are more represented than others. Ninety-two per cent of the respondents were residents of the United States. Furthermore, the vast majority of the American visitors lived in the area east of what could be called the Texas-Minnesota axis. Origin of pilgrims seems to be a function of distance and urbanization. The South Eastern states ranked highest, accounting for thirty-two per cent of the respondents. The Great Lakes and South West Regions placed second and third with nineteen per cent and sixteen per cent, respectively.

Presley 'pilgrims' and Presley 'tourists' came from the same areas. The relative importance of pilgrims, however, was not necessarily related to the total number of people emanating from a particular region. For instance, the Middle Atlantic Region sent very few people to Graceland, but proportionately many were pilgrims. Similarly, three of the five people from England who were interviewed were pilgrims. In other words, as distance increased, commitment to Presley became a more important inducement to travel.

Although roughly fifty-five per cent of the people surveyed were female, the proportion increased when the pilgrim population was isolated from the total. Two thirds of the transient pilgrims were female. Only a few individuals belonged to visible minorities, indicating that Elvis Presley is a symbol of white ideals. Relatively few were teenagers or elderly.

A significant minority of the respondents considered Elvis Presley to be a central aspect in their lives. How could a man who has been dead since 1977 still exert profound influence over the lives of many people? By examining the significance of Elvis to them we can begin to understand why visiting Graceland was truly a pilgrimage to them rather than "a trip down memory lane".

1. The Significance of Presley to Pilgrims

The meaning and hence the importance of Presley varied significantly across individuals, as the comments by Elvis' associates, pilgrims and tourists indicate. KENNETH BRIXEY, the manager of Graceland stated:

> I knew Elvis. He rented rides at Libertyland at night when I was the manager over there. My experiences were pleasant and warm ...the same kind of charisma that Billy Graham and the major evangelists had ...he had mass appeal.

Presley's relatives and associates agreed that the singer had special qualities. The singer's uncle, VESTER PRESLEY, stated in an interview:

> Elvis had talent coming out of the ears ... very few have that magnetism ... it draws people ... At home he was just old Elvis, but when he went on stage I said, "that ain't no kin of mine" ... like changing into another man.

A similar comment was made by BILLY SMITH, the singer's maternal cousin:

> When Elvis started singing I didn't have any idea that he would be as big as that ... just an older cousin. [The media did not invent Elvis.] He had a God-gift. The first time I heard him on the radio, I couldn't believe it was Elvis. I thought the world was crazy! He was a different person on stage.

People who personally knew Elvis agreed that although he became popular thirty years ago, he will remain a household word because he was a talented and generous person. Media hype gave the singer recognition very early in his career, but they felt he still would have become a star because of his talents. However, the present Presley pilgrimages have been deemed an "unexplainable phenomenon" by these same people.

a. Immigrant Pilgrims

Let us turn next to those people who knew Presley well enough by being exposed to him through the mass media and concert appearances that they subsequently chose to live in Memphis. Seven such "immigrant pilgrims" were identified; six were interviewed. Like Presley's friends, the immigrate pilgrims viewed Elvis as a magnetic and charitable human being. A woman belonging to this group stated:

> Elvis is a person I would like to have met ... like a son. He is somebody I've felt very protective of. I haven't always been this way. It all started then I went to a concert in 1976. Once you saw him live you were hooked ... I have Elvisitis. I have to have everything.

Likewise, DENIS WISE, a Presley illusionist who moved to Memphis in 1983 to be in close proximity to Graceland and other fans like himself, examined and stated his feelings:

Elvis meant a lot to me . . . like a family . . . a father-figure. [My own father was always on the road driving a truck.) . . . Elvis had the ability to care about another human. He loved his fans . . . he never lost that. (Other people in his position] didn't give two dimes or a nickel to give you an autograph (yet he did).

This appreciation of Elvis's humanness was also observed in the appartments of two immigrant pilgrims. The house of one young man was decorated with photographs of Presley mailed by the singer himself. Presley began answering letters in the early 1970s after learning that this young man had a severe kidney ailment.

On the whole, the immigrant pilgrims felt a kinship with Elvis because he directly or indirectly provided them with an object of affection. At some point in their lives they were without loved ones. Presley filled that void. In return for the friendship and entertainment which Elvis continued to give them even after his death, the immigrant pilgrims were quick to defend his honor. These people indicated that even though Elvis was dead in a physical sense, his spiritual essence flourished in the vicinity of Graceland, and it was this presence which drew them to Memphis. Not surprisingly, BROCK (1979, 116) found that many Presley fans believe his ghost exists.

b. Transient Pilgrims

Feelings of kinship toward Presley were not limited to the immigrant pilgrims. One fifth of the transient pilgrims also reported what can be described as a personal relationship with Presley. A middle-aged woman from New York passionately stated:

PRESLEY was not part of this world . . . loved by everyone . . . appreciated what he had . . . honest and sincere. He thought he was nothing. I love Elvis the person first, the entertainer second. He was more than that . . . the brother I never had.

An elderly woman from England viewed Elvis as a spiritual mediator. She stated:

I'm a spiritualist . . . I prayed to Elvis to ask God to allow me to come to Graceland. Now that I have been here I can die in peace . . . I love Elvis as an entertainer. He told me to come here.

Roughly half of those who felt a special kinship with Presley indicated that they had a spiritual encounter with Presley since his death. The remaining members of the transient pilgrim group had no such experience and did not express the belief that his spirit still lives in the vicinity of Graceland. The major difference between these two subgroups is that one feels that their friend or hero was swept from their lives by death, whereas the other believe that even though this is true, his soul has remained near Graceland because he loved his home. Nobody went as far as to profess that Elvis was a god, but then neither did the immigrant pilgrims.

Half of the transient pilgrims stressed Presley's personal qualities. Most commonly, these people admired his willingness to give of himself and his money to his family, friends, fans and charitable institutions. His ability to remain a humble person despite his great wealth and popularity also impressed many people. A young woman from England explained: "He didn't act stuck-up ... kiddin' around all the time ... took care of his parents. He's just great!" Although a few of the people interviewed thought that Elvis had charismatic qualities, the vast majority viewed him as a normal person, but one with ideal personality traits and a great musical talent.

The final subgroup of transient pilgrims, which constituted one eighth of the total, considered themselves mainly fans of his music. It should be stressed that this group were totally enthralled with the entertainment side of Elvis. Statements were given such as, "I am very much an Elvis Presley fan," and "He's a legend in his own time". These people journeyed to Memphis to investigate his musical roots, but did not display the same degree of interest in the personal side of the late singer as the other pilgrims.

To sum up, then, transient pilgrims exhibited a wide range of reactions to Elvis, but all were intensely interested in at least one aspect of him.

c. Tourists

Of the entire sample of 209 people interviewed at Graceland, only a few were there simply because they were curious to see the interior of a star's home or had accompanied somebody who liked Elvis Presley. The overwhelming majority were interested in Elvis, the person. In general, what differentiated pilgrims from tourists was the duration and primary purpose of their visit, as well as the intensity of feelings toward Presley. Pilgrims were much more enthusiastic about Elvis than tourists. Tourists mainly admired Presley's musical talents. Other significant feelings of tourists towards Elvis were nostalgia (18%), historic figure (8%) and tragedy (6%).

Elvis Presley obviously meant different things to different people. He influenced the lives of the immigrant pilgrims by far the most. These people have adopted his home town as their own. To the majority of the respondents in this study, Elvis was important enough for them to visit his home, but then only enough to stay for a few hours. This suggests that the importance of Elvis in visitors' lives varied substantially.

If the significance of Elvis is based on people's perceptions, then this would suggest that the meaning of Graceland and the experiences of that place were also a function of those same interpretations. In other words, if Presley, based entirely on his own merits, prompted his followers to make a pilgrimage to his home, then why were those people vastly outnumbered by the more casual tourists? Ideally, everyone visiting Graceland should have had pilgrim tendencies, but they did not.

Because Graceland was visited by people from all over the world, the possibility existed that different cultures would form different types of Presley fans. Overall, however, the range of meanings assigned to the late singer by the 209 respondents did not differ notably by place of origin.

Let us turn next to the meanings and experiences of Graceland sites on visitors. That is, what was it about these places which is alluring to the devout Elvis Presley fan?

2. The Significance of Graceland to Pilgrims

Just as a diversity of meanings were assigned to Elvis Presley by pilgrims, so were a variety of meanings assigned to traveling to his mansion.,

Associates of Elvis Presley were not in awe of Graceland. To them, it was their home which they had shared with a dear friend for many years. A member of Elvis' band, who did not wish to be identified, explained that other houses which Presley and his friends occupied while they were in Hollywood were also important, but Graceland had given them roots. BILLY SMITH, the singer's maternal cousin, recalled with excitement:

> Elvis and I were just a couple of poor ol' Mississippi boys ... [when I was invited to live in a house behind Graceland] it was like moving into heaven.

RICHARD DAVIS, Presley's valet, commented that Graceland represented ten years of things that he and the singer did together. Although the inhabitants of the mansion were allowed to continue living there after the singer's death, only Elvis's grandmother, Minnie Mae Presley, and his paternal aunt, Delta Mae Biggs, choose to remain there. Elvis was central to the meaning of Graceland to those who knew him personally. Presley had been their friend and a dynamic individual whom they all admired. When Elvis died, their lives were jolted. BILLY SMITH stated sadly:

> I couldn't stand it there after Elvis died ... there were too many memories. I had to get away. I packed my bags and stayed away for a couple of years ... I came back to Memphis because I belong here.

a. Immigrant Pilgrims

The immigrant pilgrims considered Graceland to be the most important place on earth. One, DENIS WISE, stated that "If there is a heart of the world it's Graceland ..." A very similar statement was made by another young man. "I always wanted to move to Memphis ... like I was always meant to be here ... Graceland could be the heart of the world ..."

The immigrant pilgrims considered Graceland to be much more precious than their own homes, which they left behind. Interestingly, these people did not have familial ties to bind them to their former residences. Feelings of isolation were alleviated by moving to Memphis because Graceland attracted other people who were equally committed to Presley. Graceland symbolized feelings of love and association with other people. Fraternal bonds were embodied in the phrase, "Elvis fans can move mountains". Moreover, the sentiment was expressed that because everybody loved Elvis, anyone who loved Elvis would also be loved. Most immigrant pilgrims would go so far as to claim that the Presley mansion was not just a meeting place, but also that is was the domain of their hero's spirit.

b. Transient Pilgrims

In contrast to the immigrant pilgrims, the transient pilgrims tended not to advocate the view that Graceland was the centre of the earth. Unlike the immigrant pilgrims who were in need of a surrogate home, the meaning of life for the transient pilgrims was based in their occupations and/or families in another place. However, a few individuals made statements such as, "coming to Graceland is like coming home". Although the transient pilgrims did not identify with the mansion quite as closely as the immigrant pilgrims, they did consider Elvis's home to be an extremely important and electrifying place. By journeying to Graceland, people in this group experienced a sense of closeness and identification with their hero. A woman from Barrie, Ontario, expressed it as follows:

> It's him, his home ... That's the closest I'll ever get to him. By being here I can get a feel of what it was like when he was alive.

Graceland was loved by Elvis and it gave him a sense of belonging and meaning. Similarly, it is loved by both immigrant and transient pilgrims. The home is also a major physical remnant of Presley's life — a life which the pilgrims needed to know more about. For some, the personal meaning of Graceland was linked to religious beliefs. One person commented: "Graceland is the closest we can get to him until we die and go to heaven with him."

For the majority of transient pilgrims, Graceland was just physical space, but for others it had a very pronounced spiritual dimension. One person declared: "I don't care about going anywhere else ... He's still in that house (in a spiritual sense)." It seems that the transient pilgrims differed from immigrant pilgrims in that the latter internalized Elvis's own religious beliefs of spirits roaming the earth.

c. Tourists

The tourist population substantiated the concept that a place can be assigned vastly different meanings. Although all pilgrims attributed great importance to Graceland, roughly one third of the tourists stated that Presley's home was devoid of any meaning to them. One such visitor stated that his coming to Graceland was "just an opportunity to stop ... wouldn't want to go through Memphis without stopping [yet] ... not truthfully an Elvis fan". An additional one tenth of the tourists were neutral toward Graceland. These people saw the Presley mansion as "the home of a famous star" or "the symbol of a bygone era in music". Even though some visitors valued and admired Elvis, this esteem did not necessarily carry over to this home. An inverse relationship exists too: one quarter of those who showed little appreciation of Graceland also lacked interest in Elvis Presley.

Respondents who indicated that the mansion did have meaning for them — recall that the entire sample is comprised of both pilgrims and tourists — can be seperated into two groups based on the meaning they assigned to Graceland. One group, which included only tourists, assigned rather superficial meanings to Graceland such as "it was simply Elvis's home". The other group identified with two responses: Graceland is a "memorial" to the late singer, and it is a "symbol" of his importance. Although the answers supplied by this second group seem similar to those given by the first, the underlying meanings differed. The second group considered Graceland to be a very significant place in history and probably in their lives.

The vast majority of people traveling to Graceland were not devoted pilgrims but rather curiosity seekers. The home attracted many people who at this stage of their lives had only casual interest in Presley, and it also attracted many devoted Elvis Presley admirers who did not place any real meaning on the externalities of the singer's life as manifested by Graceland. However, many Elvis fans visited Graceland because of the sanctity they saw in that place.

3. Experience of Place: Graceland

Experiences inside the Presley mansion also varied among visitors. By examining these experiences, one can gain further insights into the varying degrees of importance attached to being in that place.

Approximately one fifth of the transient pilgrims and one third of the tourists were impressed by the physical aspects of the dwelling. Some of these people thought that the mansion exuded wealth and beauty. A man from Fort Worth, Texas, stated, "I can't visualize anyone having enough money to buy anything he wanted ... fabulous taste ... I'm sure he enjoyed living." Other people were less than impressed, especially with his taste in home furnishings.

Transient pilgrims frequently concentrated on the aesthetic aspects of the home and tended to admire what they saw. A commonly uttered phrase by them was, "you just can't get enough of it. Each time that you go through you notice something different." In other words, by continually viewing the relics of their hero's life, the transient pilgrims felt that the secrets of his existence gradually unfolded to them.

Emotional experiences inside the home were reported by one quarter of the tourists and one third of the transient pilgrims. Although sadness was the predominant response, a number of individuals felt honored, happy and excited to actually be inside Elvis Presley's home. For instance, a female pilgrim from New York exclaimed, "It was overwhelming ... my hands were shaking ... too much of an emotional thing." By contrast, many people were not moved at all. Hence one can conclude that emotional experiences or responses must originate within the individual rather than being an instinctive reaction to an environment.

Earlier it was pointed out that one quarter of the transient pilgrims as well as all the immigrant pilgrims assigned meaning to Graceland because they were able to feel close to Presley there. Of the people who considered Elvis a friend, even though they had never actually met him, one third stated that they had spiritual encounters inside the house. For instance, an immigrant pilgrim indicated that she had acquired a photograph in which Elvis's ghost was plainly visible and seated on the living room sofa. "I have a feeling he's still here? ...I believe in a hereafter." "I believe he'll always be here", claimed another woman from England. Belief in Presley's spiritual existence, however, did not necessarily mean that this ghost would be felt within the house itself. Some people experienced him at the grave site or elsewhere on the estate. An interesting graffito written on the brick wall which surrounds the Presley property read, "I know you're up there smiling down on all of us. Edith sends her love and knows you'll be there on her wedding day."

Some people made a pilgrimage to Memphis because the soul of the person whom they revered was there. That Elvis's spirit seemingly made itself known to only a relative few of his loyal followers, and that the precise nature and location of the revelations varied between individuals, suggests that people perceive and interpret environments differently. Even though the majoritiy of interviewees were oblivious to it, Presley's ghost was very real to those people who claimed to have experienced it. The majority of people who felt close to him inside the mansion, however, did not report a spiritual interaction. Comments included: "It gives the chills to know that he once lived here" and "It's a thrill to be able to walk were he once walked."

Immigrant pilgrims viewed Graceland as sacred space, and so they resented its commercial exploitation. Tourists should not be allowed inside the Presley home, they thought, and the managers of the mansion promote tours against the wishes of the singer. This view was expressed in part as follows:

> Graceland [Enterprises] is pushing Graceland. They don't care about Elvis. People are here to see Elvis.

Two important points are reiterated by this quote. First, Graceland would be nothing without its associational link with Elvis, and because that link did exist the house is sacred. Second, the sacredness of Graceland dictates that the home should be treated with respect. Living and working in the vicinity of the mansion enables the immigrant pilgrims to monitor any ill proceedings there.

A small minority of both transient pilgrims and tourist groups shared the opinion of the immigrant pilgrims that their presence in the Presley mansion was an invasion of privacy. Transient pilgrims who felt like intruders in the home generally wanted the house closed to tours, and themselves to be given back the privilege of walking through the music gates and up the driveway into the estate rather than riding on a sterile tour bus. Still other transient pilgrims were ecstatic about having toured through Graceland, and a few wanted to see even more of the mansion than was open to the tours.

The data suggest, then, that people visited Graceland for vastly different reasons. The majority of people wished to have something akin to a tourist experience, whereas others wanted to feel physically or spiritually closer to their hero. Divergent experiences inside the Presley mansion also revealed that a site can be different things to different people. In general, people experienced different things in the same environment because they assigned different meanings to that place.

4. The Significance of Meditation Gardens to Pilgrims

For most pilgrims regardless of religion, the burial site of the person revered is important. For Elvis fans too this is so, but as with the mansion, the degree of importance attached to Presley's grave site varied among individuals. One fifth of the pilgrims and a few other respondents were ecstatic to be actually at his grave. For example, a male tourist who perceived Presley as a tragic figure said, "Meditation Gardens looked and felt nice . . . I enjoyed it the most because it's the closest you can get to him physically." Again, a substantial portion of these respondents felt Elvis' presence on the grave. A card on one of the floral arrangements placed on the grave read "You have been part of our lives. We will continue to love you for all eternity and do good works in your name."

This and other statements had strong religious connotations. Pilgrims involved in charitable projects dedicated to Presley did so to support the singer's own philosophy of giving to others. They did not see it as a form of idolatry of Presley. Even though Elvis was physically dead, he was still very real to them. They wanted to express their undying admiration by perpetuating his good name. In a sense they were his disciples, but they never lost sight of their leader's now famous proclamation, "There's only one king and that's Jesus Christ . . . I 'm just an entertainer, and that's that". As in the case of the mansion, the people who experienced his spirit in Meditation Gardens were among those who had the deepest emotional ties with him.

Half of both the tourists and pilgrims reported that they had emotional experiences at the grave. A pilgrim who journeyed from England stated, "Being Catholic I feel I must go to the grave . . . very emotional for me . . . I might as well say I have met him."

It should be noted that the vast majority of respondents, even those who were neutral toward Elvis, did feel sad at his grave. Statements such as, "a wasted life" and "it was a bitter reminder of my own lost youth" were common. For someone who was deeply involved in understanding the singer's life, visiting the grave was an emotional experience, one that was looked forward to from the outset of his or her journey.

Still, one tenth of the tourists and a similar proportion of the transient pilgrims were unmoved by Meditation Gardens. Two common responses uttered by these tourists were, "it's just another grave to me" and "I was not aware that he was buried there". To these transient pilgrims, the grave marker was little more than a memorial because they believed that Elvis was buried elsewhere on the estate. One such woman stated:

> I enjoy spending time in Meditation Gardens. It's a beautiful spot but it really doesn't mean very much because he is not really buried there. They wouldn't leave his body unguarded like that when there are so many people around ... He's buried in an unmarked location somewhere on the estate where he can be at peace.

Whereas the vast majority of pilgrims regarded Meditation Gardens as sacred space, a few cherished what was to them Elvis's true grave site. That Presley's grave site was too commercialized was expressed by about ten percent of the tourists. A statement which captured this sentiment was, he had to die to escape the public ... he'll never be in peace as long as they're here."

Further evidence of the various meanings assigned the grave site may be obtained from people's behaviour there. Between 9:00 A.M. and 6.00 P.M., Meditation Gardens was the final exhibit on the mansion tours. During that period people lined up quietly to see the graves of Elvis and his family. The vast majority stood respectfully at the foot of Elvis's final resting place for a few moments and then proceeded to the van area to be shuttled off the property. By the time one group had nearly gone, the next group would arrive. Children tended to be more fascinated with the large water fountain in the centre of Meditation Gardens, and with the many shiny coins beneath the vertical streams of water, than with the grave. A few adults dropped cigarette butts on the ground each day, an indication of lack of respect, but on the whole the visits took place in an air of reverence for the dead.

During the anniversary week of Presley's death, such behaviour in Meditation Gardens remained the same from 9.00 A.M. till 6.00 P.M., as tourists still grossly outnumbered pilgrims. But during the early morning visitation period, before the tours began, a vast change occured. Until August 7th, tourist behaviour such as picture taking and coin tossing predominated even during the early part of the day. A few people, however, sat quietly on the steps near the foot of the grave. Most notably, two women from Europe arrived at Meditation Gardens at precisely 6.50 A.M. each morning and stayed for the remaining forty minutes of the early visitation period. They were in Memphis for the entire duration of the field research. Because they seldom spoke or took photographs, their behavior indicated that they had great respect for Elvis and cherished the peaceful moments which they could spent at his grave. Never dissuaded from keeping their daily vigil; these women seemed almost oblivious to the weather and the antics of some of these tourists. The beauty, tranquility and sanctity which these two women must have assigned to Meditation Gardens were probably largely unknown to the tourists who were there at the same time.

When the pilgrims began arriving in Memphis for the festival week, the behaviour exhibited by the two European women in Meditation Gardens became the norm rather than the exception during the early morning visitation. The number of people who kept an early morning vigil at the grave gradually increased from a half dozen in early August to approximately three hundred on the day prior to the anniversary of Elvis' death. Several people brought elaborate handmade floral arrangements on the 16th of August. Personal sources indicated that some of these projects were a year in the making. A kite which was presented by one oriental woman, and a detailed replica of Presley's private airplane, set in a background of clouds, both symbolized life. Yet, the creator of another floral tribute stated in an interview, "Elvis is dead and that's it". In other words, similar overt behaviour at the grave site and comparable gift commitments to Presley did not necessarily reflect the same kind of experience. Floral tributes were set in place in a very sincere and meticulous manner. Somewhat similarly, on August ninth, people who had been sitting in Meditation Gardens helped to place flowers back on the grave after the yard men cut the grass. Earlier that morning a woman from Toronto, Canada, commenced picking up litter which was strewn around the grave yard. This kind of behaviour exemplified the sanctity of that place to the people under consideration. Prior to the influx of pilgrims, visitors were not observed taking flowers to the grave, nor did anyone kiss the commemorative plaque. Those were actions of the devout followers. The vast majority of pilgrims also arrived at the front gates of Graceland at least fifteen minutes before the visitation period commenced and were rather reluctant to leave as its conclusion. It was a very special time for them. Two days, in particular, were very emotional. These were the anniversary of Elvis' death, on August 16th, and August 19th when everyone was preparing to leave for home.

Pilgrims were very obvious in Meditation Gardens during the early part of the morning because of their sombre behaviour and dress. One day, a small group of women did sit at the grave for roughly half an hour during the tour hours, but they promptly left after they were interviewed for television. Although these women may have welcomed the opportunity to vocalize their feelings for Elvis, the cameras may also have invaded their sacred space. Another woman, who wished to spend some time at the grave one afternoon, was upset by the behavior of the tourists:

> This morning [at the pilgrims' vigil] everybody understood what everybody else felt. When I was there during the tour a little kid said, "Mommy, is Elvis dead?" I didn't like that.??

Although the pilgrims wished to visit Presley's final resting place, they chose not to stay more than a few moments unless the sanctity of that place was agreed upon by everyone present. Because Elvis' mansion and grave site together were a very popular tourist attraction, the pilgrims congregated on the property during the solemn hours of the morning. The devoted Presley fan also did not feel comfortable spending an entire day at the grave because of the tours, and the organized Presley related events throughout Memphis were undoubtedly alluring to him or her as well.

5. Repeat Journeys by Pilgrims

No behaviour is more revealing of a person's continuing strong feelings for Elvis, as well as of having superior experiences at his home, than making a return trip there. According to the survey, pilgrims and tourists could not be more different: the typical tourist was a first time visitor, whereas the typical pilgrim was not only a returnee but an annual visitor.

Again, immigrant and transient pilgrims showed some differences. The immigrant pilgrims, although not moving to Memphis until after Presley's death, had typically frequented Graceland during his lifetime in hopes of glimpsing their hero. Of the transient pilgrims, approximately two-thirds had not been to the mansion during Presley's lifetime.

Place of origin was an important factor in repeat visitations. In absolute numbers, most returing pilgrims to Graceland hailed from regions of the United States in close proximity. Of particular interest was the South West Region, which accounted for a significant number of tourists and transient pilgrims in the survey, but the only visitors from there before Elvis died were two now immigrant pilgrims. Interesting, too, were the Middle Atlantic Region and the United Kingdom: their relatively few visitors according to the survey had not been to the Presley home during the singer's lifetime, but these two areas of origins showed notably higher rates of return visits than did other areas.

IV. Discussion

Four kinds of people have been identified with the Graceland phenomenon: associates of Presley, tourists, transient pilgrims, and immigrant pilgrims, in order of their increasing emotional involvement with Elvis. Within each group there was a wide range of reaction as numbers permitted. Variables such as age, sex, and place of origin had little influence on the range of feelings. LYNCH (1960), however, suggests that people falling within the same age, sex, or socioeconomic category tend to have similar perspectives, although individuals do vary from one another within these parameters. According to this Graceland survey, the devout followers of Elvis Presley tended to be members of the working class, but their group also consisted of business and professional people. The tourists exhibited a similar profile. The range of experiences within each group, then, transcended occupations. Similarly within each group, visitors were typically middle-aged, but attitudes towards Presley and his mansion varied tremendously within each age group. For instance, there was a thirty year age gap between the youngst and oldest immigrant pilgrim. And although female pilgrims greatly outnumbered males, there was no real evidence that experiences were based on gender. The literature indicates that the most notable variations in perceptions occur among individuals within any given group (BACHELARD 1964, 74; DONOVAN 1979, 1; RELPH 1976, 24; ROWLES 1978, 160). This was certainly confirmed by this Graceland survey.

ALLEN [1976, 56) and RENWICK and CUTTER (1983, 30) state that visitors to any destination arrive with preconceived notions of the place which are not readily abandoned when further information is available. The Graceland findings do not support this, relatively few visitors to Graceland found what they expected. But the importance of Graceland did not change because the mansion was more elaborate or smaller than expected. The meaning of Graceland was founded on the visitors' intepretations of Elvis Presley.

Visiting a famous place does not necessarily constitute a pilgrimage. Tourists and pilgrims have different expectations, experiences, and behaviours. For the individual visiting Graceland, the significance of the journey as well as of the experience of being there depended primarily on the interpretation of the heroic figure of Elvis Presley. By far, the majority of visitors viewed him as an interesting historic figure, famous as "The King" who made rock and roll music widely acceptable and who perhaps was responsible for many memories for them. These "tourists", although having as a group a wide range of reactions, as did the pilgrims, did not share with the pilgrims the sense of personal identity with Elvis. The pilgrims viewed Elvis not just as a great singer but also as a most admirable human being, almost perfect, and so placed great meaning on the tangible evidence of his life. By contrast, the tourists were little aware of his personal life and attached little importance to his home.

The pilgrims wanted to experience and perpetuate the memory of their hero, whereas the tourists just wanted to see an historic site. Accordingly, the pilgrims both expected and found more in Graceland than did the tourists. The tourists tended to be passive observers in a static setting, while the pilgrims found tremendous vitality in that same setting.

Moreover, although there were interactions between the tourists and Graceland, and between the pilgrims and Graceland, there were also interactions between the two groups. The tourists ended to be oblivious to the deep meanings which Graceland held for pilgrims, but the very presence of numerous "unfeeling" tourists underlined for the pilgrims the sanctity of the place and reinforced their feelings of cameraderie with other like-feeling persons. The activities of the pilgrims, in turn, generated curiosity amongst many tourists, and amongst the general public as well which generated still more visitors.

One of the influential pilgrim activities was a spectacular candlelight vigil which was picked up by the media and televised nationwide. This raises an important question: to what extent are modern pilgrimages beholden to the media? According to the present survey, the vast majority of the tourists had never been to Memphis before. A few mentioned that they had been in Memphis when Elvis was living there, but they had no interest in seeing his house then, nor knowledge of its location. Such information suggests that the media stimulated interest among tourists by bringing the mansion to national prominence at the time of the singer's funeral.

The pilgrims, too, seem to have been influenced by the media. The emotionalism which surrounded his death prompted significant numbers of people to visit Graceland because they could extend their Presley experience to meaningful surroundings. True fans did not cherish everything Presley equally; they focused their attention on those things which he had held most dear. Understanding that Graceland and his only child, Lisa Marie, were the only things in life he had truly loved, they journeyed to the mansion because it was accessible. On the other hand, there was insufficient evidence to conclude that the varied and deep meanings of Graceland then held by the survey responding pilgrims were due to the media. The pilgrimage was an avowed act of love. If the media did have an effect on the pilgrims' perceptions, then it was at a much earlier stage in their Presley experience.

These ambiguous findings and conclusions correspond to published literature on the importance of the media. For example, SANN (1967, 317) claims that the public's overwhelming response to the death of Rudolph Valentino resulted from an intense publicity campaign, whereas MOELLER (1979, 43) holds that the media probably does not generate new trends but rather takes notice of existing activities. Although numerous people were attracted to Graceland during Presley's lifetime, widespread media attention to this occurence did not take place until the emotionalism surrounding Elvis' death had emerged.

Camaraderie was a major facet of the pilgrim's collective experience. The literature indicates that individuals who initially join social movements are lonely and in need of other people whom they can derive meaning in their lives (TURNER and KILIAN 1972, 362). This was particularly supported in the Graceland survey by those pilgrims who viewed Elvis as their surrogate partner and felt his spiritual presence there. Also the pronounced tendency of the pilgrims to congregate in Memphis during Elvis International Tribute Week indicated the importance of being with similar others.

If socialization is not a significant aspect of the pilgrimage, then one must question why comparatively little of the pilgrims' time was actually spent at Graceland. Once they were in Memphis, so meaningful because Presley loved Graceland more than any other place in the world and was buried in Meditation Gardens, the pilgrims saw the opportunity to perpetuate Elvis' memory by organizing tributes as well as by creating a familial atmosphere among themselves. Similarly, BARBER (1972, 328) states that when people congregate at a war memorial, common ideals are strengthened because there are enough people to propagate these notions.

RELPH (1976, 31) states that rituals, customs, and myths enjoin the members of a group with their surroundings. TUAN (1974, 98, 108) states that people cannot establish meaningful relationships with their physical surroundings without long-term residency and working with the land. DURKHEIM (1975, 131) and TANAKA (1977, 113) hold the sacredness is an assigned status, which is maintained through continued usage. The pilgrims in the present study were in Memphis to express the value they placed on Graceland, Meditation Gardens, and other sites associated with the life of their hero. These places did not acquire meaning through frequent visits by individual pilgrims; they were already meaningful places. Implied, then, is that commitment to a specific cause, rather than residency or continued usage, may be the underlying determiner of the meanings which we assign to our surroundings.

How long is Elvis's home likely to remain a pilgrimage destination? The survey suggests an unequivocal answer, "as long as Elvis remains a folk hero!" How long will that be? "A long time", according to indications from the survey and from literature on heroes. Throughout the research, devoted Presley fans were encountered who only really became aware of the singer after his death because they were too young to recall his heyday. AQUILA (1982) and THARPE (1979, 7) state that deceased celebrities are remembered by the public because of the publicity they receive after their deaths. The pilgrims in this study recognized the media's ability to introduce their hero to new generations. Many mentioned that they had frequently contacted their local radio and television stations in order to keep Elvis in the forefront. Having been an innovative singer, Elvis may have an advantage over subsequent derivative singer. Because there has been continuity in popular music trends for the past three decades MARSH (1984), young people exploring the roots of their own generation's music will return to Elvis.

Perhaps it is fitting to conclude with words from "Graceland", by another famous contemporary singer, PAUL SIMON:

> "I'm going to Graceland
> Memphis Tennessee
> Poorboys and Pilgrims with families
> And we are going to Graceland
>
> For reasons I cannot explain
> There's some part of me wants to see
> Graceland
> Maybe I've a reason to believe
> We all will be received
> In Graceland"

Summary

Graceland, the home of the rock 'n roll superstar Elvis Presley, has been visited by more than three million people since it was opened to the public in 1982. They comprise of two groups: tourists, by far the most numerous, and pilgrims, according to a random sample of 209 visitors interviewed there over a five week period which includes the week of special acitivities commemorating Presley's death in 1977. Pilgrims and tourists may also be distinguished from two smaller groups also found there and interviewed: former associates of Presley, and persons who have moved to Memphis permanently because of Elvis and Graceland and who may be termed immigrant pilgrims to distinguish them from the transient pilgrims. Both the mansion and the adjacent grave of Elvis occasioned different expectations, experiences, behaviour, and satisfactions in the pilgrims and tourists, although a wide range occured within each group. For pilgrims, devotion to Elvis and camaraderie with each other were particularly pronounced. A pilgrimage is much more than an journey to a significant site.

Zusammenfassung:

Die Pilgerfahrt nach Graceland

In Graceland, dem früheren Wohnort des Rock 'n' Roll Superstars Elvis Presley, sind seit 1982, als der Ort für die Öffentlichkeit zugänglich gemacht wurde, mehr als drei Millionen Besucher gezählt worden. Diese lassen sich in zwei Hauptgruppen unterscheiden, wie eine Zufallsbefragung von 209 Besuchern ergeben hat, die über einen Zeitraum von fünf Wochen hinweg durchgeführt wurde. In diesen Zeitraum fiel auch die Erinnerungswoche an Presleys Tod im Jahre 1977. Bei den beiden Hauptgruppen handelt es sich einerseits um Touristen, die mit Abstand die größte Zahl der Besucher stellen. Die zweite Gruppe kann man mit Recht als "Pilger" bezeichnen, da ihr Verhalten starke Ähnlichkeit mit den traditionell religiös begründeten Pilgerwanderungen aufweist. Touristen und Pilger müssen noch gegen zwei weitere kleinere Gruppen abgegrenzt werden, nämlich die Gruppe der früheren Mitarbeiter von Presley und Personen, die wegen Elvis und Graceland ihren Dauerwohnsitz nach Memphis verlegt haben und die man somit als Pilgerimmigranten bezeichnen könnte, um sie gegenüber den Pilgerbesuchern abzugrenzen. Sowohl das Haus als auch das daneben liegende Grab von Elvis löste die unterschiedlichsten Erwartungen, Gefühle, Verhalten und Befriedigungen bei den verschiedenen Gruppen aus, wenngleich sie in vielen Punkten auch übereinstimmten. Bei den Pilgern stand die Verehrung von Elvis und die Kameradschaft untereinander im Vordergrund. Insgesamt wurde deutlich, daß diese Art von Pilgerwanderung weit mehr ist als lediglich der Besuch eines bekannten Ortes.

Bibliography

ALLEN, J. L. (1976): Lands of myth, waters of wonder: the place of the imagination in the history of geographical exploration. In: D. Lowenthal and J. J. Bowden (eds), Geographies of the Mind: Essays in Historical Geosophy. Oxford University Press, New York. 41 – 56.

AQUILA, R. (1982): Not fade away: Buddy Holly and the making of an American legend. Journal of Popular Culture, 15 (4): 75 – 80.

BACHELARD, G. (1964): The Poetics of space. Translated by M. Jolas, with a Forword by E. Gilson. Orion Press, New York.

BARBER, B. (1972): Place symbol, and utilitarian function in war memorials. In R. Gutman (ed.), People and Buildings. Basic Books, New York, 327 – 334.

BRIXEY, K. H. (1984): Graceland Enterprises, Memphis, Tennessee. Interview, 27 July.

BRIXEY, K. H., and DIXON; T. (1983): Elvis at Graceland. Cypress Press Inc.: Memphis, Tennessee.

BROCK, V. K. (1979): Images of Elvis, the South, and America. In: J. L. Tharpe (ed.), Elvis: Images and Fancies. University Press of Mississippi, Jackson, Mississippi, 87 - 122.

DAVIDSON, James W. (1985): The Pilgrimage to Elvis Presley's Graceland.: A Study of the Meanings of the Place. Master of Arts Thesis, Wilfried Laurier University, Waterloo, Ontario, Canada.

DAVIS, R. (1984): Elvis Presley Museum, Memphis, Tennessee. Interview, 18 July.

DIXON, T. (1985): Graceland Enterprises, Memphis, Tennessee telephone correspondence May 8th.

DONOVAN, P. (1979): Interpreting Religious Experience. Issues in Religous Studies, P. Baetz and J. Holm (eds.), Seaburg Press, New York.

DURKHEIM, E. (1975): The elementary forms of religious life: the totemic system Australia. In: J. Redding and W. S. F. Pickering (trans.), Durkheim on Religion: A Selection of Readings with Bibliographies. Routledge and Kegan Paul, Boston, 131.

MEMPHIS TOURIST REPORTER (1984): Facts from Graceland, 2 August, 8.

GRACELAND ENTERPRISES (1982): Graceland: The Legendary Home of Elvis Presley. Graceland Enterprises,Memphis, Tennessee.

GREGORY, N. and GREGORY, J. (1982): When Elvis Died, Washington Square Press: New York.

LICHTER, P. (1978): The Boy Who Dared to Rock: The Definitive Elvis. Doubleday and Company: Garden City, New York.

MARSH, D. (1982): Elvis. Rolling Stone Press/Warner Brothers, New York.

MOELLER, L. G. (1979): The big four mass media: actualities and expectations. In: R. W. Budd and B. D. Ruben (eds.), Beyond Mass Media: New Approaches to Mass Communication, Hayden Book Company, Inc. Rochelle Park, New Jersey, 14 – 51.

NEW YORK TIMES (1978): New York. 9 January, 12 August, 14 August.

PRESLEY; V. (1984): Graceland Enterprises, Memphis, Tennessee. Interview, 18 July.

RELPH, E. C. (1976 a): The Phenomenological Foundations of Geography. University of Toronto, Toronto, Dept. of Geography. Discussion Paper, series, no. 21.

RELPH, E. C. (1976 b). Place and Placelessness. Pion Ltd, London.

RENWICK, H.L. and CUTTER; S. (1983): Wish you were here. Landscape, 27 (1),: 30 – 38

ROBERTS F. (1982 a): Graceland. Elvis in Canada, 2 (4): 4 – 10.

ROWLES, G. D. (1978 a): Prisoners of Space? Exploring the Geographical Experience of Older People. West View Press: Boulder, Colorado.

SANN, P. (1976): Fads, Follies and Delusions of the American People. Crown Publishers: New York.

SIMON, P. (1986): Graceland. Warner Bros. Records, BMI.

SMITH, B. (1984): Graceland Enterprises, Memphis, Tennessee. Interview, 26 July.

TANAKA, H. (1977): Geographic expression of Buddhist pilgrim places on Shikoku Island, Japan. Canadian Geographer. 21 (2): 111 - 132.

THARPE, J. L. (1979): Will the real Elvis Presley ...? In J. L. Tharpe (ed.): Elvis: Images and Fancies. University Press of Mississippi, Jackson, Mississippi, 3 – 10.

TIME (1988), New York, 19 December.

TUAN, YI-FU (1974): Topophilia: A Study of Environmental Perception, Attitudes and Values. Prentice-Hall: Englewood Cliffs, New Jersey.

TURNER, R. H. and KILLIAN, L. M. (1972): Collective Behavior. 2nd ed. Prentice-Hall: Englewood Cliffs, New Jersey.

WISE D. (1984): Stage 45, Restaurant Lounge, Memphis, Tennessee. Interview, 26 July.

WORTH, F. L., and TAMERIUS; S. D. (1981): All About Elvis, Bantam Books: Toronto.

Wilbur Zelinsky

Nationalistic Pilgrimages in the United States*

This essay is based upon the simple, but admittedly touchy, premise that *civil religions* have displaced the traditional supernatural faiths as the dominant belief-systems in the highly developed nation-states of our Twentieth Century world. Such an assertion does not ignore the fact that large fractions of the populations in question adhere, at least nominally, to Christianity, Islam, Buddhism, or other inherited creeds, or that a devout minority are observant in ritual matters — including *pilgrimages*. What it does convey is the reality that for nearly all of us, including the conventionally religious, the most precious of social and spiritual values are those represented by the nation or state, that it is in the arms of the motherland that we seek the ultimate meanings of modern existence. Thus, "by civil religion we can mean any set of beliefs and rituals, related to the past, present, and/or future of a people ('nation') which are understood in some trandscendental fashion" (HAMMOND 1976, 171).

The latterday ascendancy of civil religion is not limited to such extreme cases as Nazi Germany; it is perfectly visible in the United States of America to anyone who cares to look. Indeed one can demonstrate a truly uncanny similarity between the workings of the fully matured American civil religion and the operations of orthodox Christianity during its heyday (HAYES 1960, 164 – 168).

The individual is born into the state and remains a member of the national congregation until his death unless he elects the difficult apostasy of emigration. The compulsory registration of birth, marriage, divorce, and death by the state usurps the very same functions once performed by the parish priest. Schooling in public, that is, government-controlled, schools is mandatory for all those children not enrolled in parochial institutions. A strong case can be made to the effect that, locally managed though they may be, the public schools of America, in the words of D. W. BROGAN, serve as the country's "formally unestablished church" (MICHAELSEN 1970, 62), and is the single most important instrument of the inculcation of public piety (CARLSON 1975;

MICHAELSEN 1970; WILSON 1971, 7 – 9). The tax-supported schoolroom of today serves precisely the same purpose as did the cathedral and parish classes of an earlier day, for in both instances the transmission of knowledge and skills is really secondary to immersion in religious and societal norms.

The modern nation-state has made its flag into a literally holy object, the equivalent of the cross or communion wafer; and nowhere is such an observation more pertinent than in the United States. Furthermore, national anthems and related compositions have displaced church hymns. National heroes, martyrs, and villains have preempted the emotional space once occupied by the Holy Trinity, the saints, and Satan and his imps. The birthdays of Washington, Lincoln, Jackson, and other revered leaders have replaced the saints' days, while Independence Day, Memorial Day, and other nationalistic commemorations have rivaled church holidays on any scale of public excitement. The deaths and funerals of the greatest of the national greats have touched off convulsions of religious fervor, the like of which no traditional religious event has ever matched in America. Throughout the land graven images of the national demigods, related eidolons, and miraculous events and their portrayal on paper, wood, canvas, glass, ceramics, and every other conceivable medium have upstaged a more venerable iconography featuring Jesus Christ, the Virgin Mary, the saints, and biblical episodes.

Like any proper faith, the American civil religion venerates its sacred documents. Chief among them, of course, has been the Declaration of Independence, which underwent apotheosis soon after its signing (ALBANESE 1976, 182 – 183; HAZELTON 1906; MAASS 1976; MALONE 1954, 248 – 268; WILLS 1978, 232 - 236). It matters little that only a small minority of the population have ever read all of its noble language or are familiar with more than a couple of its incantations. Sacredness is enhanced rather than lessened by inaccessibility or by being vested in archaic, even incomprehensible tongues. Also numbered among the most divine of national scriptures are Washington's (or Hamilton's) Farewell Address (FORGIE 1979, 25), two or three of Lincoln's major addresses, and preeminently, the Constitution, whose symbolic radiance far outshines the literal import of the words. And, of course, holy writ must have its duly ordained priesthood to interpret inner meanings. If the President embodies the godhead of the civil religion, if historians act as lay clergy, it is the federal courts that furnish the regular clergy, most of all the robed justices of the Supreme Court who preside as high priests to proclaim dogma and explicate talmudically the hidden sense of divine writ. If we seek the temples in which the rites of our national creed are enacted, they are to be found in the form of public buildings at the ceremonial, and governmental, centers of our nation, states, counties, and cities, while nationalistic monuments fulfill the role of wayside shrines.

Thus there is literally no aspect of a fully constituted supernatural church that lacks its direct counterpart in the American civil religion. This is true even in the realm of missionary effort. In terms of cash, personnel, and number of establishments, no nation-state has been more active, or hyperactive, in sending church missions beyond its borders than has the United States. Whether they do so knowingly or not, the missionaries, be they Catholic or Protestant, preach not only the Christian gospel but also, implicitly, that of the American civil religion smuggled within the technological, cultural, and other precepts dispensed to their flocks. And that is also the function performed by the lay missionaries we know as the Peace Corps.

2. Is it surprising, then, that Americans, along with citizens of other modern nation-states, revere, and perform worshipful pilgrimages to a number of sacred places? If such a practice has become a standard feature of modern *nationalism* (BOEHM 1933, 234), it has developed only rather recently, within the past 130 years or so. In the case of Colonial and early Republican America, no special localities dedicated to the civil religion had yet materialized. Such a phenomenon was to develop concurrently with the passage from a relatively spontaneous peoplehood, a "bottom-up" nationalism, to a top-down, relatively regimented *statism*. Thus it was not until the mid-nineteenth century and later, with the rise of historic preservation, monument building on a grand scale, the institutionalized celebration of the national past, improved transportation, and greater affluence, that such lay pilgrimages to nationalistic shrines became a conspicuous feature of American life. Unlike most other forms of symbolic behavior, this is one phenomenon on which we can hang relatively firm numbers.

Predictably, it was Mount Vernon that attracted the first significant contingent of pilgrims, and did so at the urging of its curators (FORGIE 1979, 172). After a sluggish start in the 1850s, visitations to this great national shrine have increased steadily and remarkably, at least until the 1970s (Fig. 1). Among other things, these figures suggest that a quite appreciable fraction of the American population, along with an undetermined number of foreign guests, have visited the Washington homestead at least once during their lifetimes.

Mount Vernon is not an isolated example. As the railroad and, most especially, the motorbus and personal auto made such places readily accessible to the traveler, patronage became substantial. Thus 134,080 persons were admitted to Lincoln's Tomb in 1927 (D. L. LEWIS 1929, 25); the stream of visitors to Valley Forge swelled from 40,000 in 1906 to 600,000 in 1926 (BURNHAM 1982, 92); and during the early 1950s approximately 100,000 persons viewed the painting of 'Washington Crossing the Delaware' at Washington Crossing Park (HUTTON 1959, 171). Greenfield Village set its all-time attendance record in

256

1976 when it received 1,751,126 visitors (D. L. LEWIS 1976, 280). There were 1,289,302 paid admissions to Colonial Williamsburg in the Bicentennial year, while Valley Forge State Park drew 2,581,443 persons and Monticello 671,487. The number of individuals paying their respects at John F. Kennedy's grave in Arlington National Cemetery is nothing short of astonishing: 700,000 in the first month alone, a value exceeding the 616,406 pilgrims to Lincoln's Tomb during all twelve months of 1963. By June 1971, still arriving at the rate of 10,000 a day, no fewer than 28 million persons had made their way to the graveside (WOLFE 1975, 395).

We now have hundreds of historical parks, museums, birthplaces, famous residences, tombs, battlefields, and other buildings and plots of ground that can be called nationalistic shrines, including many administered by state and local agencies and private organizations as well as by the U. S. National Park Service (Fig. 2). If both the number of such places and the volume of visits to them have increased markedly in recent decades, as indeed they have, one might contend that their popularity is simply another manifestation of the boom in domestic tourism. A good many of these hallowed sites are also 'fun places', for there is undoubtedly plenty of entertainment value at such spots as the Statue of Liberty, Monticello, Mount Vernon (where relatively few visitors bother to see the tomb), Williamsburg, Sturbridge Village, the Washington Monument, or the breathtaking arch at St. Louis' Jefferson National Memorial.

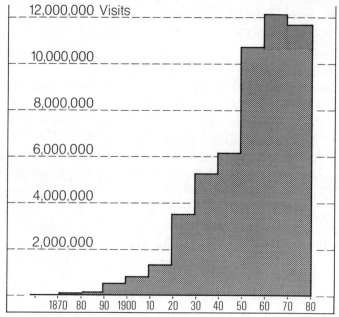

Fig. 1: Visits to Mount Vernon, 1858 – 1980
Source: MOUNT VERNON LADIES ASSOCIATION, 1983

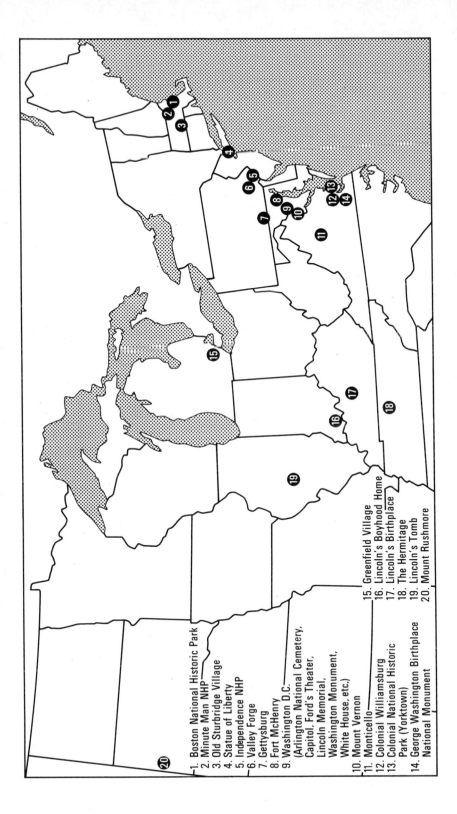

1. Boston National Historic Park
2. Minute Man NHP
3. Old Sturbridge Village
4. Statue of Liberty
5. Independence NHP
6. Valley Forge
7. Gettysburg
8. Fort McHenry
9. Washington D.C.
   (Arlington National Cemetery,
   Capitol, Ford's Theater,
   Lincoln Memorial,
   Washington Monument,
   White House, etc.)
10. Mount Vernon
11. Monticello
12. Colonial Williamsburg
13. Colonial National Historic
    Park (Yorktown)
14. George Washington Birthplace
    National Monument
15. Greenfield Village
16. Lincoln's Boyhood Home
17. Lincoln's Birthplace
18. The Hermitage
19. Lincoln's Tomb
20. Mount Rushmore

Fig. 2: Major American Nationalistic Shrines

Tab. 1: Visits to National Park Service Areas, by Type of Area, 1930 – 1981
(in thousands)

Period	(1) Nationalistic Areas	(2) Civil War Areas	(1) + (2)	(3) All Other NPS Areas	(4) Total
	(N = 7)	(N = 8)	(N = 15)	(N = 45)	(N = 60)
1930 – 34	1,429	1,083	2,513	17,852	20,365
	(17)	(9)	(26)	(68)	(94)
1935 – 49	18,659	8,233	26,892	39,770	66,662
	+1205.7 %	+660.2 %	+970.1 %	+122.8 %	+227.3 %
	(24)	(12)	(36)	(87)	(123)
1940 – 44	20,589	4,405	24,994	31,337	56,331
	+10.3 %	-46.5 %	-7.1 %	-21.2 %	-15.5 %
	(28)	(13)	(41)	(102)	(143)
1945 – 49	31,601	6,051	37,652	82,944	120,596
	+53.5 %	+37.4 %	+50.6 %	+164.7 %	+114.1 %
	(31)	(12)	(43)	(109)	(152)
1950 – 54	51,152	10,634	61,786	144,931	206,717
	+61.9 %	+75.7 %	+64.1 %	+74.7 %	+71.4 %
	(34)	(12)	(46)	(122)	(168)
1955 – 59	65,334	14,229	79,563	206,142	285,705
	+27.7 %	+33.8 %	+28.8 %	+42.2 %	+38.2 %
	(38)	(13)	(51)	(133)	(184)
1960 – 64	113,566	32,955	146,521	289,778	436,299
	+73.8 %	+131.6 %	+84.2 %	+ 40.6 %	+ 52.7 %
	(43)	(15)	(58)	(177)	(235)
1965 – 69	153,016	51,513	204,529	462,989	667,518
	+34.7 %	+56.3 %	+39.6 %	+59.8 %	+53.0 %
	(52)	(16)	(68)	(199)	(267)
1970 – 74	146,853	68,347	215,200	647,665	862,865
	-4.0 %	+32.7 %	+5.2 %	+39.9 %	+29.3 %
	(57)	(15)	(72)	(195)	(267)
1975 – 79	183,633	40,876	224,509	806,475	1,030,984
	+25.0 %	-40.2 %	+4.3 %	+24.5 %	+19.5 %
	(58)	(15)	(73)	(198)	(275)
1980 – 81	69,093	14,584	83,677	454,971	371,294
Total	854,925	252,910	1,107,835	3,101,178	4,209,013

Source: U.S. NATIONAL PARK SERVICE, Annual Reports

An examination of National Park Service (NPS) statistics for a recent half-century period imparts some color to the proposition that the massive surge in the number of persons frequenting historic and nationalistic sites is part of an even larger, more inclusive phenomenon: touristic or pleasure travel to all manner of recreational opportunities. The number and acreage of national parks, battlefields, historic sites and parks, memorials, monuments, seashores, recreation areas, and other types of real estate managed by the NPS have increased enormously since the establishment of Yellowstone National Park in 1872. It seems reasonable to assume that NPS areas and their traffic not only account for a large share of aggregate recreational experiences in the United States but are also a reasonably representative sample of public preferences for travel-related leisure activities.

In Table 1 I have displayed visits to three classes of NPS areas by five-year periods during an era when both the numbers of such places and their visitors expanded enormously. Two species of places are of special interest: those that can be considered fully nationalistic; the total of which has climbed from 1 in 1930 (George Washington Birthplace National Monument) to 58 in 1981[1]; and the Civil War sites that one might classify as marginally nationalistic. Ignoring the 1940 – 1945 period, when every variety of civilian travel was curtailed, the general trend for all types of NPS areas has been sharply upward. The grand 52-year totals of 854,925,000 visits to nationalistic areas, 252,910,000 to Civil War sites, and 3,101,178,000 to other NPS areas are impressive, to say the least.

On closer inspection, however, the dynamics for the two main categories: nationalistic, broadly defined, and other areas (mostly scenic and recreational), diverge in suggestive fashion. The non-nationalistic areas have enjoyed truly spectacular growth, and evidently have not yet reached their maximum levels of traffic. On the other hand, the relative increments for both varieties of nationalistic areas have been more irregular. Indeed, in two quinquennia (1970 – 74 for nationalistic areas; 1975 – 79 for the Civil War locations) there were actual decreases. The NPS data may suggest that the phase of genuine expansion in pilgrimages to national shrines reached its climax in the 1960s, and that, since then, the volume of such movements has been virtually at a stand-still. Indeed, the total number of visits to such places taken as a fraction of the national population has oscillated around the same level since 1967, while the comparable value for recreational/scenic NPS areas has moved ever higher to stratospheric levels. The temporary surge in the Bicentennial quinquennium was just that: temporary, and artificial, and less than expected. Although 1976 was indeed a banner year for most nationalistic shrines, attendance generally failed to live up to expectations, and was only moderately greater than in proximate years. For example, Valley Forge anticipated 30,000 visitors each day during the Bicentennial, but only 15,000 showed up (POWELL 1983, 213).

Table 2: Aggregate number of visitors to selected, nationalistically significant Historical Parks and Sites: United States, 1936 – 1980

Group I (1936 – 1980)[a]								
Years	Number of visitors (in thousands)	Percentage of U.S. population	Year	Number of visitors (in thousands)	Percentage of U.S. population	Year	Number of visitors (in thousands)	Percentage of U.S. population
1936	2,413.0	1.88	1951	3,845.7	2.48	1966	12,237.3	6.22
1937	2,884.3	2.44	1952	4,372.7	2.77	1967	13,089.4	6.59
1938	2,665.5	2.05	1953	4,832.8	3.02	1968	12,809.0	6.37
1939	2,637.8	2.02	1954	4,723.3	2.90	1969	13,583.2	6.70
1940	2,930.3	2.21	1955	4,690.1	2.83	1970	13,532.7	6.60
1941	3,252.9	2.43	1956	5,018.4	2.97	1971	13,270.5	6.41
1942	1,973.5	1.46	1957	6,001.5	3.49	1972	10,881.6	5.21
1943	1,232.2	0.90	1958	5,007.1	2.90	1973	11,483.6	5.46
1944	1,441.7	1.04	1959	5,396.3	3.04	1974	10,734.3	5.07
1945	1,859.6	1.32	1960	7,333.1	4.06	1975	11,494.5	5.38
1946	2,669.4	1.88	1961	9,885.2	5.38	1976	13,114.5	6.10
1947	2,940.3	2.03	1962	10,310.0	5.53	1977	12,126.9	5.59
1948	3,216.2	2.18	1963	10,668.2	5.64	1978	12,491.6	5.73
1949	3,447.3	2.30	1964	11,607.8	6.05	1979	11,927.5	5.42
1950	3,525.2	2.31	1965	11,825.5	6.09	1980	11,266.6	4.97

Group II (1954 – 1980)[b]								
1954	8,290.2	5.09	1960	11,629.6	6.44	1971	20,682.9	9.99
1955	8,259.9	4,98	1961	14,853.0	8.09	1972	17,113.6	8.20
1956	8,795.0	5.21	1962	16,164.9	8.66	1973	17,074.1	8.12
1957	10,040.5	5.84	1963	16,775.6	8.87	1974	17,065.0	8.05
1958	9,139.2	5.23	1964	18,591.1	9.69	1975	17,894.2	8.38
1959	9,738.4	5.48	1965	18,920.5	9,74	1976	21,199.7	9.86
			1966	19,384.5	9.86	1977	17,610.3	8.12
			1967	20,360.0	10.25	1978	18,245.8	8.37
			1968	19,304.3	9.62	1979	17,248.9	7.84
			1969	20,557.9	10.14	1980	16,735.7	7.39
			1970	20,589.3	10.05			

Group III (1972 – 1980)[b]								
1972	21,812.8	10.45	1975	24,117.5	11.32	1978	23,818.1	10.92
1973	21,847.5	10.38	1976	29,322.7	13.63	1979	22,573.1	10.26
1974	21,943.9	10.36	1977	23,170.6	10.69	1980	22,177.5	9.76

[a] Group I consists of: Lincoln's Birthplace (Ky.); Colonial National Historical Park (Va.); Washington's Birthplace (Va.); Statue of Liberty (N.Y.); Washington Monument (D.C.); Monticello (Va.);* Mount Vernon (Va.).*

[b] Group II consists of Group I plus: Independence National Historical Park (Pa.); Mount Rushmore (S.D.); White House (D.C.); Lincoln's Tomb (Ill.);* Old Sturbridge Village (Mass.).*

[c] Group III consists of Group II plus: Lincoln's Boyhood Home (Ind.); Minute Man National Historical Park (Mass.); The Hermitage (Tenn.);* Greenfield Village (Mich.);* Colonial Williamsburg (Va.)*; Valley Forge (Pa.); Ford's Theater (D.C.).

Sources: U.S. National Park Service, annual reports; unpublished tabulations furnished by organizations indicated by asterisk.

"In Philadelphia, officials anticipated anywhere from 14 to 15 million visitors at the shrines of the chief city of the Revolution. Somewhere between 7 and 10 million came. In Boston, planners projected more modest numbers and got but a fraction of those ... Surveys showed that travelers were celebrating the bicentennial in California, the Southwest, and Hawaii instead" (ZUCKERMANN 1978, 225). Visitor levels in 1980 – 81 at nationalistic sites returned to the pre-1976 situation.

In order to provide additional insights into temporary trends in American nationalistic pilgrimages, I have compiled Table 2 (Fig. 3) covering the years 1936 – 80 for some of the more notable shrines, and have indicated the number of visits as a percent of the national population. Unfortunately, figures are not available for the entire group of nineteen for the entire time span. Consequently, I have segmented the nineteen and the table into three subgroups in

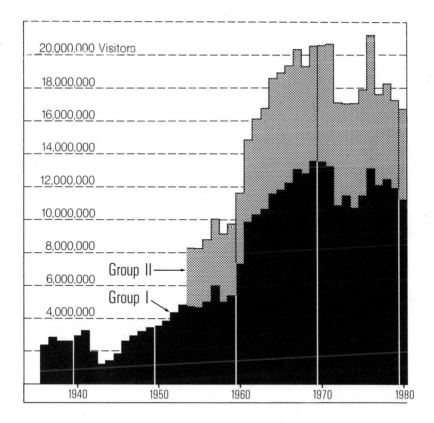

Fig. 3: Number of visitors to selected nationalistically significant Historical Parks and Sites in the U.S.
Source: U.S. NATIONAL PARK SERVICE, Annual Reports, unpublished tabulations furnished by different organizations

order to ensure stable universes within each of the designated time periods. In each of these subgroups there is consistent growth in absolute values (the war years excepted) and in percentile values in two cases, but with some suggestion of stasis by the late 1960s, until the attainment of maximum amounts in 1976. During the subsequent four years, we find a significant decline in both absolute and relative values; and this diminution, it should be recalled, took place during a period when general tourism was still expanding quite healthily. There are grounds for suspecting that such popularity as nationalistic shrines may have enjoyed in recent years is as much a matter of nostalgia and a sort of voyeuristic titillation as an exercise in true devotion. This post-1976 slump is intriguing. Are we seeing post-Bicentennial fatigue? Or is it the onset of a long-lived trend that will persist well into and beyond the 1980s? Obviously, it is too early to do more than speculate.[2] Still, the recent trends do appear to be general and consistent among the major attractions. Thus, for example, attendance at Old Sturbridge Village has declined from 667,961 in the peak year of 1972 to 518,968 in 1978, while Greenfield Village has suffered a drop from 1,751,126 in 1976 to 953,670 in 1982, a loss of 45.5 percent.

Most revealing perhaps are recent developments at Lincoln's Tomb in Springfield, Illinois. The person who travels to that structure, one that is lacking in architectural distinction, is engaged in the closest approach to absolute nationalistic piety that may be conceivable under American conditions. The tomb stands near the corner of an unremarkable cemetery in an unremarkable residential neighbourhood. No one wages an advertising campaign on its behalf; there are no other attractions or distractions in the vicinity; no satellite enterprises, no souvenir or refreshments stands, no amusements for the bored traveler. After many years of steady increments in visitations, 1968 recorded the maximum number to date: 756,432. Since then, the volume of visits has decreased steadily until it amounted to only 296,056 in 1982. I suspect that these numbers may be telling us something important, but just what is, is not yet clear.[3]

3. No discussion of nationalistic pilgrimages in the United States can pretend to be complete without contemplating the extraordinary drawing power of the *Washington, D.C.* area. Within the District of Columbia and neighbouring communities we find the greatest aggregation of nationalistic objects, sites, and activities in the entire country, if not the entire world. The throngs of pilgrims who come to gaze or join in ritual, and thus, in a sense, engage in nationalistic communion, are too vast for confident enumeration. The Capitol and White House are only the oldest of hundreds of government buildings that can suffuse the onlooker with wonder and awe. Sightseers enjoying New York City, San Francisco, or New Orleans can, with a little luck, entirely avoid any reminders of American nationhood or statehood, but such cultural amnesia is literally impossible in Washington.

Beyond all the federal structures, there are the countless monuments and memorials, awesome tombs, the burial grounds for the historically illustrious, military installations, foreign embassies, the museums and libraries, unreasonable numbers of flags, headquarters of numerous national (and international) organizations, and those insistently nationalistic names of streets and traffic circles. The capital city is the setting for rituals and demonstrations large and small and for national conventions of every imaginable sort of group. Washington is as much a theater for the flaunting of symbols as a place for the conduct of government, perhaps more so. And to its streets and corridors come the swarming businessmen, lobbyists, petitioners, diplomats, scholars, scientists, college students from near and distant states and countries, and above all, the worshipful tourists. Throughout the year, they stream in endless procession, much as they do in Paris, Moscow, Beijing, or Mexico City, but, unquestionably, in greater hordes. Or perhaps the analogy should be with Jerusalem, Rome, or Mecca.

Tourism in Washington, which, inescapably, is tourism with a thick coating of nationalism, is more than a major industry; it is a rite of passage for old and young, but especially for the young. During and between sessions of the school year, entire classes of students and troops of Girl Scouts and Boy Scouts jam the well-trodden circuit of sacred stations. In spring and early summer, hundred of buses disgorge the graduating seniors from high schools in every corner of the land. These are students who have scrimped and saved for months or even years, scraping up travel funds via all manners of ingenious projects for what might be the first extended trip away from home and parents and an experience that will remain deeply imprinted in their memories.

Just how many tourists, with whatever intentions, have been flocking to Washington is quite difficult to ascertain or guess (NATIONAL CAPITAL PLANNING COMMISSION 1948 b, 18). We do have several estimates for what is surely an enormous quantity; but "the statistical basis for such estimates are somewhat unreliable as a statistically significant survey of visitor traffic in the Washington Area has never been conducted" (NATIONAL CAPITAL PLANNING COMMISSION 1978, 12). A plausible figure for total number of visitors in 1974 was fourteen million (WASHINGTON POST, August 24, 1975, A12); and the National Capital Planning Commission (1984 a, 2) has assumed a continuing average annual increment of 3 to 5 percent in numbers of visitors to the 'Monumental Core'.[4] The values cited include not only tourists but also business, convention, and social visitors as well as demonstrators, many of whom may also have taken in some incidental sightseeing while in the area. An estimate of 4,650,000 tourists in 1980 (GREATER WASHINGTON BOARD OF TRADE, N. D., 20; WASHINGTON CONVENTION AND VISITORS ASSOCIATION 1981, 1) seems unduly conservative when one considers that the recorded admission for just one popular attractio, the Air and Space Museum, was 10,014,892 in 1983 (NATIONAL CAPITAL PLANNING COMMISSION 1984 a, 9). The only safe inference is that the traffic has been immense and has probably been increasing, at least until quite recently.

The Washington saga could be repeated for many American state capitals, albeit on a more modest scale. However, it must be noted, that, in terms of sheer grandiosity, Nelson Rockefellers's Empire State Plaza in Albany, NY challenges anything to be seen in the District of Columbia.

4. This introductory sketch, evidently the first frontal assault on the topic of nationalistic pilgrimages, leaves more than one question unanswered. Perhaps the most significant problem is the reality of the apparent post-1976 slump in visits to American nationalistic shrines and what this may portend for the future evolution of nationalism. Also high on the research agenda is a series of detailed field studies, on the order of those reported elsewhere in this volume, on pilgrimages to individual localities in the United States and other countries to which faithful citizens throng in great numbers. We need to know much more about the economic and social implications of such devotion as well as the political and cultural.

Notes

* The observations reported here and related matters are presented in much greater breadth and detail in the author's NATION INTO STATE: SHIFTING SYMBOLIC FOUNDATIONS OF AMERICAN NATIONALISM (Chapel Hill: University of North Carolina Press, 1988).

[1] Abraham Lincoln Birthplace (BPL); National Historic Site (NHS); Adams NHS; Andrew Johnson NHS; Arlington House, R.E. Lee National Memorial (NMem); Booker T. Washington National Monument (NM); Boston National Historic Park (NHP); Carl Sandburg NHS; Clara Barton NHS; Colonial NHP; Cowpens National Battlefield (NB); Custer Battlefield NM; de Soto NMem; Edgar A. Poe NHS; Edison NHS; Eisenhower NHS; Federal Hall NMem; Ford's Theater NHS; Fort McHenry NM and Historic site (HS); Fort Necessity NB; Fort Stanwix NM; Fort Washington Park; Frederick Douglass Home; General Grant NMem; George Washington BPL NM; George Rogers Clark NHP; Golden Spike NHS; Guildford Courthouse National Memorial Park (NMP); Hamilton Grange NMem; Harpers Ferry NHP; Herbert Hoover NHS; Home of F. D. Roosevelt NHS; Independence NHP; Jefferson Memorial; John F. Kennedy NHS; Kings Mountain NHP; Lincoln Boyhood NMem; Lincoln Home NHS; Lincoln Memorial; Longfellow NHS; Lyndon B. Johnson NHS; Minute Man NHP; Moores Creek NB; Morristown NHP; Mount Rushmore NMem; National Visitor Center, Perry's Victory and International Peace Memorial (IPMem); Sagamore Hill NHS; Saint Gaudens NHS; Saratoga NHP; Statue of Liberty NM; Theodore Roosevelt BPL NHS; Valley Forge NHP; Washington Monument; White House; William Howard Taft NHS; Wright Brothers NMem.

[2] KAMMEN (1980) had also found some evidence of a falling off in museum patronage after the Bicentennnial and following the 1972 – 76 period, one of "greatest intensity in the contemporary American boom". He also hints at the possibility that parallel trends might be found in other countries.

[3] In its Planning Report concerning visitors to Washington, the National Capital Planning Commission (1984 a) assumed that the upward trend in volume would continue indefinitely. But inspection of a graph entitled "Visits to Selected Facilities Administered by the National Park Service in the Core Area, 1960 – 1982" (NCPC, 1984 a:6) reveals a sharp, possibly persistent decline since 1976. The most benign interpretation of the statistics is that the volume of visitors may have begun to level off around 1980.

[4] "In 1980 the District received over 11 million domestic visitors, almost 2 million foreign visitors, and nearly 4 million day visitors (those not staying overnight in the area and/or living within 100 miles of D.C."(District of Columbia, 1981:1).

Summary

This paper is based on a simple, but controversial, premise: that civil religion has replaced the traditional supernatural faiths as the dominant belief-system of the citizens of advanced 20th Century nation-states. In support of this contention, one finds close parallels between all significant aspects of the two types of religion — in their sacred figures, music, holiday, holy documents, holidays, monuments and priesthoods, inter alia. Singled out for special attention here are the visits, literally pilgrimages, by many millions of persons annually to nationalistically important sites in the U.S.A. The volume of such traffic to homes and tombs of national heroes, major battlefields and cemeteries, and, most particularly, to the many historically and symbolically meaningful attractions of Washinton, D.C., has increased enormously during the present century or at least until the 1970s. The implications of the apparent dropoff, in both absolute and relative terms, of such pilgrimages since about 1976 is a topic awaiting further investigation.

Zusammenfassung:
Nationalistische Pilgerstätten in den USA

In den modernen Nationalstaaten des 20. Jahrhunderts, so die einfache und gleichwohl strittige Prämisse des vorliegenden Aufsatzes, wird die vorherrschende Glaubensanschauung nicht länger mehr durch diesen oder jenen traditionell-übernatürlichen Glauben, sondern durch bürgerliche Religionen geformt. Gestützt wird diese Behauptung u. a. durch auffallende Parallelen zwischen verschiedenen Aspekten beider genannter Religionspraktiken, sei es in der Art ihrer geheiligten Abbildungen, ihrer Musik, Feiertage, Monumente, Priester oder auch nur in ihrem jeweiligen Umgang mit spezifischen heiligen Dokumenten. Unter diesen Ausdrucksformen gilt das besondere Augenmerk dieses Aufsatzes jenen Besichtigungen oder buchstäblichen Pilgerfahrten, die Jahr für Jahr von mehreren Millionen Menschen zu wichtigen nationalen Stätten in den USA unternommen werden. Das Ausmaß solcher Fahrten zu Heim oder Grab verschiedener Nationalhelden, größeren Schlachtfeldern und Begäbnisstätten oder auch und insbesondere zu den zahlreichen, historisch und symbolisch bedeutungsschwangeren Attraktionen von Washington, D.C., hat in diesem Jahrhundert bis in die 70er Jahre stark zugenommen. Die deutlich sichtbare Abnahme solcher Pilgerfahrten, sowohl in absoluten wie relativen Zahlen, seit ungefähr 1976 ist hingegen ein Phänomen, das noch weiterer Klärung bedarf.

Bibliography

ALBANESE, Catherine (1974): Sons of the fathers: The civil religion of the American Revolution. Temple University Press. Philadelphia.

BOEHM, M. H. (1933): Nationalism: Theoretical aspects. — In: Encyclopedia of the Social Sciences. Macmillan. New York. Vol. 11, p. 231 – 40.

BURNHAM, I. (1982): Making history out of artifacts: An interpretive exhibit at the Valley Forge Museum. - In: Valley Forge Journal, 1 (1), p. 82 – 96.

CARLSON, R. A. (1975): The quest for conformity: Americanization through education. Wiley. New York.

DISTRICT OF COLUMBIA, OFFICE OF BUSINESS AND ECONOMIC DEVELOPMENT (1981): District of Columbia tourist development policy study. Washington.

FORGIE, G. B. (1979): Patricide in the house divided: A psychological interpretation of Lincoln and his age. W. W. Norton. New York.

GREATER WASHINGTON BOARD OF TRADE (n. d.) The case for Washington: Our resources. Washington.

HAMMOND, P. E. (1976): The sociology of American civil religion: A bibliographic essay. — In: Sociological Analysis, 2, p. 169 – 82.

HAYES, C. J. H. (1960): Nationalism. A religion. MacMillan. New York.

HAZLETON, J. H. (1906): The Declaration of Independence: Its history. Dodd Mead. New York.

HUTTON; A. H. (1959): Portrait of patriotism: "Washington Crossing the Delaware". Chilton. Philadelphia.

KAMMEN, M. (1980): In search of America. — In: Historic Preservation, 32, p. 30 – 39.

LEWIS, D. L. (1976): The public image of Henry Ford: An American folk hero and his company. Wayne State University Press. Detroit.

LEWIS, L. (1929): Myths after Lincoln. Harcourt, Brace. New York.

MAASS, J. (1976): The Declaration of Independence. — In: Antiques, 110(1), p. 106 – 10.

MALONE, D. (1954): The story of the Declaration of Independence. Oxford University Press. New York.

MICHAELSEN, R. (1970): Piety in the public schools. Macmillan. New York.

NATIONAL CAPITAL PLANNING COMMISSION (1978): Tourist, business visitor and convention activities, 1976. Phase I. Washington.

NATIONAL CAPITAL PLANNING COMMISSION (1984 a): Comprehensive plan for the National Capital. Visitors to the National Capital. Planning. Report. Washington.

NATIONAL CAPITAL PLANNING COMMISSION (1984 b): Comprehensive plan for the National Capital. Visitors to the National Capital. Proposed Federal Element. Washington.

WILLS, G. (1978): Inventing America: Jefferson's Declaration of Independence. Doubleday. Garden City, N. Y.

WILSON, J. F. (1971): The status of 'civil religion' in America. — In: E. A. Smith, ed. The religion of the republic. Fortress Press. Philadelphia.

WOLFE, J. S. (1975): The Kennedy Myth: American civil religion in the sixties. Ph. D. dissertation. Graduate Theological Union. Berkeley.

ZUCKERMAN, M. (1978): The irrelevant revolution: 1776 and since. American Quarterly, 30, p. 224 – 42.

Addresses of the editors and authors

Prof. Surinder Bhardwaj, Ph.D.
Dept. of Geography
Kent State University
KENT, Ohio 44242
USA

Carol Cameron
Dept. of Geography
Kent State University
KENT, Ohio 44242
USA

J. W. Davidson, M.A.
Dept. of Geography
Wilfried Laurier University
WATERLOO, Ontario
Canada   N2L 3C5

Martin E. Donach
Centro Ricerche Socio Religiose
Via del Seminario, 29
I-35122 PADOVA
Italy

Prof. Gregory E. Faiers, Ph.D.
Dept. of Geography
University of Pittsburgh
JOHNSTOWN, PA 15904
USA

Prof. Dr. Paolo Giuriati
Centro Ricerche Socio Religiose
Via del Seminario, 29
I-35122 PADOVA
Italy

Prof. Alfred Hecht, Ph.D.
Dept. of Geography
Wilfried Laurier University
WATERLOO, Ontario
Canada   N2L 3C5

Prof. Richard H. Jackson, Ph.D.
Dept. of Geography
Brigham Young University
PROVO, Utah 84602
USA

Jill Knapp
Dept. of Geography
Brigham Young University
PROVO, Utah 84602
USA

Prof. Phyllis M. G. Myers, Ph.D.
Northern Illinois University
DEKALB, Illinois 60115
USA

Prof. James J. Preston, Ph.D.
Dept. of Anthropology
State University of New York
ONEONTA, New York 13820
USA

Prof. Carolyn V. Prorok, Ph.D.
Dept. of Geography
Slippery Rock University
SLIPPERY ROCK, PA 16057-1326
USA

Prof. Dr. Gisbert Rinschede
Math.–Geogr. Fakultät
Katholische Universität Eichstätt
Ostenstr. 26

D-8078 EICHSTÄTT
F. R. of Germany

Prof. Herbert A. Whitney, Ph.D.
Dept. of Geography
Wilfried Laurier University

WATERLOO, Ontario
Canada   N2L 3C5

Prof. Wilbur Zelinsky, Ph.D.
Dept. of Geography
The Pennsylvania State University

UNIVERSITY PARK, PA 16802
USA

GEOGRAPHIA RELIGIONUM

Interdisziplinäre Schriftenreihe zur Religionsgeographie

Band 1

GRUNDFRAGEN DER RELIGIONSGEOGRAPHIE
Mit Fallstudien zum Pilgertourismus
Herausgegeben von M. Büttner, K. Hoheisel, U. Köpf,
G. Rinschede, A. Sievers

286 Seiten, 49 Abbildungen und 1 Faltkarte. 1985
Brosch. DM 48,– / ISBN 3-496-00832-6

Band 2

RELIGION UND SIEDLUNGSRAUM
Herausgegeben von M. Büttner, K. Hohcisel, U. Köpf,
G. Rinschede, A. Sievers

268 Seiten, 43 Abbildungen und 2 Faltkarten. 1986
Brosch. DM 38,– / ISBN 3-496-00869-5

Band 3

Reinhard Henkel
CHRISTIAN MISSIONS IN AFRICA
A social geographical study of the impact of their activities in Zambia

236 Seiten, 45 Abbildungen und 25 Tabellen. 1989
Brosch. DM 48,– / ISBN 3-496-00934-9

Band 4

S. M. Bhardwaj and G. Rinschede (eds.)
PILGRIMAGE IN WORLD RELIGIONS
presented to Prof. Dr. Angelika Sievers on the occasion of her 75th birthday

200 Seiten, 30 Abbildungen und 3 Faltkarten. 1988
Brosch. DM 38,– / ISBN 3-496-00959-4

DIETRICH REIMER VERLAG BERLIN
Unter den Eichen 57 · 1000 Berlin 45

Band 5

G. Rinschede and S. M. Bhardwaj (eds.)
PILGRIMAGE IN THE UNITED STATES

256 Seiten. 1989
Brosch. DM 48,– / ISBN 3-496-00379-0

Band 6

Rudolph, K. u. G. Rinschede (Hrsg.)
BEITRÄGE ZUR RELIGION/UMWELT-FORSCHUNG I
Erster Tagungsband des Interdisziplinären Symposiums in Eichstätt,
5. – 8. Mai 1988

264 Seiten. 1989
Brosch. DM 48,– / ISBN 3-496-00377-4

Band 7

Rinschede, G. u. K. Rudolph (Hrsg.)
BEITRÄGE ZUR RELIGION/UMWELT-FORSCHUNG II
Zweiter Tagungsband des Interdisziplinären Symposiums in Eichstätt,
5. – 8. Mai 1988

207 Seiten. 1989
Brosch. DM 48,– / ISBN 3-496-00378-2

DIETRICH REIMER VERLAG **BERLIN**
Unter den Eichen 57 · 1 000 Berlin 45